The Complete Guide to Film and Digital Production

The Complete Guide to Film and Digital Production

The People and the Process

Second Edition

LORENE M. WALES

Regent University

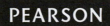

Boston   Columbus   Indianapolis   New York   San Francisco   Upper Saddle River
Amsterdam Cape Town   Dubai   London   Madrid   Milan   Munich   Paris   Montreal Toronto
Delhi Mexico City   Sao Paulo   Sydney   Hong Kong   Seoul   Singapore   Taipei   Tokyo

Editor-in-Chief, Communication: Karon Bowers
Project Editor: Ziki Dekel
Assistant Editor: Stephanie Chaisson
Associate Managing Editor: Bayani Mendoza de Leon
Project Manager: Pat Brown
Marketing Manager: Wendy Gordon
Art Director: Jayne Conte
Production and Composition Services: Element-Thomson North America
Cover Designer: Suzanne Duda
Text Printer and Binder: Courier Westford
Cover Printer: Courier Westford

Library of Congress Cataloging-in-Publication Data

Wales, Lorene M.
    The Complete Guide to film and digital production : the people and
the process / Lorene M. Wales.
        p. cm.
    Rev. ed of: The people and process of film and video production.
    Includes bibliographical references and index.
    ISBN-13: 978-0-205-07862-2 (alk. paper)
    ISBN-10: 0-205-07862-1 (alk. paper)
    1. Motion pictures—Production and direction.   I. Wales, Lorene M.
People and process of film and video production.   II. Title.
    PN1995.9.P7W344 2011
    791.4302'32--dc22
2011013379

1 2 3 4 5 6 7 8 9 10— —14 13 12 11

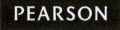

ISBN-13: 978-0-205-07862-2
ISBN-10:   0-205-07862-1

This book is dedicated to Dad who taught me the value of hard work, integrity and counting your blessings, I will always count him a blessing, and to the film-makers, the ones who do it because they love it, because they want to make great films and because they love the crazy chaotic process that it takes to get there.

CONTENTS

CHAPTER 6

The Director's Team & 2nd Unit   96

CHAPTER 7

Casting, Actors, Extras, and Stunt People   117

CHAPTER 8
The Art Department   133

CHAPTER 9
The Camera Department   141

PREFACE

The first edition of this book laid out the production process, who does what on low- to high-budget films. When it came to working on this revision, I realized a lot has changed. Sure, most of the process itself is still the same, but the parameters have changed, the industry climate has changed, and, because of digital technology, the process has changed. Paperwork can be distributed more quickly through cell phones and email. Special effects can be created in monitors on set, instead of in post-production. People still do what they do, but it is how they do it that has changed.

What's more, budget levels have changed somewhat. Low-budget is still low budget. The student level is still a little or no budget at tall. Professional low budget can still be as low as $50,000 but can go up to $200,000. In certain markets less than $10 million is considered low budget. Medium budget has grown too anywhere above $10–$50 or $60 million. High budget has hit record highs, landing at greater than $200 million. These ultra-high budgets are usually the special-effects films. These are big action movies that require a lot of digital work to make men in iron suites fly or to create an entire new planet with a race of blue people.

The important point still is that whatever the budget level, while some of the people and process can be the same, the number of people involved and the procedures for completing a project are different. One or two people in a low-budget project may handle a department that would take an entire team of twenty people in a medium-budget project. It is even more essential to know going into a production how the process will work, and how it will work can be determined by the budget level. The golden rule is still do it yourself—until you can afford to hire someone else to do it.

NEW TO THIS EDITION

This second edition starts with a new chapter on different media. Students are not only graduating to work in one field anymore. The new chapter expands their knowledge to cover production in the field, live events, mobile content, and animation. The broader range of coverage in this new edition will provide students with a more marketable set of skills and experiences, necessary for an ever-expanding and converging industry. In addition, as distribution avenues grow, this edition covers how to keep up with the latest trends in Internet distribution and the effect of the digital revolution on traditional distribution. Finally, as the process of production may somewhat stay the same, digital formats and tools have changed the way some of the process is done. Students will get updated information about the recent changes to the process as well as online access to updated and expanded production forms for all their production needs. Another update to this book is the production forms. These forms have been updated to reflect digital production needs and can be found online for easy access. The new pdfs can also be filled out electronically (instead of printing them out first). Finally, this new edition was updated and expanded to cover the process for different media, all with the goal to make students' production knowledge broader and current, and therefore make them more marketable.

This new edition still approaches the process from the angle that the budget level can affect how you make your movie. What is also central to know about this new edition is that just as the industry climate has changed, so the scope of the book had to as well. Anyone starting out in filmmaking will find themselves not just making films, that is, if they want to make a living. There are more forms of media now than ever before. You can find yourself working in documentary one day and feature film the next. Content for the Internet has become a huge part of the filmmaker's resume. Almost everyone needs content for their Websites, and contrary to what some believe, they do not want cheap material. They want professional quality production and will pay handsomely (in most cases) for it. Any aspiring director or producer would do well to plug into this market. There is also producing live events, an area which has been around forever but is now open to the filmmaker as more people want their events filmed. The process here is a little different and requires shooting in the field, more time constraints and pre-planning. Documentary and animation are also more profitable and worthy of tapping into.

The structure of this edition remains pretty true to the first edition. Each chapter (with the exception of Chapter 1) examines each department on a production and covers what you can expect at the different budget levels. This is still best described as a reference book that shows you how to put a production together, but this time expands to cover the script process on the front end and distribution at the end.

Give Your Students Choices

In addition to the traditional printed text, *The Complete Guide to Film and Video Production, 2/e* is available in the following format to give you and your students more choices—and more ways to save.

The **CourseSmart eTextbook** offers the same content as the printed text in a convenient online format—with highlighting, online search, and printing capabilities. **www.coursesmart.com** CourseSmart eTextbook: ISBN: 0205209858, $22.50

Prep and Production

Producing Media

THE PRODUCER'S JOB

The producer of any media is, or should be, a leader. He is the one person on a project who is responsible for everything, the process, the budget, the people, and ultimately the final product, whether it be feature film, documentary, mobile content, or live events. Notice I don't say the producer *does* everything because a good producer knows how to delegate. The producer definitely has to have the ultimate vision for what the project needs to be and also the ability to communicate that vision to the director. A producer is the type of person who is highly self-motivated, who can take a great idea and transform it into a great film or show. Being a producer is seeing all the possibilities of a project and having the ability to put together the right people and elements that will make it work. What makes a good producer great is a combination of many factors:

- Knows how to handle people. A producer not only deals with paperwork such as budgets and cost reports but also must lead a large group of people in often stressful situations. If someone does not perform well, the unit production manager (UPM) or producer may need to handle the situation and either help the person improve or, if necessary, fire that person.
- Able to handle confrontation and personality conflicts. The business of making a film or any show involves a large group of people working extremely closely for long hours. Conflicts are bound to arise and usually do.
- Able to handle a large volume of details and people all at once.
- Able to handle stress.
- Good at motivating people, able to get them to work in tough situations.
- Knows what makes a good script, and how to get the story on the screen.
- Good at rewriting, as is usually necessary on any project.
- Able to match a script with the director that would be best for that project. I once produced a short film about the Holocaust. I had two very able directors up for the position. My final decision was based on the sensitivity and maturity of one of the directors, even though the other director had better technique.

- Able to deal with prima donnas. Unfortunately, the industry is full of them, and it is hard to see them coming. You may find a prima donna in the form of a director of photography (DP), or even in a production assistant (PA). A good producer knows how to handle these kinds of people.
- Able to fire people. Ability to hire the right people for the right positions and fire the ones that don't work out.
- Knows how to delegate. While it is sometimes good for a producer to be hands-on, a good producer gets a lot done in a short period of time by knowing what should be delegated.

The producer generally is the final authority of a project, but there are some exceptions.

For instance, in some cases the producer of a film is the final creative authority, even over the director. However, this is not always true. You may use a well-established director with much power but have a producer who is just starting out. In this case the director would have greater creative authority.

There are many different kinds of producers. In single-camera production the **executive producer** (EP) is most likely the person who puts a project together. This person creates a "package" that may include certain stars and a director. In other productions the EP may be the person who is actually funding the film. People who are investors and may not have any experience in the film business could also fill this position. Or, the producer could be someone in the business who is hired to supervise the production for the investors. Having this title helps them retain fiscal control. In higher budget films the producer could be the representative of a company that has invested in a film, and hired to oversee the production. Or, he could be a wealthy investor who has put a significant amount of money into the film (in this case millions). In some cases, though rare, this position could be what is known as a **courtesy credit.** This means it is someone who may have invested heavily but takes little part in overseeing the production, relying instead on a good line producer.

There are many different styles to producing. Some EPs prefer to oversee at a distance, merely reading **production reports** and watching **dailies** on video or digitally. They would still have the right to approve or not approve significant budget or script changes, anything that would significantly change the original essence of the project. Their authority is still in place, and they have the right to step in at any moment if there is trouble, but they rarely come to the location. In fact, if you have this kind of EP, and he does show up at your location, you can bet there are problems somewhere, perhaps with the budget or dailies. If that same EP is actually seen on set, there is an even greater level of trouble, most likely with the director.

Then there are the more hands-on EPs. These kinds of producers are frequently on location, and may occasionally be on set. They scrutinize the **rushes,** sending notes to the producer and director daily. Some films may have more than one EP. I once worked on a picture that had three EPs. Two of them were people who had invested money in the film, and one was a representative of a production company that invested money in the film. Having multiple EPs can get complicated, depending on their involvement. It is easier to get approval for something from one person, rather than tracking down three. In addition, the three members must agree on certain issues related to the production, which is no small feat. Just remember that each situation is different. Following is a list of possible duties for the EP during pre-production, production, post-production, and wrap.

Pre-Production

- Approves the budget based on the amount of money invested in the project.
- Approves or hires the producer and sometimes the director.
- Holds meetings with producer and director to discuss vision of the project.
- If it has not been done already, may secure **distribution** for the project.

Production

- Reviews production reports (if shooting film) to monitor the progress of the shoot.
- Steps in if there appear to be problems, such as using too much overtime, or maybe the director shooting too much film. Usually the EP will rely on the producer to deal with most problems.
- Approves more funds if warranted. For instance, I worked on a film once where there was so much rain in the city in which we were shooting that we lost a full week of shooting over a two-month period. The EP was consulted and deemed it necessary to shoot another full week, which cost the production extra money.
- May review footage to monitor the progress of the project.

Post-Production

- Reviews all cuts of the project to see how it is taking shape and makes recommendations.
- Works with the producer to spend out the budget.
- May review/approve marketing materials for distribution.
- Works with the distribution company to assure delivery of the project.
- Works on her next project.

There are certain qualities that make for a good EP. An EP:

- Is a self-starter. This is not someone who is sitting around waiting for someone to hire her.
- Is entrepreneurial enough to create her own job.
- Is a good leader, able to be perceptive with deals and people.
- Understands the industry, has a vision for it, and yet has business expertise.

LINE PRODUCER

The producer, also often called the **line producer,** works directly under the EP. Sometimes in low-budget film productions the producer may even be the same person as the EP, if she has put the package together and secured funds for the project. Just like the EP, there are different styles to producing. Some producers are very hands-off, hardly ever showing up on set. However, some producers like to go to set every day.

If the producer is also the EP, she is responsible for everything. One rule of the industry is that if the film succeeds, the director is praised. If the film fails, the producer is blamed. This is why in some cases the producer may have ultimate creative power. Keep in mind this is especially true for television work. Also keep in mind that in certain situations the producer may have less creative power than the director. The creative power resides in the person with the most influence or experience in the industry.

How much a producer does in terms of responsibilities may depend on the budget. The rule is that you do everything until you can hire someone else to do it. The kind of project you do also can determine the producer's level of involvement. For instance, if the project is a documentary, the producer often functions also as the director and often the editor. When producing live events, the producer must be hands-on with all the many details to pull off any type of event. If you are producing animation, you can afford to be less hands-on and rely more on your director of animation to pay attention to the details of the process. Following is a list of duties for the producer during pre-production, production, and post-production.

Pre-Production

- Puts together the budget. This process, discussed in Chapter 2, may involve receiving bids from various department heads. For instance, a production designer may submit a budget for the art department. The producer will review this bid and approve or make changes as the overall budget permits.
- May hire the director.
- Hires the UPM.
- May hire an assistant, if the budget allows.
- Works with the director to define the vision of the project.
- Meets with director and production team to assure pre-production matters are being handled.
- May work with director and director's team on the scheduling of the shoot.
- Sometimes makes the distribution deal.
- Goes on **location scouts.** The producer does have the power to veto a location if she feels it does not fit the overall vision of the project.
- Approves cast.
- Approves script changes (this goes on during the production as well).

Production

- Answers to the EP.
- Helps support the director to get the vision they have discussed. Again, different producers have different styles when doing this. The approach depends on the relationship with the director. There must be a certain level of trust between both parties. Some producers tend to be overbearing. A good producer will find a way to bring the best work out of a certain director, still maintaining control without being domineering.

- Oversees management of the budget with the UPM.
- Attends dailies.
- Discusses footage with director to ensure progress of the project.
- Approves budget expenditures.
- Approves the production report (if shooting film).
- May visit the set to ensure the shoot is progressing well.

Post-Production and Wrap

- Reviews all cuts of the project and makes recommendations.
- Oversees wrapping up the final budget with the UPM.
- May pay for the **wrap party**. The funds for the wrap party may also be covered under the production budget.
- Pays for **crew gifts.** Crew gifts can be as simple as a T-shirt or ball cap with the project's title, or as expensive as a quilted jacket at $100 per person. Some crew gifts are more creative. I once worked on a film that was about a duffle bag of money that fell off a Purolator truck. Each crew member received a duffle bag and money clip decorated with the project's title. What and how expensive the crew gift is depends on the resources of the producer.
- Approves the final cut of the project.
- Delivers the project to the appropriate personnel.

ASSOCIATE PRODUCER

The position of **associate producer** is one of the most misunderstood in the industry. This is because the position varies so greatly from project to project. In low budget you most likely will not have this position. In medium to high budget this position could be many things. In television the role is clearly defined, but not in film and digital work. I once worked on a high-budget film where the associate producer was a friend of the producer who typed script changes. I have even seen an associate producer who was the producer's nephew and needed a film credit. Historically the associate producer is the person who guides the picture through post; however, these days that position is being called the **post-production supervisor.** The associate producer may also be someone who consults on the picture, in a certain area of expertise or technical acumen. The role of the associate is often a judgment call, a courtesy credit. This should not be surprising. Read the credits on many films and you will constantly see new titles. Producers are thinking up new titles all the time. I once worked on a film where I received credit as a production associate. I was given this title because I had done two different jobs on the picture but could receive only one credit.

ASSISTANT TO THE PRODUCER

Becoming a producer can happen pretty quickly if someone is motivated enough. Some people, however, choose to learn the ropes by working for a producer first. In this case, becoming an **assistant to the producer** is a great job for newcomers to the industry. This position allows the person to sit in on important meetings and, if aspiring to be a producer, learn firsthand how to produce. The assistant gets to know what is going on all the time. This puts the assistant in a very valuable position, as communication is extremely important on a production. The main job, obviously, is to assist the producer. This assisting could involve a variety of duties, depending on the proclivity of the producer. Different producers give different responsibilities to their assistants. The assistant may begin work at the discretion of the producer and continue working through post-production, budget permitting. Following is a general description of the range of duties that may be required of an assistant:

- Answers the telephone for the producer and screens calls. This is a position that requires discretion.
- Could type script pages for the producer, if the production is not using a script service. A good knowledge of the different screenwriting programs is essential.
- May schedule meetings with a variety of crew members, the director, and possibly studio executives, if it is a studio shoot.
- Sits in on production meetings, usually to take notes for the producer, execute conference calls, and get coffee.
- Becomes the voice of communication with the studio and/or certain crew. This is merely to save time for the producer.
- May be involved in more personal matters such as picking up the dry cleaning, walking the dog, or scheduling a haircut.

Qualities of a Good Assistant

- Reliable, resourceful, and respectful of the producer's position.
- Understands production well enough to be discrete at appropriate times.
- Has adequate scheduling and secretarial skills: typing, faxing, and telephone.
- Is willing to learn and work without attitude.

ACQUIRING THE SCRIPT

The first step in producing any project begins with the script. Even in documentary a partial script is often used to flesh out the story or provide some structure to a piece. Whatever the format, the producer may either need to option or buy the script, if it is not an original work, written by the producer. Sometimes the producer hires a writer to write something for a show. In this case the writer becomes a work-for-hire, meaning that the producer, by hiring and paying the writer, now owns the script. Depending on the format, residual payments to the writer may be in order (union work mostly). If a producer wants to acquire an already written script, but has not yet raised the funds for a project, then she may buy an option on the script. This means that the producer essentially keeps the "option" of producing the project for a certain period of time. The writer cannot let anyone else try to produce the script while it is optioned. If at the end of the option period the producer has secured funding, great, the project gets made. If at the end of the option the producer has not raised the money to produce the project, the rights to the script may go back to the writer, who will then have the choice of optioning the script to someone else. At this point the producer could renew the option, or walk away.

If the producer already has funding, she may buy an already written script outright. In this case the writer may give up all of his rights to the script and the producer can do whatever she wants to it. There are no rules here in terms of how the deal can be made. Each situation and deal is different depending on how much money is involved, what kind of project it is, whether the writer is union or nonunion, and how good the script is. Often a producer will acquire a script, but not be entirely happy with it. The script may need rewrites, which can be done by the writer (if hired and paid to do so) or the producer. Even later in the process the director sometimes also rewrites scenes or dialogue once the project is underway. As a producer you need to remember you are acquiring a product, which means you need to have the right contracts in place whether you are commissioning a script or buying an already written script. You may need an Option and Purchase Agreement, a Writer Agreement, or maybe a Collaboration Agreement if you are co-writing with someone. Each of these contracts outlines the parameters of the agreements such as how long the contract is for, what work it is for, how credits will be given later, what the compensation is, whether the contract is renewable, and more. Make sure a lawyer is involved in this part of the process to insure you get everything you want and need. See the online forms for some examples of these contracts.

WORKING WITH WRITERS

If you hire a writer to write or rewrite a script for you, it is important to know how to communicate with a writer, in order to get the best work out of him and to ultimately get what you need, a great script. Writers are artists who will sometimes spend hours pondering a line of dialogue or story point. They often work alone (except in some cases such as comedy writing teams or co-writers) and are comfortable living inside their stories. What many writers have in common is the passion for their work. That passion can translate to someone who is easy to work with, or someone who requires a lot more patience. I've worked with writers who are very easygoing, and will keep rewriting until they give you what you want. I've also worked with writers who can't imagine why you would want to change a single word of their script, and fight you to do so. The key here is personality management. Writers can be insecure and sometimes need lots of encouragement and positive feedback. Some writers do better if you give them very specific notes on the script, while others do better if you only give them a general direction to go in. Know your writer and not only how she likes to work but also how she works in a way that will give you the best script possible.

WORKING WITH FIRST-TIME DIRECTORS

As a producer, you may be shooting in low budget and run across first-time directors. First-time directors have a few qualities that a producer needs to watch out for. Here are some things to keep in mind:

- First-time directors always try to shoot too much. The reason for this is that they have not yet learned the economics of shooting. Also, they are most likely nervous, and figure the more they shoot, the more footage they will have, and the better their chances of making a good film. A good producer needs to weigh this trend in a new director to allow some freedom while retaining control so as to protect the budget.

- Some first-time directors are more concerned with shots than story or acting. This is very common. Many directors think the cool shot will showcase great creative talent. Seasoned directors have gained perspective on this and understand the importance of good performances and storytelling.
- First-time directors get tunnel vision. Tunnel vision is the ability to see in only one direction, and narrowly. It is not necessarily bad. This trait allows directors to attend to the detail of a scene, a performance, and a moment with great intensity. The problem with tunnel vision arises when a director cannot see outside his own world, and this sometimes translates into budgetary nightmares. Directors are not hired to watch the budget, nor do some of them feel responsible for it, which is another reason why good producers are so important. A good producer is adept at keeping the wider, overall vision of the project, which may be desperately needed to ensure the final vision is achieved.
- Some first-time directors don't do **shot lists**. This is usually because they don't know how. I've worked with many a director who did not do shot lists. However, these seasoned professionals had gained enough experience to shoot confidently "off the cuff." A good producer will encourage, and even sometimes demand, shot lists from a new director.
- Many first-time directors have little endurance. They tend to relax after **principal photography** because they are not used to the long days and weeks it takes to shoot a project. A good producer will keep on the director through his contracted role in post-production, and keep him on a timely schedule.

PRODUCING IN THE FIELD

While the general responsibilities of a producer cover lots of different media, there are some important differences in shooting various kinds of projects. Shooting in the field is a term often used for television applications where an interview is conducted with some sort of expert in an office location, or it can be doing an interview "MOS" or with a man on the street. Sometimes producing in the field is for short **features** or stories that will be used later as part of another show. Shooting in the field is also synonymous with documentary work. The key to successful field producing is planning. Here are some issues that will need to be dealt with:

> *Crew:* The type of material you need to get will determine the kind of and how much crew you need. In some cases, such as short features, you may only need a cameraperson and possibly one sound person. If you are doing only interviews, it will be just you and the cameraperson. If you are shooting some reenactments, you may need camera, sound, lighting, and grips. Some of this crew can be hired locally, such as sound, lighting, and grips. Check with the film office where you are shooting as they often have directories of local crew people.

On the road: In the field more than likely means you will be going somewhere, whether it is locally, or across the globe. If your company does not have coordinators arranging your travel, you may need to do it yourself. Make sure that hotel, airfare, and per diem for the crew are secured before you head out. Also make sure your crew are securing the necessary equipment you will need. In addition, in case of equipment failure, have backup equipment, or the location of the nearest equipment rental houses, should you need them. If you are shooting internationally, be aware of that country's requirements for visas and/or immunizations before entering the country.

Location issues: As with location shooting for feature films, shooting in the field means shooting on location. This kind of shooting has much of the same policies regarding location agreements and permits. See Chapter 15 for a more detailed explanation of dealing with your locations. That said, because shooting in the field generally takes a small crew, many people try to shoot "on the fly" or "drive-by" meaning they simply pull up, set up the camera, and grab some footage without dealing with location agreements or permits. While this is highly successful, it's not entirely legal. It's better as the producer to cover all the bases legally so you don't incur any fines or break the law.

PRODUCING LIVE EVENTS

Producing live events is where many future film and television producers start out. A live event, of course, differs from producing a media show in that there is usually no post-production. However, the process of going through pre-production is somewhat the same. Then, the actual event is much like doing a live television show or theater production. Everything should be in place enough that the event runs itself. There are two kinds of live events: those that are filmed, either for DVD, web, or television, and those that are not filmed. For both there are many considerations and steps to take, starting with pre-production:

The final outcome: Live events is such a broad format that you could be producing anything from an awards show to a fundraiser to a retrospective or festival. An important element of all of these is the final outcome. What will your attendees leave the event with? One element that can cement the event in their minds is branding the event. There should be some sort of logo, slogan, or phrase that sums up what the event is about, its purpose. Part of that branding lies in the design you choose to brand it. That design is then carried through to items such as the invitations, posters, programs, and advertising. This gives the event an aesthetic continuity and also an identity.

Publicity and advertising: The scope of the event usually determines how much and what kind of publicity and advertising needs to take place. If the event is public, then you will want to advertise with commercials, local businesses, radio, cable, and public television. You should first draw up a press release that contains all the relevant information about the event, time, place, purpose, etc. In addition, creating posters flyers and mailings (email and snail mail) that are strategically distributed could make the difference in your turnout. Consider timed announcements at various intervals, increasing them as you get closer to the event. Of course, if the event is not public and invitation only, your advertising is minimal.

Budget: As with all production the budget you have will determine many things, such as what kind of venue you can afford and how much crew and/or production design you can afford. If appropriate, consider sponsors for the event. Sometimes businesses will donate funds to an event, in exchange for having their advertisement appear in the program, or appear in some of the elements of the venue (on a screen, stage, or banner). Sponsors will want to know that the event will give their company exposure to the right audience. Obviously a nonpublic event would only appeal to certain sponsors who still might want to target a certain audience, the one you are inviting. Other sponsors might be seeking more of a public exposure, which then works well with public events.

Venue: When deciding on a venue, there are the logistical considerations such as setup, how long will the event take to set up in a particular venue, is there good access for equipment and services, etc. In addition, consider cleanup, emergency services, or any security that might be needed. Ultimately, though, the venue has to match the scope and purpose of the event. I once produced an event that was to be a forum with panels and speakers. The venue was more of a screening room for films, so there were challenges in acquiring the right on stage equipment for forum panels and speakers. We chose to trade the practicality of a different venue, in place of a beautiful screening room, which again, produced some challenges, but worked out in the end.

The crew: Your crew could consist of many people, depending on your needs. Certainly you need to hire a **stills photographer** to capture the event. Be sure to discuss with your photographer what specific shots or people to capture. You could also hire a videographer. Be sure to understand and communicate what the cameraperson should shoot. To answer that, think about why you would want the footage. Do you want to create a promo piece later to promote an annual event or raise funds? Do you just want a recording of the event for its own sake, or something that may be distributed to those who took part in it? Answer these questions and you will know what to tell your videographer to shoot. Other crew you might need is determined by the venue itself. Whether the event is public or not, when people show up, they need to know where to go. You should have greeters and ushers to guide people to where they need to go. In addition, participants in the event need to come early and perhaps rehearse. Assigning someone to escort and monitor the talent ensures they will be where you need them, when you need them. Finally, if your event involves local or national celebrities, as is often the case, consider hiring security to protect them from unwanted approaches by well-meaning fans.

The cast: Any live event needs a host or hosts. Choosing the right one for your event is crucial. The host should be professional but more importantly, appropriate for the event. Do not get a comedian for an event that honors victims of some tragedy. Think about what kind of personality is appropriate.

Production design: Some events are bare bones because of the budget, while some can have high "production value" if affordable. If the venue needs some aesthetic touch-ups, you will need to hire a production design team or decorators to embellish the venue. This could mean anything from flowers and plants to make the room look nicer, to building dozens of displays that take up the entire venue. Make sure the venue owners know and approve exactly what you want to do ahead of time. In addition, it is good to have these changes to the venue outlined in the venue contract to avoid confusion and conflict later.

Invitations: Invitations, if your event calls for them, are something that should be done early in the process to allow for RSVPs if needed. Generally you should send out the invites via snail mail or Evite a month before the event. If the event is larger, such as a charity ball, the invitations should go out more like three months in advance. Make sure you are clear on the invite regarding the RSVP date and how guests are expected to respond (email, RSVP card, etc.).

Programs: Most live events need some sort of program to let attendees know how the event will go. The program should use the same branding and aesthetic theme of the event. Be sure to allow time for printing (or copying if on a low budget) before the event.

Admissions: If the event is free, you won't need tickets; if it is not, you will need tickets printed, for admittance. Make sure your ticket takers tear them in half so that you can keep a count of how many people attended. Low-budget events use regular tickets that can be bought at an office supply store. Bigger budget events may use elaborate invitations with formal custom tickets that guests bring to the event. Determine what kind you will use as per your budget.

Logistics: If your event has seating, pay attention to general seating, assigned seating, or reserved seating. Your ushers can escort guests for reserved seating as they enter. Make sure the reserved section is securely cordoned off. You also need to make sure you have proper accommodations for any physically challenged attendees with adequate access for wheelchairs.

Parties and food: Your event may have a pre-event party that could involve the host, talent, presenters, etc. Make sure you allow enough time for these people to travel from the party to the event, along with enough time for a walk-through or rehearsal. Many times people also have an after-event reception. Typically the caterer will set up as the event is taking place. Be sure to have someone monitoring the caterer so that they are ready in time. You don't want people walking into a reception when the caterer is still setting up.

Legal matters: You will need to do a contract with the venue that outlines the parameters, date, and time of the event. You would be wise to have a lawyer go over the contract to make sure there are no hidden stipulations. Most venues will also require insurance from you. This is in case any damage is done to the venue, and then your insurance would cover the damages. If your event is outside or on public property, you may need permits to hold the event, and possibly for parking vehicles at or for the event. Your local convention and visitor's bureau should be able to help with this. Other legal paperwork you may need is releases. If the event is being filmed for other media distribution, you may need release forms for your talent and perhaps the audience. For the audience a crowd release placed in a conspicuous area (see the online forms for an example) will suffice.

Props: If your event has some form of awards tied to it, you will need to acquire the awards or plaques well before the event. Simple plaques may only take a couple of days, but elaborate awards could take quite a few weeks, so allow for plenty of turnaround from the time you order them to when you need them.

The script: Even free-flowing events need a script. The script could be for a show with general timings for each element of the event, or, if the event is being filmed, could be a very detailed outline of each element as per each camera with audio cues. Either way, the script needs to show each component to insure the event runs smoothly. All personnel, including the host, guests, camera, and audio people, need this script to keep track of how things need to go. The script should be ready in pre-production and gone over with each person in advance of the event.

Transportation: Some events provide private cars, airfare, and maybe even hotel for talent, hosts, or crew. It's a good idea to have a production coordinator to take care of these details for you. That person will make sure they know where these people are at all times and get where they need to be.

Production: Now that everything should be in place, you need one more check to make sure the event runs smoothly.

The walk-through and rehearsals: It is imperative that you either do rehearsals for an event, if warranted, or hold a **walk-through.** A walk-through takes all personnel (host, talent, camera, and audio crew) through the event, element by element. This should be done right before the event and can take anywhere from 30 minutes to a couple of hours. Always budget for more time than you think you need.

Craft services: You should provide some sort of craft services for people working or taking part in the event. This could include just water and some snacks to something more elaborate such as drinks, coffee, and hot hors d'oeuvres.

Payroll: All events will cost something. Be sure to be prepared to pay personnel, the venue, and services the night of the event. Some venues and caterers may require partial payment in advance and full payment the date of the event. This is normal. Just be prepared to provide checks at the end of the event to complete payment.

PRODUCING DOCUMENTARY

Certainly there are volumes of books that explain the process of documentary production. This section does not intend to go into that amount of detail but rather to discuss documentary from the producer's perspective. In other words, what is important about producing documentary, as opposed to other content? With documentary it starts with a problem. The way to look at and explore that problem, in a documentary starts with research.

Research: Most will agree that research is the most important part of the documentary process. For a producer it is crucial not only to identify your problem but also to make sure that your research reflects accurately the context of the problem. You will find after doing lots of research that your perspective as the producer will begin to shape how you want to present the problem. Are you trying to expose a certain issue that no one knows about? Are you examining a well-known issue, but in a new way that viewers will find not just interesting but also fascinating? In this phase you should have some idea what viewpoint you will be taking. That is not to say that it may not change down the road. One of the beauties of doing documentary is that it is much more an "organic" process than narrative film. As you progress through the process you may find information or events that change the way you were looking at the problem. That's okay. As the producer it will be your job to make decisions about these new directions, exploring some while disregarding others.

Pre-production: Once the research is at a good point where you have enough information to proceed (research is never really complete until the final edit), you can proceed with pre-production. This part of the process for the producer consists of hiring a great production manager who can take care of the day-to-day running of the production. In many cases a director is hired, although many a documentary is completed by a producer/ director. If that is you, great, but be prepared for the work. Doing so, you will live and breathe the project for many months, which is actually not difficult if you are passionate about the subject. During this time your team should be acquiring equipment, setting up interviews, and coordinating travel and any reenactments that might be needed. What you should be doing is continuing to work on the script.

The partial script: Obviously in documentary you do not start out with a script in the traditional sense of the word. Some documentaries go out with no script at all, and end up with wonderful footage. However, that is risky and creates much more work during post-production. A partial script is what many experienced documentary filmmakers use to provide some sense of the structure of the piece. Again, not that the structure might not change later, but it's always better to start out with some sense of direction than none at all. The partial script is also meant to make sure what you are trying to say with the film reaches the audience. Seeing the "film" on paper allows you to see what areas might not be clear and require more research. This will help you in the field to insure you get all the footage you need. Sometimes the partial script also helps you as the producer formulate your viewpoint into a communicative form.

Production: As you begin getting footage for your film, keep aware of many of the ethical issues involved with documentary filmmaking. You are going into people's lives or situations and they may or may not like what they could see as an intrusion. As the producer you need to be the diplomat, the person who can make people feel at ease and open to the camera. You often will need to negotiate access to people or places in order to get the story you are looking for. You need to be assertive, yet tactful and respectful.

Travel: If you are in low-budget land and doing much of the work yourself, you will need to take care of travel for your crew, and possibly your talent. As with bigger budget productions, if you can afford coordinators to handle these details, it will make your life much easier. Chapter 4 has more detailed information about what's involved in traveling crew.

Interviews: Most documentaries have interviews with either experts or people who have experienced the problem of your film. Conducting an interview is an art, and not to be taken lightly. As the producer it will usually be your job to do the interview, or, maybe your director. Make sure you hire a director who knows how to do an interview well. A good interviewer will have questions beforehand that have been gone over and revised as needed. However, do not feel the need to stick to the questions. As the interview proceeds you may find subjects touching upon something interesting. Take them down that path to see where it leads. If it leads nowhere, then get back to your questions. Certainly you want to ask the questions you need to, in order to get the information you want for the film; however, frequently you may find wonderful bits of knowledge, conflicts, or unresolved emotions that come up by just having a conversation. Get what you need, but be open to what may come. Also, consider alternatives to the sit-down interview. Have your subject doing something they love, or walking as you talk. The more visually interesting, the better.

B-roll: If all you did for a documentary were interviews, you would end up with "talking heads" for the length of your film. Nothing is more boring! You need footage to cut into and out of the interviews. This **B-roll** may take the form of stock footage, reenactment, or other footage you have shot. Either way, B-roll should be visually interesting, and add commentary or meaning to the interview. If much of the B-roll is outlined in the partial script, you will be sure to get it and have much more to work with in the editing room. Even if your piece does not use interviews, or uses very little interviews, getting good B-roll to add to your production footage is always a good idea.

The importance of conflict: As your filming progresses, do not lose sight of the importance of conflict in a documentary. If there is no conflict, then you may end up with something that is just informational or educational, which may be desirable, or not. A good documentary retains conflict throughout, sometimes never really resolving it in the end. As the producer, it's your job to keep an eye on the big picture, to insure that everything you or your director is shooting keeps that conflict going.

Post-production: The wonderfully creative thing about documentary is that post-production can reveal what is called "the found story." This may be a story that you never intended to tell, but that came about as a result of the footage and/or interviews. As the producer you need to stay open to this, in case it happens; it may just be a better story to tell than the one you originally started with.

The paper cut: With all the footage you may acquire, assembling it can be daunting. Many documentarians swear by the **paper cut.** This document lays out your footage on paper in its final version, from cut to cut, including audio cues or narration. It gives you the chance to organize the content and see how the structure of the overall piece is working. You can rework and rearrange sequences until you are happy with them, before doing so with your footage, which is a lot more time-consuming.

Screenings: As with many media, screening of your work is important. It is especially important in documentary. As the producer, you have a certain viewpoint to the project, and, if you edit it yourself, it can be easy to lose perspective. Hold screenings for people whose opinion you trust, who will be honest with you about the work. Then, go back and rework it, until it's the best it can be.

PRODUCING MOBILE CONTENT

Producing mobile content is an ever-growing field as more and more smart phones and portable devices flood the market. Currently there are many companies jumping on the mobile content bandwagon. And that's good news for producers who are needed to provide that content. Providers want content that is specifically made for mobile viewing; usually no more than 2–3 minutes that helps create or promote brands. This kind of content is impactful because it uses actors and characters that people can identify with quickly. Sometime mobile content can be produced for creative advertising campaigns. Sometimes mobile content provides a lot of interactivity in the form of games. Still other mobile content can be educational, or informational, as in news and sports features.

To produce mobile content is much the same as typical film production in terms of putting together a crew, shooting it, and editing it. Legal issues in terms of copyright, clearances, and releases also apply. Funding can be a little different in that sometimes producers need to self-fund mobile content and then sell it, like a feature film. However, some mobile content providers are dying for content and have started funding or partial funding of some content. The key is in finding the right mobile operators for the right content and then producing what their audience or subscribers want.

Producing mobile content is more than just filming something with a flip camera. It's staying on top of mobile trends and having an eye for what specific content is needed. Whereas film content originates from a producer, from some inspiration or story to tell, mobile content is consumer based, attempting to provide the public with entertainment or information needed for a specific audience.

PRODUCING ANIMATION

There are many good books on producing animation that cover the process and technical details at length. To outline all of that here, again, would be outside the scope of this book. However, there is something specific about producing animation that the producer should be aware of. The process of animation has been around for a long time and has been changing rapidly over the last decade. A good producer will keep up with the latest trends and techniques in producing either 2D or 3D animation, or a combination of both. Animation productions can take the form of educational or narrative projects, gaming, and even scientific applications. Whatever the form, the producer, as with most projects, is the leader. One difference in producing animation is the time factor. Most animations take much longer to complete than typical live action productions. Keeping track of your director and director of animation is crucial.

With animation there is not just one production schedule, there are animator's schedules as well to deal with to make sure that your backgrounds and characters are being completed in a certain amount of time. As the producer you have to have the endurance to keep the vision going, not only for yourself but also for the crew. You will be asked to view a lot of character models, rigged models, and digital or painted backgrounds, and mostly in the early part of the process, as separate elements. Keeping the original idea for the project in mind is your job, to make sure that all of the separate elements are in line with that vision.

DISTRIBUTION

Again, there are entire books on the distribution process, which really is a business of its own. A good producer will keep up with these trends as they may affect how your project is produced. Traditionally there has been theatrical release for feature films, followed by television distribution and the home video market. Producers were mostly dependent on distribution companies who had the money and advertising power to promote the film. That model still exists today, but there are additions and alternatives.

Web distributors such as Netflix and Hulu provide further distribution to the home market, which then provides an additional revenue stream to the producer. These are deals that can be made before the film is produced or after. Each deal is different depending on what kind of film you have and if these companies feel your film will do well with their audiences.

Other kinds of productions, including educational, promotional, and industrial video, have also usually depended on a distribution company to promote, advertise, and get their projects to their intended audiences. This method is still in use and valid today. However, many independent filmmakers are beginning to self-distribute through various websites. These websites, which are too numerous to mention, will create a space online where your film or shows can be rented, sold, or subscribed to. There are also services that will encode your project so that it can play on a multitude of platforms such as computers and mobile devices. Keep in mind each of these companies handles its deals differently in terms of the revenue stream. Some companies will air projects for free and then retain revenue from advertising. Some companies create revenue streams through their subscription services. Producers can use Internet sites such as YouTube, iTunes, and Facebook to promote their own works as well or to find festivals and distributors that operate through social networks. There is no magic formula here. You need to find the company or Internet distributor or site that works best for your project and that will reach your particular audience and provide the greatest probability for a successful revenue stream.

SUMMARY

The producer's job is to be a leader, to guide a crew through a production to its completion. In today's market the producer should be well versed in the latest trends and technologies as they relate to producing in the field, live events, documentary, mobile content, or animation. The first step is acquiring the right script and working with writers (if you don't do it yourself) to get the best script possible. Remember producing is not just managing the process but also, more importantly, managing people. A good producer will be just as good, if not better, with leading, inspiring, and motivating people to do the best job they can do. If that can be accomplished, you will achieve much more success with your productions.

Script Breakdown and Scheduling

Completing a script breakdown and schedules for your project are two of the most important processes in pre-production. Here is where you will determine exactly what is needed to shoot your film, and when it is needed. This chapter will sketch out this process, which involves breaking down a script into various **elements**, getting that information into the computer, and deriving a realistic schedule from which to work. In addition, the chapter outlines which schedules are appropriate for all crew members and which schedules should go only to certain crew members, such as heads of departments.

To begin with, you should break down your script only when it is **locked**. A script is locked when you are finished making major changes. Minor changes to dialogue or some elements are bound to occur. At the end of this chapter you will find information about how to incorporate those minor changes into schedules you may have already printed.

The process of breaking down a script and creating schedules is pretty much the same from low budget to high budget. The only difference may be in the length of your schedule, which could be shorter because of your budget. Student films can be shot in a couple of days or weeks, depending on the length of your script. For instance, a 20-minute project can be comfortably shot in ten days or less if shooting digitally. Many feature-length low-budget films are shot in four to six weeks because they can only afford a crew for that amount of time. Medium-budget films can usually be shot in two to three months. Some high-budget, special-effects films may take up to a year to shoot. A longer schedule means paying crew for a longer period. When completing your schedule, stay within the confines of your budget, but make sure you have enough time to shoot all you need.

So, who does the breakdown? In low-budget films, the producer most likely will do the breakdown, unless he has hired the **unit production manager** (UPM). In some television applications the first **assistant director** (1st AD) will do the script breakdown, and then have a production assistant enter the data into the scheduling program. Then, the 1st AD most likely will take over the actual scheduling of scenes.

SCHEDULING A FILM: A STEP-BY-STEP OVERVIEW

1. First, read the script. You will find that the first step to a breakdown, marking *elements*, is easier when you know the entire scope of the film. Second, make sure it is in **standard screenplay format**. This is important because in standard screenplay format, one page equals approximately 1 minute of screen time. This formula provides a way for you to make decisions as to how long your final project will be, which is important in the budgeting as well as the scheduling process. Using standard screenplay format also establishes a standard for how long each scene is, which is important in the scheduling process.
2. Break down the script by marking elements either one of two ways. First, use colored pencils. You should have at least ten different colors. You may need more, depending on your script. Alternatively, break down the script using a **tagging** process with screenwriting software.
3. Break down the pages into **eighths** to establish a page count and the length of each scene.
4. Transfer the elements and page count onto **breakdown sheets** (with scheduling software the computer will do this for you).
5. Turn the breakdown sheets into **strips** (the computer can do this). These strips form the **production board**.
6. Arrange the strips on the production board by various parameters.
7. When the strips have been arranged, you will have formed the bones of the schedule.
8. Print out your schedules in readable formats and distribute them to the crew.

THE SCRIPT BREAKDOWN

The script breakdown is a valuable tool for examining and bringing out the different elements of a script. Besides schedules, the breakdown also helps you to create lists of elements such as cast, props, set dressing, stunts, and wardrobe. The breakdown also ensures that these elements show up on set. For this reason, accuracy in the breakdown is crucial. Let's say you mark a scene but forget to mark a character who walks into the room at the end of the scene. That character will not get on the breakdown sheets, which means he will not show up on the strips, which means he will not get on the **day-out-of-days** (DOOD) (a schedule of actors), which means he will not show up on the **call sheet**, which means he will not get called with a **call time**, which means he will not show up on set the day you shoot that scene! It is wise to always double-check your work.

There are two ways of completing a breakdown: by hand and electronically, using screenwriting software. Each has its own advantages and disadvantages. Both methods will be covered in this chapter.

Electronically—Scheduling Software

There are a few programs for scheduling. The software most widely used is Movie Magic Scheduling. It is also the most expensive, but definitely worth it.

Breaking down the script electronically involves the process of **tagging** elements. If you are using Movie Magic Screenwriter or Final Draft, the program describes how to do it. Essentially what you do is go through the script and mark each element with a "tag." The tag tells you what category the element is. For instance, you would tag the word "watch" as belonging to the wardrobe category. When you are finished tagging all the elements, you can then import the file into Movie Magic Scheduling. The program will create breakdown sheets for you, with each element in its proper category on the sheet. Breaking down your script electronically can be advantageous in that the process is fast. There is one major disadvantage to this process. The computer does all the work. There may be nuances in the words of the script that the computer will not translate accurately. The major disadvantage for breaking down a script electronically is that the computer will miss some elements because, frequently, elements are carried over from scene to scene, although the script may not state that explicitly. A computer does not know how to read into a scene to determine if the element *should* exist, only if it does.

Second, it is important to know your script inside and out. Having the computer do all the work for you eliminates the process of getting to know the script intimately, which doesn't happen if you break down your script by hand. One way to make the electronic process work to your advantage is to tag your elements, import the broken-down script into the scheduling program, print your breakdown sheets, and then double-check the sheets against the script. This way you can know for sure how the computer interpreted the elements, and you can find any elements the computer may have missed.

By Hand

In order to break a script down by hand, you will need your script and colored pencils. Start with the first scene. Read through the scene and underline or mark the appropriate elements with the appropriate color or notation. This can be time-consuming, so allow yourself about 6–8 hours for a feature-length screenplay.

WHAT ARE THE ELEMENTS?

Elements are items in a script that need to be identified, such as cast members, props, and wardrobe. By identifying these elements, you can later see them in various lists and schedules, which ensures they will be available on set. The schedules also put the elements into a form that makes them easy to find and organize. Following is a list of elements you need to identify and their descriptions. There are two ways of marking the elements: Either you go through the entire script, marking one element, or you mark all of the elements scene by scene. The golden rule here is: *Mark elements only one time per scene.* The different colors you use to mark each element listed below are standard for the industry. However, you can use different colors if you choose, as long as you do a key to tell yourself which colors refer to which elements. If you are marking elements electronically, you will find a list of these elements in the software.

Speaking Cast (Underline in Red)

Speaking cast are characters who have dialogue. If characters do not have dialogue in one scene, that does not mean they are not speaking cast. They may have dialogue in a following scene. This is why it is wise to read the entire script beforehand. If a character *ever* speaks in the film, she is considered speaking cast, and you should tag her name or underline it in red pencil. If a character is written as speaking offscreen (O.S.), you should still mark her as being in the scene. Whether the character is actually seen on screen is irrelevant. The director may still want the actor on set to "play off" the on-screen actor. It is better to have everyone there and maybe not need them than to not have them there and absolutely need them.

Extras/Atmosphere (Underline in Green)

Atmosphere are **extras** who usually appear as crowd members, people walking down the street, people in the background. They do not have dialogue and do not have any special skills or physical anomalies that would qualify them as **silent bits**.

Silent Bits (Underline in Yellow)

Silent bits are extras who have some form of physical characteristic or skill that would separate them from being normal extras, or atmosphere. For example, a silent bit may be a juggler in a circus scene or the musicians in a quartet.

Props (Underline in Lime) and Set Dressing (Underline in Purple)

The traditional definition of a prop is any item that an actor touches or uses in a scene. Do not get this confused with set dressing. Just because an actor touches a television set to turn it on does not make the television set a prop. The TV is set dressing because it dresses the set. If you were shooting a dinner scene, the plates, silverware, table, and chairs would all be set dressing. However, the food items on the table would be props.

Wardrobe (Circle the Item)

You mark wardrobe when there is any specific type of wardrobe mentioned. For instance, the script may say the character looks at his watch. Draw a circle around the word *watch* (regular pencil is okay). Alternatively, the script might say the character enters the room wearing a long evening gown. Circle the words *evening gown*. Other items, besides clothing, that are included under wardrobe are purses, glasses, jewelry, and hats.

Makeup (Mark with an Asterisk)

You mark makeup when either the script refers specifically to a certain style of makeup such as sweat or heavy makeup or there is occasion for **special-effects makeup**, such as blood or a gunshot wound.

Stunts (Underline in Orange)

Sometimes it is hard to determine if an event in the script is a stunt. Perhaps you have a character who trips over a bucket and falls down. Is that a stunt? Well, it definitely is a stunt if the character is a ninety-year-old man. However, it probably would not be a stunt if the character were a twenty-year-old woman. The best thing to do is to always mark an event as a stunt, even if you are not sure. Later, the producer, director, and/or **stunt coordinator** will make a final determination on stunts. At this point, it is only your job to point them out.

Special Effects (Underline in Blue)

Traditionally, special effects were anything from a car explosion to a building catching on fire. With the advent of computer-generated images (CGI), special effects can include anything from dinosaurs eating people to a bullet that can be seen traveling slowly through the air. Mark as special effects anything that cannot be created in real life or that requires **pyrotechnics**. In addition, because more special effects are being done with CGI, one trend is to delineate between on-set special effects and CGI. If you think you might have the budget to do CGI, mark these effects with a different color.

Sound Effects (Underline in Brown)

If a script is written properly, sound effects will appear in capital letters. The script may say that a character hears a telephone "RING." Underline the word *ring* in brown. A script may also have an O.S. narrator, who would qualify as a **sound effect**. Generally, these sound effects are ones that you do not expect to record on set, but that will be added later, in post-production. Be careful: There is a difference between *narration* and *O.S.* A character speaking O.S. is not a sound effect, but a narrator is.

Special Equipment (Draw a Box around the Action)

Special equipment refers to events that might not be photographable with equipment that you would normally have on set. For instance, a scene may describe a bird's-eye view that follows someone walking down the street. Getting that shot will probably require a crane and that is special equipment. After you draw a box around the action, make a note in the right-hand margin of the page or in the notes section about what kind of special equipment will be required. You will then put that piece of equipment on the breakdown sheet.

Vehicles and Animals/Livestock (Underline in Pink)

Anytime the script indicates the presence of an animal, whether it is as large as an elephant or as small as a fly, underline it in pink. Also, when the script indicates that a certain vehicle is present, underline that in pink. Remember, a vehicle can be more than just a car. Any motorized vehicle, such as a boat, plane, train, motorcycle, or spaceship, qualifies as a vehicle. For instance, the script might say that a character leaves his house, gets into his van, and drives away. Underline the word *van* in pink. Because **picture vehicles** (vehicles seen on-screen) fall under the transportation department and animals fall under the casting department, you may mark them in different colors as well.

Music (Underline in Aqua)

If your script identifies a place where music is heard, you would mark it as music. There are three different kinds of music that could appear in your final project. These are production, source, and **underscore**. Underscore is the music that plays under a scene. It is usually composed specifically for a project and is added in post-production. **Production music** is music that may be recorded live on set or pre-recorded and played back on set. People singing a song or a musician playing a piano are examples of production music. **Source music** is music that comes from a specific source, such as a radio or jukebox. Production and source music are the elements you want to break down. When marking music, it is also a good idea to identify on the breakdown sheet the name of the song or piece. This way you can begin the process of music **clearance** early in the production.

OTHER CATEGORIES

There are more elements that can be broken down in a script, depending on the amount of detail the producer would like. These elements can be underlined in the script with additional colors of your choice. Since the breakdown is an internal document and not distributed to crew, as long as you know which color is being used for a certain element, you can choose any additional colors you like. Following is a list of additional elements that may be marked in a breakdown.

Animal Handler

In many cases, when an element in the script is tagged as animal or livestock, it is assumed that an **animal handler** will be employed. However, some prefer to specifically identify when an animal handler will be required. The advantage of also marking for an animal handler is that, if you know you need many handlers, this point can be delineated in the breakdown. For instance, if your script calls for a herd of horses, you will most likely need more than one animal handler to wrangle them. You can then put the number of wranglers needed next to the element on the breakdown sheet.

Greenery

Greenery is any plant or foliage that is specifically identified in the script. For instance, the script may call for a garden full of white roses. Since finding a location that specifically has a garden full of only white roses could be difficult, the roses will have to be placed in the location by the greens department. Some people prefer to mark greenery under set dressing. If you are marking greenery, make sure that the elements are not being doubled up under set dressing.

Security

Breaking down in your script where security is needed is a judgment call. For instance, if the script calls for a scene to take place at night in a dangerous neighborhood, you may want security to ensure the safety of your crew. If you are not sure whether security would be required, it is always best to mark the element and then decide later.

Additional Labor

Additional labor could mean additional **camera operators**, assistant camerapersons, makeup, hair, wardrobe, drivers, construction crew, and more. Additional labor is usually needed on days when there are large numbers of cast or major stunts and special effects. For instance, the script calls for a large battle scene with hundreds of soldiers. You will need additional makeup people to make up these soldiers, additional wardrobe people to dress the soldiers, additional weapons people to arm the soldiers, and additional stunt personnel to handle any of the fighting that qualifies as stunts.

Optical Effects/CGI or Visual Effects

Optical effects, CGI or visual effects, are elements that call for effects to be created in post-production or on a computer in production. The traditional title for this category has been *optical effects*. However, as *CGI* has become a more popular term, many people are using it in their breakdowns. Additionally visual or digital effects can also be used. At this point in the process, you may not know whether an effect will be attempted on set or if CGI will be used. In some cases the use of CGI will be obvious. For instance, if a scene calls for a person to morph into a robot, you would mark this occurrence as CGI. In another case the scene could call for a spaceship to crash into a mountain. You may not know whether this effect will be accomplished with models or CGI. You make the judgment call based on what you know of your budget. CGI can be expensive. Unless you know for sure that you will be able to afford CGI, mark the element as a special effect instead.

Miscellaneous

This category is left for anything you might find in your script that does not qualify as another element.

Notes

The notes category is for any notes you might want to make during the course of your breakdown. For instance, I once worked a show in which, halfway through the story, the lead character dyes his hair blond. We made notes on each break-down page where he appeared, of what his hair color needed to be. This way, when it came to scheduling the actor, we could find and shoot all of the scenes with his hair one color, and then plan to dye his hair and shoot the scenes with the other hair color.

A NOTE ON CONTINUITY

Be aware of **continuity** of elements. A script could say that a character walks into a scene with, for example, a briefcase. The script may then cut to the next scene, which is continuous (meaning one scene happens immediately after the other in real time). In this next scene the script might not stipulate that the character is still carrying his briefcase, but he should be. You need to watch for these kinds of continuity nuances. What you do is make a note in the right-hand margin of this next scene. Just writing the word *briefcase* is sufficient. You will find many elements that need to be carried over like this.

You also need to be aware of character names that may change. For instance, the writer may have a character called Jim in the first scene. In this scene the character is four years old. Later in the script, when the character is twenty years old, he could still appear in the script as Jim. What you need to do is delineate the four-year-old Jim from the twenty-year-old Jim. You can do this by calling the four-year-old Young Jim and the twenty-year-old, Jim. Be sure to check with your writer and producer on this, as changing character names qualify as a script change, which must always have the approval of the producer.

BREAKING THE SCRIPT INTO "EIGHTHS"

Now that you have finished marking the elements, you will need to determine how long each scene is. Breaking down the script into eighths is the process of taking each scene and determining how many pages long it is. A scene can be a portion of a page long, a whole page, or more than a page. Because scenes are different lengths, there is a minimum unit of measurement that is used to determine a scene's length, and that is *eighths*. The use of eighths as opposed to some other fraction comes from the calculation that there are approximately 8 inches of typed copy on one page of script in standard screenplay format. Therefore, the minimum unit of measurement, eighths, was created.

To begin, draw a straight horizontal line between each scene, as in Figure 2.1, for the entire script. Next, you need to determine how long each scene will be. The standard formula for the page is that *eight-eighths equals one page*. The standard formula for the length of an eighth is that one-eighth (1/8) equals 1 vertical inch on the page, indicating that this scene may not take long to shoot. However, that approach does not allow for the content of the scene. Here, some of your own judgment needs to come into play. A scene may only be 1 inch long, yet it may involve stunts and special effects that require a whole day to shoot. What you need to do here is to consider not only the length the scene takes up on the page, but also the amount of time the scene might take to shoot. Again, there is no exact right or wrong here: You make the judgment call. If a scene is only 1 inch long on the page (vertically) but would take a better part of the day to shoot, make it four-eighths long. If you have more than eight scenes on a page, you will then have more than eight-eighths to a page. That is okay. Just make sure each scene has a length in eighths. You also need to be aware of scenes that may be five or more pages in length. See the section "The Breakdown Sheet."

11   EXT. FOREST—DAY

Regina, Fila and the Wochera stand in the forest with Donato and the doctor and a crowd of children.

> Regina, Fila and Donato are speaking cast, so would be underlined in RED. The Wochera and crowd of children are extras, so would be underline in GREEN.

REGINA

Thank you.

Slayvnak reacts with surprise. Fila brandishes her gun.

DR. SLAYVNAK

Well, oh, yes, well, that's quite alright.

6/8

> Notice this scene is 6/8's of a page long.

REGINA

Are we ready?

FILA

I've sent several Wochera ahead to clear the tubes. You should be safe there. Do you remember the way?

> The gun is props and would be underlined in LIME.

REGINA

How could I forget.

Regina hugs Fila as a loud CRASH, followed by SCREAMS, is heard, coming from below.

> The crash and screams are sound effects and would be underlined in BROWN.

DONATO

What's that?

REGINA

You need to trust me. Fila, make sure our good doctor gets safely back to his laboratory.

> Notice Donato and the Wochera are underlined only at the beginning of the scene. You only underline an element one time per scene.

She grabs Donato and leads him from the room. A few of the Wochera women follow.

12   EXT. WOCHERA COMMUNITY TOWER/FRONT ENTRANCE—NIGHT

2/8   Prono stands before a hole, blown into the front door of the tower. He climbs inside the hole and falls to the ground.

> Falls to the ground is a stunt, so would be underlined in ORANGE.

FIGURE 2.1
Sample Broken-Down Script Page.

13   INT. WOCHERA COMMUNITY TOWER/FRONT ROOM—NIGHT

<u>Prono</u> gets up and looks around the room. He starts to laugh. His laughter becomes hysterical as his <u>body begins to disintegrate</u>.

<u>Regina</u> and the <u>Wochera</u> climb down on some branches. They watch Prono.

Another <u>EXPLOSION</u> rips through the wall. This shakes the tower and Fila, losing her footing, falls to the ground.

4/8

REGINA

FILA!

Fila lies on the ground, her <u>leg twisted</u> and bent so that it lies next to her ear.

REGINA

(to another Wochera)
Stop them on the outside.

<u>WOCHERA #1</u>

Done. You need to get to
the castle. Use tube five.

Regina climbs back up the tree.

---

14   EXT. WOCHERA COMMUNITY TOWER/FRONT ENTRANCE—NIGHT

The <u>castle guards</u> stand in front of the new hole in the wall, not wanting to step foot inside.

Suddenly, pink sheer material flies across the hole.

The guards all step back.

A few <u>Wochera</u> appear in the hole.

The guards raise their <u>scanners</u>.

4/8

One Wochera walks slowly up to Castle Guard #2; she smiles demurely. She slowly unbuttons one button at the top of her <u>gown</u>. It falls to the ground.

Castle Guard #2 smiles.

The other Wochera come out through the hole, with their hands on their top buttons. The guards drop their weapons.

FIGURE 2.1
Continued

Once you determine the eighths, write the number of eighths for each scene on the left side of the page. See Figure 2.1 for an example of two script pages broken into eighths. After you have divided your script into eighths, you can then count how long a scene is. In the example, the first scene is six-eighths page long and the next scene is two-eighths page long. On page two of the example each scene is four-eighths page long. Later you will record the length of each scene on a breakdown sheet. You are now ready to convert these broken-down script pages into breakdown sheets.

THE BREAKDOWN SHEET

All the elements you either marked by pencil or tagged in the computer are then put into the breakdown sheet. See Figure 2.2 for an example of a breakdown sheet. If you are doing the breakdown by hand, the procedure is to take one scene and place each element from the script into its proper category on the breakdown sheet. For instance, in scene eleven *Regina, Fila, Wochera, Donato,* and *Dr. Slayvnak* go into the cast category. The gun goes into the props category, and *CRASH* and *SCREAMS* go into the sound effects category. For scene twelve, *Prono* goes into the cast category and *fall to the ground* will be put in the stunts category on the breakdown sheet. Repeat this process scene by scene until all of the scenes have a corresponding breakdown sheet.

An additional consideration when creating breakdown sheets is **cast numbering** and **multiple elements**. Cast numbering is the process of giving each character in the script a cast number. These numbers can be assigned by giving the leading character *1*. The next role down in terms of size and importance gets *2*, and so on. Continue to number all the speaking cast in this order. The more important the role is, the lower the number. It is always a good idea to leave a group of numbers between the speaking cast and extras. Let's say your last speaking cast is numbered *32*. Begin numbering extras at *57*. There is no hard rule here. Just make sure there is a gap. The reason for this is that in the course of production a cast member may be added to the script. This gap leaves room to give the new character a lower number than the extras.

Extras are considered *multiple elements*. This means that one element, extras, will actually require a multiple of people on set. When numbering extras, be sure to estimate how many extras may be required. There is no way you can know this figure for certain at this point, because the number is determined by a combination of budget considerations and the director's vision for the scene. Making an estimation is all that is needed at this point in the process. For instance, for scene eleven you would put the crowd of children in the breakdown sheet as "62. Crowd of Children (12)," where sixty-two is the cast number and twelve is the number of children in the crowd.

Generally, one breakdown sheet equals one scene, but there are exceptions. For instance, the first consideration is: What is the maximum number of pages you plan to shoot each day? If the answer is four, then you need to make sure none of your breakdown sheets contain a scene that is more than four pages long. If a scene is more than four pages long, you need to break the scene into two different breakdown pages. This way, when each of these breakdown sheets gets converted into a strip on the production board, the scene can be split up and can be shot on more than one day.

The computer may number the breakdown sheets automatically, or you may number each breakdown sheet differently. There is no set rule here. For instance, let's say scene number fifteen is eight pages long. You can split the scene into two different breakdown sheets, breaking it into four pages and four pages. Then, when you put the scene number on the breakdown sheet for the first half of the scene, you can name it "15 part 1" and the second half, "15 part 2." Or, you can name them "15 **partial**" and "15 partial." What you name each one is a matter of preference.

CODE:
DAY EXT: YELLOW   **SCRIPT**
NIGHT EXT: GREEN   **BREAKDOWN SHEET**   DATE: 4/30/03
DAY INT: WHITE   "Regina of Icelandia"
NIGHT INT: BLUE

Frame Right Films	8978978	11
Production Company	Production Title No.	Breakdown Page No.
11	Forest	Ext.
Scene No.	Scene Name	Int. or Ext.
Regina & Donato continue chasing Prono.		Day
Description		Day or Night
		6/8
		Page Count

CAST	STUNTS	EXTRAS/ATMOSPHERE
1. Regina		
2. Donato		62. Crowd of Children (12)
3. Wochera		
6. Slayvnak		
10. Fila		
11. Zana		
	EXTRAS/SILENT BITS	
SPECIAL EFFECTS	**PROPS**	**VEHICLES/ANIMALS**
	Gun	
WARDROBE	**MAKEUP/HAIR**	**SOUND EFFECTS/MUSIC**
		Crash
		Screams
SPECIAL EQUIPMENT	**PRODUCTION NOTES**	

FIGURE 2.2

When you have completed creating all the breakdown sheets, the computer will convert these sheets into your **strip board**, also known as the production board.

THE STRIP OR PRODUCTION BOARD

The strip, or production, board is a representation of your breakdown sheets where each breakdown sheet equals one strip. See Figure 2.3. These strips, which in the "old days" used to be written by hand on cardboard strips, are the bones of your schedule. If you are using scheduling software, the computer automatically creates the strips after you have completed the breakdown sheets. At this point, strips are in "breakdown order," or the order in which you created the breakdown sheets. It is unlikely that you would ever shoot your film in this order. You now need to rearrange these strips into the order in which you will shoot. This process will create your **production schedule**. The strips, whether cardboard or in the computer, are also color coded as follows:

- Yellow = exterior day
- White = interior day
- Green = exterior night
- Blue = interior night

This color-coding system allows you to see more easily what is day, night, exterior, and interior, which makes rearranging the strips easier. The strip board also contains a **header board** (see Figure 2.3). This board has information, such as the name of the director, producer, and 1st AD. The header board also lists the characters' names vertically, which allows you to locate each of them across the strip board. If you have a large cast, the board will have two columns of character names in order to fit them on the same board.

CREATING A SCHEDULE

The process of creating a schedule means rearranging your strips based on various scheduling parameters. Scheduling parameters are considerations you make when deciding what to shoot and when to shoot it. The following parameters are listed in order of importance. Keep in mind that these parameters are only guidelines. Certain situations may necessitate that you consider, for instance, cast before sets. This is rare, but it can happen. Let's say you have a cast member who can shoot only within a certain time frame. You then need to shoot all of her scenes together. This consideration places cast as a parameter ahead of sets in order of importance. Otherwise, beginning with the order below will work well.

SCHEDULING PARAMETERS

Geography

If your shoot requires you to shoot in different states or countries, start by ordering your strips by these locations.

				Sheet Number:	24	18	22		21	25
				Page Count:	3/8	5/8	2 1/8		7/8	3 2/8
				Shoot Day:	1	1	1		2	2
"Regina of Icelandia"					EXT. FOREST—DAY—Sc. 4	EXT. FOREST—DAY—Sc. 8	EXT. FOREST—DAY—Sc. 34	End of Day 1 – 4/30/03 – 3 1/8	INT. CASTLE—NIGHT—Sc. 9	INT. CASTLE—NIGHT—Sc.
Director: Darin Wales Producer: Lorene Wales Asst. Director: Joe Smith Script Dated: 4/2/01										
Character		Character								
Regina	1	Margee	2		1/2	1	1		2	1
Donato	3	Alb	4		3	3	4		3	
Wochera	5	Sino	6		7					
Helma	7	Phillippe	8							
Sinjoo	9	Reporter	10							
Slayvnak	11	Police #1	12							
Eda	13	Police #2	14							
King	15	Carter	16		15					
Tree Princess	17	Palace Guard	18							
Merla	19	Palace Doctor	20							
Zana	21	Sammuio	22							
Zuauu	23	Grumpy child	24				23			
Wochera #1	25	Suitor	26		25		25			
Wochera #2	27	Forest Guard	28				27			
			Extras:		E100		E25			
					Regina & Margee discuss plans.	Regina & Donato run away.	Regina & Donato meet others in fore		Regina & Donato hide.	Regina waits in her quarters.
Prepared by: Lorene M. Wales										

FIGURE 2.3

Sample Strip Board or Production Board.

Set

Next, order your strips according to sets. You do not want to go back to the same location more than once. Doing so is inefficient and does not make for good relations with your locations.

Cast Members

When cast members are scheduled to be on set, they are working. However, you may not need a certain cast member every day. If you are doing a union shoot, the in-between days are considered "hold" days. During **hold days** you must pay the actor, but he is not allowed to leave the location (meaning city, not set) and must be available by telephone. If an actor has more than ten hold days, you need to do what's called a **drop–pickup**. This means you will drop the actor from contract and pick him up later. In addition, you can only drop–pickup an actor one time per film. This can make scheduling multiple actors a challenge. What you want to do is to schedule your actors so that, as much as possible, all of their shooting days are together and with the least amount of holding time. In low budget, when you use nonunion actors, these rules are not mandatory but still a good idea since this practice also cuts down on travel to and from location for actors.

Day/Night

As you schedule your scenes you must pay attention to **turnaround**. Turnaround is the time between camera **wrap** (in most cases) and crew call the next morning. Most production companies use a 10-hour turnaround, but some use 12. Therefore, you should not schedule an exterior night scene and then an exterior day scene the next morning. If you were to do this, the crew would have no turnaround at all. I have seen some student films attempt to shoot without much turnaround. This situation usually leads to an unhappy and less productive crew. It is possible to have a short golden hour or evening exterior at the end of the day and then schedule an exterior day the next morning, as long as you give enough turnaround and have enough light to shoot the following day's **exteriors**.

It is usually a good idea to schedule all night exteriors together because shooting a full night of exteriors requires starting when it gets dark and filming through the night. Your crew will take about two to three days to adjust their body clocks to being up all night and sleeping during the day. If you then put a day off between the night exteriors and your next day exteriors, your crew will have time to readjust to working during the day.

EXT/INT

Because of weather, it is wiser to shoot your exteriors first. This way, if you do have to cancel a shoot day because of the weather, you will have the option of doing **interiors** until the weather clears. The interiors that you choose to go to are called *cover sets*. Cover sets should be arranged in pre-production. This means that in pre-production your location people make an arrangement with owners of interior locations that the crew have the option to shoot there if weather forbids them from shooting certain exteriors.

Sequence

There are many definitions of what a **sequence** is. In the process of scheduling, a sequence is a portion of your script that takes place at a certain time. For instance, if your script has a flashback to the 1920s, you should shoot all of the 1920s scenes together. Let's say you have a street scene set for the 1920s. Your art department dresses the shop fronts. Your transportation brings in valuable vintage cars. Your **costume designer** orders vintage clothing for the actors. These departments will certainly not want to re-dress an entire street scene like this more than once! Also when scheduling these sequences, make sure your art department gets enough prep and **strike** time.

Children

When working with children, there are many considerations. First, children are children; they have short attention spans and little patience when it comes to working all day on a film set, where the pace can appear to move pretty slowly. If you are working on a union shoot and your cast belongs to the Screen Actors Guild (SAG), you need to follow strict rules as to how long children can work and how many breaks they must have (check out www.sag.org for a full list of rules). If working nonunion, you may be required by child labor laws in most states to submit an application for a **theatrical permit** or **minor permit**. Each state is different in how strictly it requires you to stick to these permits. Check the department of labor for the state you are working in for details. In low budget, you could theoretically work them all you want. However, this is not wise. Tired children will not perform well for long hours anyway. Therefore, you want to schedule children for short periods.

Time of Year/Climate

Are you shooting during the winter months, when the amount of available light is shorter? Are you shooting in July in California, when you can be pretty much guaranteed a full 12 hours of sunlight? Granted, your script or finances may dictate when you have to shoot, but the climate and time of year can affect your shoot. Many areas of the Northeast have months when it mostly rains, such as Pittsburgh in April and May. Shoot in upstate New York in January and you will definitely have a crew working in freezing temperatures. I once worked on a film that shot in mid-July in the Mojave Desert—on a dry lake bed, no less. There was no shade anywhere, and the temperatures were above 105 degrees daily. The crew members were dropping like flies.

Special Effects and Stunts

Unless you have a script with so many stunts or special effects that these crews would be there for **run of show**, you need to schedule all stunts together and all special effects together. To have someone be there for run of show means that they are there the whole time, as opposed to just coming in when needed. Also, if you have a couple of major effects or stunts, you should not schedule them back to back, as your team may need prep time.

Second Camera/Second Unit

Some people get second camera and **second unit** confused. The second camera is the one you use either when you need another camera (or cameras) on set to get extra angles on a tight schedule or when you need extra angles of a stunt or special effect. Famous Japanese director Akira Kurosawa used to shoot with three cameras simultaneously so his actors would not know which camera to play to. However, unless you have the influence or money Kurosawa did, you will most likely shoot with one camera.

The crew shooting your main scenes is your first unit. The second unit may be a small crew that gets **"beauty shots,"** such as sunsets, panoramas, or vistas not requiring actors. Second unit also may be a small crew that shoots crowd shots or minor scenes without the main actors. Second unit can also be a large crew, such as an **aerial unit** that shoots only aerial footage that may involve your main cast or not (see more about who's involved in the second unit in Chapter 6). You determine if you need second crew by how tight or how involved your schedule is. If you find you do need a second unit, then you will need to do its breakdown sheets separately and put all second unit personnel in their own schedule, separate from the first unit.

Special Equipment

Special equipment is defined as any extra piece of equipment you may need to accomplish a shot, something you would not normally have. This equipment can be a helicopter with a special camera mount to get aerial shots, a rainmaker to create rain, an underwater camera, a shotmaker to get car interiors while driving, or, in low budget, a **steadicam** (in higher budget productions a steadicam is usually run of show because they can afford it).

PUTTING THE SCHEDULE TOGETHER

Now that you have considered these parameters, rearrange your strips. Take time and think about your schedule. There are many parameters to consider and they all must be evaluated carefully. Some other things to watch out for are key scenes that may require emotional strain on your actors. Do not schedule these scenes first because the actors may not be ready. Do not schedule these scenes at the end of a long day when your actors might be tired. It is usually best not to schedule very heavy days first in the schedule. Any crew will take a few days to "gel" and get into a smooth working mode. Easier days to begin with will allow the crew to gel better.

"Regina of Icelandia"

Shooting Schedule

Shoot Day #1—Monday, July 6, 2002

EXT. FOREST	DAY	PAGES
Scene 21	Establishing shot, the forest	1/8

EXT. FOREST	DAY	
Scene 45	Regina and Donato run through the woods	1 4/8

Cast
 1. Regina
 2. Donato

Props
 Scanners
 Bowl

Costumes
 Regina's pink gown

INT. CASTLE	DAY	
Scene 103	The King talks with Regina and the Wochera	2 4/8

Cast
 1. Regina
 5. Wochera
 6. Wochera #1
 15. King

Props
 Scanners

Costumes
 Pink hooded gowns

End of Day #1—4 1/8 Total Pages

Shoot Day #2—Tuesday, July 7, 2002

INT. LAB	DAY	
Scene 3	The future queen is chosen.	3 1/8

Cast
 1. Regina
 2. Donato
 9. Children

Props
 Medical equipment
 Computer notepad

End of Day #2—3 1/8 Total Pages

FIGURE 2.4
Shooting Schedule.

SCHEDULES TO PRINT

After you have arranged your strips according to the schedule you desire, it's time to print out readable versions to distribute to your crew.

Shooting Schedule

This schedule takes all the information on your strips and prints it in a readable format. Because it is so comprehensive, including all the elements, it is quite a sizeable document. You will distribute this schedule to heads of departments only (see Figure 2.4). Heads of departments include the following: producer, director, first AD, production manager, director of photography, **key grip**, gaffer, costume designer, **production designer**, props, makeup, **art director**, special-effects supervisor, **sound mixer, transportation coordinator**, location manager, and **second unit director** (if you have one).

Production Schedule

The production schedule takes a more limited amount of information from your strips. Typically, it will only include a scene description, scene number, a note about whether the scene is exterior or interior, whether the scene is day or night, and what cast is involved (see Figure 2.5). Because it is not as comprehensive as the shooting schedule, it is distributed to all crew members.

One-Liner

The one-liner is like a production schedule in that it has more limited information than a full shooting schedule. The distinctive thing about the one-liner is that it is sometimes in scene order. You may need to look at a scene to remember what actors

"Regina of Icelandia"

Production Schedule

Shoot Day #1—Monday, July 6, 2002

Scene				**Description**	**Pages**	**Cast**
Sc. 21	EXT.	FOREST	DAY	Establishing shot, the forest	1/8	N.A.
Sc. 45	EXT.	FOREST	DAY	Regina & Donato run thru woods.	1 4/8	1,2
Sc. 10	INT.	CASTLE	DAY	King talks with Regina & Wochera.	2 /48	1,5,6

End of Day #1—4 1/8 Total Pages

Shoot Day #2—Tuesday, July 7, 2002

Sc. 3	INT.	LAB	DAY	The future queen is chosen.	3 1/8	1,2,9

End of Day #2—3 1/8 Total Pages

Shoot Day #3—Wednesday, July 8, 2002

Sc. 43	EXT.	WO HOUSE	DAY	The Wochera prepare the queen.	5/8	1,45,46
Sc. 3	EXT.	DESERT	DAY	Wochera take Regina away.	3/8	1,45,46

End of Day #3—8/8 Total Pages

Shoot Day #4—Thursday, July 9, 2002

Sc. 5	INT.	CASTLE	NIGHT	King takes court.	1/8	1, 44
Sc. 35	INT.	CASTLE	DAY	King counsels Regina.	2 3/8	1,5
Sc. 88	INT.	CASTLE	DAY	King and Regina plot revenge.	2	1,5

End of Day #4—4 4/8 Total Pages

FIGURE 2.5
Production Schedule.

play, or whether it is a night exterior or day interior. If you tried to find the scene in the production or shooting schedule, you would need to remember what date you were shooting the scene. Obviously, flipping through twenty or so pages of a production or shooting schedule is not efficient. Since the one-liner is in scene order, you can quickly find the scene. This schedule is generally only distributed to heads of departments. See Figure 2.6.

Day-Out-of-Days

The DOOD is a schedule that shows when cast members work (Figure 2.7). Because it is in chart form, it is easy to see when an actor starts (S), works (W), and finishes (F). This schedule also gives you a chance to see when actors are being put on hold (H) or dropped (D) and picked up (P). You will notice that one day an actor might be an "SWF." This means that the actor starts, works, and finishes in one day. An actor's first day is always written as "SW," meaning it is a "start–work." An actor's last day is always written as "WF," meaning it is a "work–finish." All other days when actors work are written as "W." This form is distributed to the production team, director's team, and any heads of departments that work with cast, such as wardrobe and makeup.

"Regina of Icelandia"

One-Liner Schedule

Scene				Description	Pages	Cast
Sc. 1	EXT.	FOREST	DAY	Establishing shot, the forest	1/8	N.A.
Sc. 2	EXT.	FOREST	DAY	Regina & Donato run thru woods.	1 4/8	1,2
Sc. 3	INT.	CASTLE	DAY	King talks with Regina & Wochera.	2 /48	1,5,6
Sc. 4	INT.	LAB	DAY	The future queen is chosen.	3 1/8	1,2,9
Sc. 5	EXT.	WO HOUSE	DAY	The Wochera prepare the queen.	5/8	1,45,46
Sc. 6	EXT.	DESERT	DAY	Regina returns home.	4 2/8	1,3,6 45,46
Sc. 7	EXT.	DESERT	DAY	Wochera take Regina away.	3/8	1,45,46
Sc. 8	INT.	CASTLE	NIGHT	King takes court.	1/8	1, 44
Sc. 9	INT.	CASTLE	DAY	King counsels Regina.	2 3/8	1,5
Sc. 10	INT.	CASTLE	DAY	King and Regina plot revenge.	2	1,5
Sc. 11	INT.	LAB	NIGHT	Doctor gives test.	1/8	1, 44
Sc. 12	INT.	LAB	NIGHT	Doctor fixes test.	4 2/8	6
Sc. 13	INT.	DESERT	DAY	Regina finds Donato.	2 1/8	1,2
Sc. 14	INT.	CASTLE	NIGHT	King admonishes Prono.	6/8	5, 12
Sc. 15	INT.	FOREST	DAY	Donato & Regina chased.	2 3/8	1,2
Sc. 16	INT.	WO HOUSE	DAY	Wochera prepare.	2	44,45

FIGURE 2.6
One-Liner Schedule.

Day-Out-of-Days
"Regina of Icelandia"

Report Created Tuesday, April 29, 2002

	Day of Month	6	7	8	9	10	11	12	13	14	15
	Day of Week	Mon	Tu	Wed	Thu	Fri	Sat	Sun	Mon	Tu	Wed
	Shooting Days	1	2	3	4	5	6		8	9	10
1	Regina	SW	W	W	W	W	W		W	W	W
2	Margee	SW	W	W	W	H	H		H	H	H
3	Donato			SW	W	W	W		W	W	W
4	Alb	SW	W	W	W	W	W		W	W	W
5	Wochera	SW	W	W	W	W	W		W	W	W
6	Sino			SW	W	W	W		W	W	W
7	Helma	SW	W	W	W	W	W		W	W	W
8	Phillippe			SW	W	W	W		W	W	W
9	Sinjoo				SW	W			W	W	W
10	Reporter	SW	W	WF							
11	Slayvnak									SW	SWF
12	Police #1			SWF							
13	Eda								SW	W	WF
14	Police #2			SWF							
15	King					SW	W		W	W	W
16	Carter						SWF				
17	Tree Princess	SW	W	W	W	W	WF				
18	Palace Guard				SWF						
19	Merla	SW	W	W	W	W	W		WF		
20	Palace Doctor								SW	W	WF
21	Zana									SW	WF
22	Sammuio					SW	WF				
23	Zuauu			SW	W	W	WF				
24	Grumpy Child						SWF				
25	Wochera #1	SW	W	W	W	W	W		W	W	W
26	Suitor								SW	SWF	
27	Wochera #2					SWF					
28	Forest Guard								SWF		

FIGURE 2.7

UPDATING YOUR SCHEDULE

You have now completed scheduling your production. However, no schedule is re-ally ever completed. The nature of production is that situations change daily. You will most likely be changing your schedule several times during pre-production. This is normal. When this happens, go back to your strips, rearrange them in the new order, and reprint your schedules. There may be times when more than just the order of scenes will change. For instance, let's say the director writes a new scene that must be incorporated into the schedule. You will need to break down the scene into elements, create a new breakdown page, and insert that page into your other breakdown sheets. The computer will then create a new strip, which can be placed in the strip board at the appropriate place. As before, reprint your schedules. For another example, maybe you will decide to delete an actor from a scene. Go back to the original breakdown sheet and delete the actor. Your computer will automatically delete the actor from the strips. Reprint and distribute the new schedules. With all this reprinting you may be wondering how people know they have the most recently updated schedule. The answer is **revision colors**.

Revision Colors

Revision colors are different-colored papers that are used for different versions of a schedule, script, or DOOD. All documents start out white. When a new version is completed (or a portion as in the case of a script), you copy the page or document on the next color in the revision order and put the revised date in the upper right corner of the document along with the word *REVISED*. This assures that crew members will know they have the most recent version of a document. Most studios and production companies use six revisions colors as standard. These colors in order are as follows:

- White
- Blue
- Pink
- Yellow
- Green
- Goldenrod

If your document goes beyond five revisions (which is pretty usual for script pages), other colors used are salmon, cherry, buff, tan, and gray. If revisions go beyond these colors and you need more colors, it is at the discretion of the production to choose other colors. I have seen some productions go to neon-colored paper when necessary.

SUMMARY

Breaking down a script begins with reading the script and knowing it well. You can create a breakdown either by hand or with the use of certain screenwriting software. With either method, you must ensure accuracy in the breakdown. Forgetting to mark even one item will result in its not being on set when needed. The many categories of elements help to guarantee the breakdown will be thorough. After you break the script into eighths, you can derive an accurate scene count and continue the process of creating strips. You use the strips to construct your schedule based on parameters such as geography, cast, day or night, and more. Once the schedules are finished, they are printed and distributed to a variety of crew members. Keep in mind a production schedule will always change as locations are locked and cast schedules are secured.

The Budget

One of the first steps in getting a production off the ground is preparing the budget. By now, you probably have a script in place but may be looking for financing or beginning pre-production, ready to hire a crew. Before you shoot it you should know how much a film will cost. This is true from **low budget** to **high budget.** Yes, you can shoot a project without any budget at all; many student projects and low-budget films are shot this way. However, if you want to learn how to "do it in the real world," you need to learn how to prepare a professional **line-item production budget.**

You may begin the process of writing your budget with a defined amount, or you may need to write a budget to see how much a production will cost. Perhaps you have managed to raise $100,000 to shoot your film. You then must construct a budget that will fit this budget amount. With $100,000 you probably will not be able to afford a union crew, or **distant** locations. If you are still in the process of finding **investors,** they will want to know how much money they need to invest. Some investors will not need to see a detailed budget; they just want to know the bottom line of how much it will cost to shoot the show. If this is the case, you need to prepare a summary page, which is the first page of a budget, showing total costs for each category in the budget. At this point, these costs can be only estimates. You will still need to write a detailed line-item budget later.

This chapter outlines the process of putting together a line-item budget. While the software used for most productions goes into detail about actually typing the budget, the purpose of this chapter is to introduce issues that one would find on any budget and to present the differences you will encounter with budgets ranging from low to high. Finally, the chapter expands the subject by examining how to track a budget and manage costs during the production.

One of the frequent questions asked in preparing a budget is: "How much will it cost to shoot my movie (or video, or promo, or commercial)?" There are no formulas for how much it will cost to shoot anything. Even though there are some standards, each budget is different, based on a number of variables. These variables could include:

- What is the length of the project?
- Will it be shot on 35-mm film, 16-mm film, tape, digitally, or some other format?
- Will the project be edited on film or a nonlinear editing system?
- Will the crew and/or cast be paid?
- If the crew and/or cast are being paid, are they union, nonunion, or a combination?
- Is this a **local** shoot, or will it require traveling with the cast and crew to a distant location?
- Will the cast be made up of unknowns, name actors, or highly paid stars?
- Will the project be shot in a studio or on location?
- What will be the final delivery format? Is it for web broadcast, theaters, or straight to DVD?
- Will there be a significant number of special effects or stunts involved?

These are just a few of the major variables that significantly affect your budget. For instance, if you shoot a project on film, your raw stock costs will be significantly higher than if you shoot digitally. If you are shooting in the field at a distant location, you need to travel your cast and crew, so there will be many additional costs such as **per diem,** hotel, and airfare (per diem is a daily meal allowance for distant crew).

Perhaps one of the most significant factors affecting film budgets is the use of highly paid stars. In the union world, you would hire actors from the **Screen Actors Guild** (SAG), in which most actors are paid what is called **scale.** This means they receive the minimum SAG rate. However, many actors who have achieved a modicum of fame and power may receive quite more than scale, sometimes in the multimillion-dollar range.

Once you have an idea of the scope of your production and have answered most of the above questions, you can begin to work on your budget. The first budget you write may be only a preliminary budget. This kind of budget is very general and is meant only to give a bottom-line cost for a production. After you have completed a **script breakdown** (see Chapter 2), you will be able to construct a detailed budget. For instance, in the budget you must allot for paying an actor for a certain number of days. Without the breakdown, you will not have that information.

You should note that this chapter refers only to production budgets. There are other types of budgets such as a **prints and advertising budget** (P&A). This is a type of budget used by a **distributor** to market and distribute a project. There is also a **development budget,** which is used mainly by studios to pay for people and resources when a film is in development.

BUDGETING SOFTWARE

There are many budgeting software packages available. One of the most widely used is **Movie Magic Budgeting.** Like their scheduling software (discussed in Chapter 2), they have become an industry standard. Another software, called Gorilla, has also taken hold in the indie market. With their production software you can schedule, budget, and create other production lists, such as contact or location lists, all in one software. Be sure to get the right software for your needs. If you cannot afford any software, you can easily write a budget in any spreadsheet application. You use formulas in the cells of these programs to automatically add figures, much like you do with budgeting software. The major difference between using budgeting software and a spreadsheet is in fringes. Fringes (explained in detail later in this chapter) are taxes and employee benefits. Budgeting software lets you apply fringes as percentages of a person's wage and automatically calculates the totals for you. With a spreadsheet program you would have to calculate this individually for all personnel, which can be very time-consuming.

BUDGET STRUCTURE

While there are many different kinds of budgets available, all production budgets are divided into four sections: **above-the-line, below-the-line** (production), post-production, and "Total Other." Each section shows subtotals that appear at the bottom of your budget. Each division also contains various categories that apply to each section. You can liken these categories to the different departments in a production. For instance, there are categories such as camera, sound, lighting, and makeup.

Above-the-Line

Above-the-line refers to some of the creative force of a film. This section contains such categories as "Writer," **"Director,"** "Producer," and "Cast." These are also some of the people whom you see on movie posters. Each of these categories contains items particular to that category. For instance, the Producer category may contain line items such as the payment for the **line producer, associate producer,** and secretaries. These categories can also contain nonpersonnel items such as office expenses and **fringe benefits.** If you are traveling your crew to a distant location, there may be a separate category here for travel and living totals, or you may prefer to detail each person's travel and living expenses with each line item for that person.

Below-the-Line (Production)

Below-the-line costs can include not only departments such as camera, lighting, and sound but also resources such as production film and lab and set operations. Just as in above-the-line, each category will contain line items for paying crew and purchasing or renting various items such as camera and sound equipment.

Post-Production

The post-production section holds the costs for all of your post-production expenses, up to **delivery** of your project. Besides the typical costs of paying for your picture and **sound editors,** this category details the remainder of the post-production process, which includes items such as negative cutting, **answer prints**, and **stock footage** (if working in film). This category includes everything it takes to get your project to its final delivery format.

Total Other

This section of the budget contains miscellaneous items, such as insurance, publicity, and legal costs. Insurance and legal costs are sometimes written as **contractuals**. Contractuals are services that you contract for your project. For instance, when you purchase insurance for your project, you may pay a **flat fee** or you may pay a percentage of your total budget. There is usually a miscellaneous category as well under this section. This category may contain items such as the cost for the **MPAA seal**, bank service charges, or executive entertainment (usually found in high budgets). One last category that may appear in this section is **general expenses**. This category usually contains line items for office furniture, telephone service, or office rental.

Beneath the "Total Other" section and before the grand total are a few other items. These items may appear in "Total Other" or they may appear here. For instance, if general expenses do not appear in the "Total Other" section, they may appear here and be called **overhead**. Overhead is then budgeted as a percentage of the overall budget. All of the items in this final section are budgeted as percentages of the total budget. Other items that may appear here include the **completion bond** and the **contingency fee** (also contractual).

Each budget is structured such that the totals for each category appear on the first page, called the summary sheet. Then, each category's line items appear detailed in the remainder of the budget's pages. The section of the budget that contains individual line items is structured differently in different budgets, but there is one standard. For each line item, there are six columns of figures. These are "Amount," "Unit," "x," "Rate," "Subtotal," and "Budgeted." See Figure 3.1.

The **"Amount" column** shows how many of each line item will be budgeted. For instance, you may need to purchase many rolls of film stock. The number you write in the amount column of the "production film & lab" category dictates how many rolls of film will be budgeted. The unit column states what kind of item is being budgeted. For instance, in the above example the units would read "rolls" (for rolls of film). Therefore, forty-five rolls of film are budgeted. One rule to remember is that the rate column always refers to the unit column. In other words, each roll (unit) of film costs $140 (rate).

DESCRIPTION	AMT	UNIT	X	RATE	SUBTOTAL	BUDGETED
Film Stock	45	Rolls	1	$140.00	$6,300.00	$6,300.00

FIGURE 3.1
Line Item Columns.

DESCRIPTION	AMT	UNIT	X	RATE	SUBTOTAL	BUDGETED
Per Deim	28	Days	10	$62.00	$17,360.00	$17,360.00

FIGURE 3.2
Example Spreadsheet Columns.

The "x" column refers to how many times the item is to be accounted for. In most cases the "x" column contains a *1* or is left blank (it is still assumed to be "1"). An example of when this column would be different is shown in Figure 3.2.

In this example, under the line item "Per Diem" there are twenty-eight days in which ten people will receive per diem payments at a rate of $62 per day. Keep in mind that this is not the only way per diem expenses are budgeted. Some people prefer to budget per diem after each person, as opposed to the above example where the per diem for a group of people has been combined into one line item.

STARTING TO WRITE A BUDGET

Before you begin inputting your budget into the computer, you may need to do some research. For instance, if you don't know off the top of your head the latest rate for film stock, you will need to either call companies that sell film to find out what the rate is or check the Internet. There are two ways of beginning this process: you can print a blank budget with all the line items you need and then research the amounts for each line item, or you can input into the computer program while you are doing the research. Additionally, you need to start with the right budget template. Feature films require many more line items because more personnel and equipment may be used. A documentary budget is usually not as involved and may need to have line items for researchers and stock footage, which may not be found in a feature film budget. Furthermore, if you are doing a live event, you would have line items for crew and equipment, like the other budgets, but probably not for cast. Finally, a budget for animation is very different than a live action budget. See the online production forms, for example, budgets and templates in each of these areas. You can also find many different budgeting templates in your budgeting software.

Budgeting with Software Packages

Budgeting software makes writing a budget easy. You enter amounts for line items at what they call the detail level (or line-item level). As you enter figures, the program automatically updates your totals. This process makes entering changes to the budget very easy. You can always see how high the budget is, and it is easy to get it to the total you desire just by going in and adjusting different line items.

Spreadsheet Budgeting

Budgeting for production with spreadsheets takes a little time to set up, but once set up it makes budgeting almost as easy as using software packages. What you do is create a template within the spreadsheet that contains cells with different formulas. These cells can be linked together in such a way that when you change a dollar amount in one, it is also reflected in another. You can use the **summing tool** to create columns whose cells, when defined with the summing tool, add together, and give a total. Figure 3.3 is an example of a budget for a $3-million-dollar film (low budget), done with an Excel spreadsheet. See the online production forms for examples of student, medium, and high budgets. Keep in mind that the rates in these budgets are only an approximation. Each time you do a budget, the figures should be researched for the latest rates. This research would need to begin with the unions if the project is union.

"Regina of Icelandia"
Shoot Days: 30
Local: 0
Distant: 30
Production Co.: Frame Right Films

Shoot Dates: 4/28/03 to 5/30/03
Executive Producer: John Carter
Producer: Lorene Wales
Director: Darin Wales

Summary Sheet

Acct.	Description	TOTAL
1100	Story, Rights & Continuity	80700.00
1200	Producer's Unit	145504.00
1300	Director	117704.00
1400	Cast	348812.00
	ATL Fringe	21000.00
	TOTAL ABOVE-THE-LINE	**713720.00**
2000	Production Staff	268232.00
2200	Set Design	185462.00
2300	Extras	40325.00
2500	Set Operations	133909.00
2800	Property	56108.00
2900	Wardrobe	173916.00
3100	Makeup & Hair	127716.00
3200	Lighting	124162.00
3300	Camera	205136.00
3400	Production Sound	47608.00
3500	Transportation	147900.00
3600	Locations	90008.00
3700	Production Film & Lab	172140.00
	BTL Fringe	45000.00
	TOTAL BELOW-THE-LINE	**1817622.00**
4500	Film Editing	71200.00
4700	Post-production Sound	149600.00
4800	Post-production Film & Lab	60120.00
4900	Titles	29138.00
5000	Publicity	21600.00
	Post Fringe	56000.00
	TOTAL POST-PRODUCTION	**387658.00**
5100	Insurance	16000.00
5200	General Expenses	25000.00
5300	Completion Bond	10000.00
5400	Contingency	30000.00
	Total Other	**81000.00**
	TOTAL ATL	713720.00
	TOTAL BTL	1817622.00
	TOTAL POST-PRODUCTION	387658.00
	GRAND TOTAL	**3000000.00**

FIGURE 3.3
Three-Million-Dollar Film Budget.

Budget Detail

Acct.	Description	Amt.	Unit	x	Rate	Budgeted
1100	**STORY, RIGHTS & CONTINUITY**					
1101	Writer	1	Flat		50000.00	50000.00
1102	Research	4	Weeks		800.00	800.00
1103	Title		Allow		3000.00	3000.00
1105	Script Timing	1	Flat		500.00	500.00
1106	Xeroxing	200	Scripts		7.00	1400.00
1110	Screenplay	1	Flat		25000.00	25000.00
	TOTAL FOR 1100					**80700.00**
1200	**PRODUCER'S UNIT**					
1203	Producer	1	Flat		80000.00	80000.00
1204	Associate Producer	1	Flat		20000.00	20000.00
1205	Secretary	20	Weeks		600.00	12000.00
1206	Gratuities		Allow		2000.00	2000.00
1207	Entertainment		Allow		2000.00	2000.00
1208	Airfares	4	RT		1900.00	7600.00
1209	Hotels	42	Days		350.00	14700.00
1210	Per Deim	42	Days		62.00	2604.00
1211	Miscellaneous	1	Allow		4600.00	4600.00
	TOTAL FOR 1200					**145504.00**
1300	**DIRECTOR**					
1301	Director	1	Flat		80000.00	80000.00
1351	Secretary	8	Weeks		600.00	4800.00
1352	Storyboard Artist	4	Weeks		800.00	3200.00
1353	Dialogue Coach	4	Weeks		2300.00	9200.00
1354	Airfares	3	RT		1800.00	5400.00
1355	Hotels	42	Days	1	250.00	10500.00
1356	Per Deim	42	Days	1	62.00	2604.00
1357	Miscellaneous		Allow		2000.00	2000.00
	TOTAL FOR 1300					**117704.00**
1400	**CAST**					
1401	Stars/Leads	2	People		50000.00	100000.00
1402	Supporting Cast					
1405	Paolo	6	Weeks		5000.00	30000.00
1406	Tesha	6	Weeks		5000.00	30000.00
1407	Brad	4	Weeks		2000.00	8000.00
1408	Lucille	4	Weeks		2000.00	8000.00
1409	Miram	1	Weeks		2000.00	2000.00
1410	Brad's Wife	2	Weeks		2000.00	4000.00
1411	Day Players					
1412	Soldier #1	3	Days		600.00	1800.00
1413	Soldier #2	4	Days		600.00	2400.00
1415	Soldier #3	6	Days		600.00	3600.00
1416	Soldier #4	5	Days		600.00	3000.00
1417	Grace	1	Days		600.00	600.00
1418	Elizabeth	1	Days		600.00	600.00
1419	Cpt. Mawazo	1	Days		600.00	600.00
1420	Casting Director	4	Weeks		2500.00	10000.00
1421	Stunt Coordinator	6	Weeks		3000.00	18000.00
1422	Utility Stunts	6	Weeks	6	2000.00	72000.00

FIGURE 3.3

Continued

Acct.	Description	Amt.	Unit	x	Rate	Budgeted
1423	Welfare Worker	6	Weeks		2500.00	15000.00
1424	Purchases		Allow		500.00	500.00
1425	Airfares	3	RT		1800.00	5400.00
1426	Hotels	42	Days	3	200.00	25200.00
1427	Per Deim	42	Days	3	62.00	7812.00
1428	Miscellaneous		Allow		300.00	300.00
	TOTAL FOR 1400					**348812.00**

Acct.	Description	Amt.	Unit	x	Rate	Budgeted
2000	**PRODUCTION STAFF**					
2001	UPM/Co-Producer	1	Flat		40000.00	40000.00
2002	Production Coordinator	12	Weeks		2000.00	24000.00
2003	Asst. Production Coordinator	12	Weeks		1600.00	19200.00
2004	Office PAs	10	Weeks	4	400.00	16000.00
2005	Script Supervisor	6	Weeks		2200.00	13200.00
2006	1st AD	6	Weeks		2500.00	1320.00
2007	2nd AD	6	Weeks		1500.00	9000.00
2008	2nd 2nd AD	6	Weeks		800.00	4800.00
2009	Set PAs	6	Weeks	5	500.00	15000.00
2013	Production Accountant	16	Weeks		2500.00	40000.00
2014	1st Asst. Production Acct.	16	Weeks		2000.00	32000.00
2015	2nd Asst. Production Acct.	15	Weeks		1000.00	15000.00
2016	Airfares	3	RT		1800.00	5400.00
2017	Hotels	42	Days	3	200.00	25200.00
2018	Per Deim	42	Days	3	62.00	7812.00
2019	Miscellaneous		Allow		300.00	300.00
2020	**TOTAL FOR 2000**					**268232.00**

Acct.	Description	Amt.	Unit	x	Rate	Budgeted
2200	**SET DESIGN**					
2201	Production Designer	1	Flat		50000.00	50000.00
2202	Art Director	1	Flat		30000.00	30000.00
2203	Assistant to Art Director	14	Weeks		600.00	8400.00
2204	Art Department Coordinator	14	Weeks		1200.00	16800.00
2205	Art Department PAs	10	Weeks	3	600.00	18000.00
2206	Airfares	3	RT		1800.00	5400.00
2207	Hotels	3	People		350.00	1050.00
2208	Per Deim	3	People	42	62.00	7812.00
2209	Graphics		Allow		6000.00	6000.00
2210	Purchases		Allow		25000.00	25000.00
2211	Art Dept. Rentals		Allow		12000.00	12000.00
	Miscellaneous		Allow		5000.00	5000.00
	TOTAL FOR 2200					**185462.00**

Acct.	Description	Amt.	Unit	x	Rate	Budgeted
2500	**EXTRAS**					
2500	Stand-Ins	6	Weeks		500.00	3000.00
2501	Extras	245	Days		125.00	30625.00
2502	Wardrobe Fittings		Allow		2000.00	2000.00
2503	Wardrobe Manufacture		Allow		4000.00	4000.00
2503	Loss & Damage		Allow		500.00	500.00
2512	Miscellaneous		Allow		200.00	200.00
	TOTAL FOR 2500					**40325.00**

FIGURE 3.3

Continued

Acct.	Description	Amt.	Unit	x	Rate	Budgeted
2500	**SET OPERATIONS**					
2500	Key Grip	8	Weeks		2500.00	20000.00
2501	Best Boy Grip	6	Weeks		850.00	5100.00
2501	Company Grips	6	Weeks	7	750.00	31500.00
2501	Standby Painter	6	Weeks		700.00	4200.00
2504	Standby Greens	6	Weeks		700.00	4200.00
2505	Grip Package	6	Weeks		3100.00	18600.00
2506	Dolly	6	Weeks		400.00	2400.00
2507	Jib Arm	6	Weeks		400.00	2400.00
2508	Purchases		Allow		2000.00	2000.00
2509	Security	6	Weeks		16.00	9600.00
2510	First Aid		Allow		600.00	600.00
2511	Airfares	2	RT		1900.00	3600.00
2512	Hotel	56	Days		200.00	11200.00
2513	Per Deim	56	Days	2	62.00	6944.00
2514	Loss & Damage		Allow		3000.00	3000.00
2518	Craft Service Purchases	1	Flat		7000.00	7000.00
2519	Craft Services Person	6	Days		200.00	1200.00
2520	Catering	6	Days		40.00	240.00
2521	Miscellaneous	5	Days		25.00	125.00
	TOTAL FOR 2500					**133909.00**

Acct.	Description	Amt.	Unit	x	Rate	Budgeted
2800	**PROPERTY**					
2801	Prop master	7	Weeks		1500.00	10500.00
2816	Asst. Prop master	7	Weeks		1200.00	8400.00
2817	Airfares	2	RT		1900.00	3600.00
2818	Hotel	42	Days	2	200.00	16800.00
2819	Per Deim	42	Days	2	62.00	5208.00
2820	Prop Purchases		Allow		6000.00	6000.00
2821	Prop Manufacture		Allow		1600.00	1600.00
2822	Rentals		Allow		2000.00	2000.00
2823	Loss & Damage		Allow		1500.00	1500.00
2824	Miscellaneous		Allow		500.00	500.00
	TOTAL FOR 2800					**56108.00**

Acct.	Description	Amt.	Unit	x	Rate	Budgeted
2900	**WARDROBE**					
2901	Costume Designer	1	Flat		55000.00	55000.00
2909	Asst. to Costume Designer	12	Weeks		500.00	6000.00
2911	Wardrobe Supervisor	10	Weeks		2200.00	22000.00
2912	Men's Costumer	6	Weeks		1000.00	6000.00
2913	Women's Costumer	6	Weeks		1000.00	6000.00
2914	Purchases		Allow		30000.00	30000.00
2915	Seamstress	6	Weeks		800.00	4200.00
2916	Airfares	1	RT		1900.00	1900.00
2917	Hotel		Allow		200.00	200.00
2918	Per Deim	42	Days	4	62.00	10416.00
2919	Outside Rentals		Allow		18000.00	18000.00
2920	Manufacturing Labor		Allow		9000.00	9000.00
2921	Cleaning & Dyeing		Allow		3000.00	3000.00
2922	Loss & Damage		Allow		2000.00	2000.00
2923	Miscellaneous		Allow		200.00	200.00
	TOTAL FOR 2900					**173916.00**

FIGURE 3.3

Continued

Acct.	Description	Amt.	Unit	x	Rate	Budgeted
3100	**MAKEUP AND HAIR**					
3101	Key Makeup Artist	6	Weeks		2300.00	13800.00
3102	Asst. Makeup Artist	6	Weeks		1800.00	10800.00
3103	Key Hair	6	Weeks		2000.00	12000.00
3104	Asst. Hair	6	Weeks		2000.00	12000.00
3105	Additional Hair	4	Weeks		1000.00	4000.00
3106	Additional Makeup	4	Weeks		1000.00	4000.00
3107	Prosthetics		Allow		3000.00	3000.00
3108	Body Makeup	1	Weeks		1900.00	1900.00
3110	Wigs		Allow		10000.00	10000.00
3111	Airfares	4	RT		1900.00	7200.00
3112	Hotel	42	Days	4	200.00	33600.00
3113	Per Deim	42	Days	4	62.00	10416.00
3114	Purchases		Allow		1500.00	1500.00
3116	Rentals		Allow		2000.00	2000.00
3117	Box Rentals	6	Weeks		200.00	1200.00
3118	Misc. Expenses		Allow		300.00	300.00
	TOTAL FOR 3100					**127716.00**

Acct.	Description	Amt.	Unit	x	Rate	Budgeted
3200	**LIGHTING**					
3201	Gaffer	6	Weeks		250.00	1500.00
3204	Best Boy	6	Weeks		125.00	750.00
3205	Electrics	6	Weeks		100.00	600.00
3206	Rigging Crew	2	Weeks		5000.00	10000.00
3207	Generator Operator	6	Weeks		2600.00	15600.00
3209	Purchases		Allow		12000.00	12000.00
3210	Other Rentals		Allow		10000.00	10000.00
3211	Loss & Damage		Allow		2000.00	2000.00
3212	Lighting Package	6	Weeks		3000.00	18000.00
3213	Airfares	3	RT		1900.00	5700.00
3214	Hotel	42	Days	3	200.00	25200.00
3215	Per Deim	42	Days	3	62.00	7812.00
3216	Globes/Gels		Allow		2000.00	2000.00
3217	Electric Current		Allow		3000.00	3000.00
3218	Generators	6	Weeks		1500.00	9000.00
3219	Miscellaneous		Allow		1000.00	1000.00
	TOTAL FOR 3200					**124162.00**

Acct.	Description	Amt.	Unit	x	Rate	Budgeted
3300	**CAMERA**					
3301	Director of Photography	1	Flat		65000.00	65000.00
3302	Camera Operator	6	Weeks		3500.00	21000.00
3303	Additional Camera Operators	3	Weeks		2000.00	6000.00
3304	1st Asst. Camera	6	Weeks		1600.00	9600.00
3305	2nd Asst. Camera	6	Weeks		800.00	4200.00
3306	Camera PAs	6	Weeks	2	400.00	4800.00
3307	Steadicam	6	Weeks		2000.00	12000.00
3308	Airfares	4	RT		1900.00	7600.00
3309	Hotel	42	Days	4	200.00	33600.00
3310	Meals	42	Days	4	62.00	10416.00
3312	Camera Package	6	Weeks		3500.00	21000.00
3314	Still Photographer	60	rolls		12.00	720.00
3317	Loss & Damage		Allow		500.00	500.00
3318	Miscellaneous		Allow		200.00	200.00
	TOTAL FOR 3300					**196636.00**

FIGURE 3.3
Continued

Acct.	Description	Amt.	Unit	x	Rate	Budgeted
3400	**PRODUCTION SOUND**					
3401	Sound Mixer	6	Weeks		2300.00	2200.00
3402	Boom Operator	6	Weeks		1200.00	300.00
3403	Sound PA	6	Weeks		500.00	3000.00
3405	Airfare	2	RT		1900.00	3600.00
3406	Hotel	42	Days	2	400.00	16800.00
3407	Meals	42	Days	2	62.00	5208.00
3408	Sound Package	6	Weeks		100.00	15000.00
3409	Loss & Damage		Allow		1000.00	1000.00
3410	Miscellaneous		Allow		500.00	500.00
	TOTAL FOR 3400					**47608.00**

Acct.	Description	Amt.	Unit	x	Rate	Budgeted
3500	**TRANSPORTATION**					
3501	Transportation Coordinator	20	Weeks		2500.00	50000.00
3502	Transportation Captains	20	Weeks		2200.00	44000.00
3503	Drivers	15	Weeks		1000.00	15000.00
3504	Vehicle Rental		Allow		7000.00	7000.00
3506	Vehicle Purchase		Allow		24000.00	24000.00
3507	Gasoline, Oil & Mileage		Allow		4000.00	4000.00
3508	Parking/Permits/Taxis		Allow		3000.00	3000.00
3509	Loss & Damage		Allow		500.00	500.00
3510	Miscellaneous		Allow		400.00	400.00
	TOTAL FOR 3500					**147900.00**

Acct.	Description	Amt.	Unit	x	Rate	Budgeted
3600	**LOCATIONS**					
3601	Location Manager	10	Weeks		2300.00	23000.00
3602	Asst. Location Manager	10	Weeks		2000.00	20000.00
3603	Location PAs	7	Weeks		500.00	3500.00
3607	Scout	3	Weeks		400.00	1200.00
3608	Airfare	2	RT		1900.00	3600.00
3609	Hotel	42	Days	2	200.00	16800.00
3610	Meals	42	Days	2	62.00	5208.00
3611	Location Site Rental Fees		Allow		15000.00	15000.00
3612	Courtesy Payments		Allow		1000.00	1000.00
3614	Shipping-Customs		Allow		500.00	500.00
3615	Miscellaneous		Allow		200.00	200.00
	TOTAL FOR 3600					**90008.00**

Acct.	Description	Amt.	Unit	x	Rate	Budgeted
3700	**PRODUCTION FILM & LAB**					
3702	Negative Raw Stock	90000	Feet		0.60	54000.00
3703	Developing	90000	Feet		0.42	37800.00
3704	Printing	90000	Feet		0.55	49500.00
3705	Negative Prep	90000	Feet		0.10	9000.00
3706	Video Dailies	90000	Feet		0.24	21600.00
3707	Stock-Behind-the-Scenes	30	Tapes		8.00	240.00
3708	**TOTAL FOR 3700**					**172140.00**

Acct.	Description	Amt.	Unit	x	Rate	Budgeted
4500	**FILM EDITING**					
4501	Editor	10	Weeks		3000.00	500.00
4502	1st Asst. Editor	10	Weeks		2000.00	20000.00
4503	2nd Asst. Editor	10	Weeks		1000.00	10000.00
4504	Editing Apprentice	8	Weeks		400.00	3200.00
4506	Avid Rental	10	Weeks		2500.00	25000.00
4507	Masters		Allow		2000.00	2000.00

FIGURE 3.3

Continued

Acct.	Description	Amt.	Unit	x	Rate	Budgeted
4508	Projection		Flat		4000.00	4000.00
4509	Shipping		Allow		3000.00	3000.00
4510	Film to Tape Transfers		Allow		20000.00	2000.00
4511	Miscellaneous		Allow		1500.00	1500.00
	TOTAL FOR 4500					**71200.00**

Acct.	Description	Amt.	Unit	x	Rate	Budgeted
4700	**POST-PRODUCTION SOUND**					
4707	Re-recording Mixer	2	Weeks		4000.00	8000.00
4708	Sound Editor	8	Weeks		3000.00	24000.00
4709	Sound Effects Editor	8	Weeks		3000.00	24000.00
4710	Music Editor	8	Weeks		2800.00	22400.00
4711	Dialogue Editor	8	Weeks		2900.00	23200.00
4712	Sound Mix	3	Weeks		2500.00	7500.00
4713	ADR Editor	7	Weeks		2000.00	14000.00
4715	Foley	2	Weeks		2000.00	4000.00
4716	Pro Tools Rentals	8	Weeks		2500.00	20000.00
4718	Stock		Allow		2000.00	2000.00
4719	Miscellaneous		Allow		500.00	500.00
	TOTAL FOR 4700					**149600.00**

Acct.	Description	Amt.	Unit	x	Rate	Budgeted
4800	**POST-PROD FILM & LAB**					
4801	Answer Print	20000	Feet		0.67	13400.00
4802	Optical Track	20000	Feet		0.35	7000.00
4803	Negative Cutting	2000	Cuts		7.00	14000.00
4804	Setup Fee		Allow		400.00	400.00
4805	Reels	4	Reels		30.00	120.00
4806	DVD Authoring		Allow		5000.00	5000.00
4807	Video Dubs	200	Dubs		10.00	2000.00
4808	Stock Footage	400	Feet		45.00	18000.00
4809	Miscellaneous		Allow		2000.00	200.00
	TOTAL FOR 4800					**60120.00**

Acct.	Description	Amt.	Unit	x	Rate	Budgeted
4900	**TITLES**					
4901	Main & End Titles		Allow		10000.00	10000.00
	TOTAL FOR 5000					**10000.00**

Acct.	Description	Amt.	Unit	x	Rate	Budgeted
5000	**PUBLICITY**					
5001	Unit Publicist	6	Weeks		2000.00	12000.00
5003	Still Develop & Print	60	Rolls		10.00	600.00
5004	Previews		Allow		7000.00	7000.00
5005	CD-RT		Allow		2000.00	2000.00
	TOTAL FOR 5000					**21600.00**

FIGURE 3.3
Continued

Each union has a minimum pay scale for their members, called *scale*. If a show is non-union, then rates for a particular location or state would apply. The local **film office** or commission should have the latest information on these rates. For services, equipment rental, and office rental, you would need to contact the specific vendors for their rates.

PADDING THE BUDGET

To say that you are going to pad your budget may be construed as bad or sneaky. However, as many filmmakers know, **padding** a production budget is good practice. The nature of the production process is that it is fraught with problems.

Even the most experienced producers find it hard to anticipate every contingency that may come along requiring payment. I once produced a project where two months had been spent on pre-production in a foreign country, arranging for location approvals on a military base. During those two months, we had every indication from the officials that our plans would proceed. However, when our crew arrived, they ran into resistance from the military. The only way for the trip not to have been a waste was to pay more "fees" to the military officials. Luckily, there were certain padded line items in the budget that ate these costs.

There are two places where the budget can be padded: in the line items called "Miscellaneous" and **Loss and Damage**. *Miscellaneous* appears in almost every category of a budget. This line item is for extraneous costs that may be incurred. In higher-budget films, this line item may contain thousands of dollars. In low-budget films, where you most likely need to cut costs wherever you can, this line item may contain only hundreds of dollars or not appear at all. "Loss and Damage" is a line item that usually appears in categories where equipment or goods are budgeted. For instance, in the wardrobe department this line item is reserved for costumes that may be damaged on set or lost by an actor.

THE CONTINGENCY

The contingency is an amount reserved for unexpected or unanticipated costs. The standard contingency for most productions is 10 percent of your budget and is included in the cost of your total budget. On larger shoots this 10 percent is required by the completion bond company. For example, if your budget is $5 million, your contingency will be $500,000.

FRINGE BENEFITS

A fringe benefit is an item that is attached to a certain crew member, in addition to the original cost of that person. There are several kinds of fringe benefits. For personnel, fringe benefits are taxes, **payroll fees**, and employee benefits. For goods and services, there may be sales tax. For example, if you are paying a nonunion gaffer and doing fringes, you will pay what his rate is, and you will also pay a percentage of taxes. If you are paying a union gaffer and doing fringes, you will pay a rate, a percentage of taxes, and a percentage of employee benefits. Individual unions determine these percentages.

Taxes

In the United States there are several kinds of taxes. There is the **Federal Insurance Contributions Act** (FICA), the **State Unemployment Tax** (SUI), the **Federal Unemployment Insurance** (FUI), Workers' Compensation, and Medicare. Specific rates for each of these vary. You should always check for the latest rates. In addition, some states do not have a state wage tax. Therefore, you would not take state taxes out of their pay. The rule for state taxes is that you pay the taxes according to where the person resides, not where you are shooting. For goods and services you would pay sales tax for the state where the production is shot.

There are two ways of budgeting your film when it comes to fringes. In most higher-budget films, fringe benefits are attached to any person who is being paid. In low-budget films, where fringe benefits are too expensive to incur, fringe benefits may not be included. However, either way has implications.

If you plan to do fringe benefits, this is what it means for your budget: You will need to take taxes out of everyone's pay. If you do not do fringe benefits, you will hire your crew as **independent contractors**. Therefore, no taxes will be taken out, and everyone will receive a **Form 1099** from the government at the end of the year and will have to take care of the taxes then. Some of your employees may prefer to be paid this way because they may be incorporated. When an employee is incorporated—meaning he is treated legally as a corporate body—you pay the company. The employee then pays himself from the company. Many freelance crew members do this, as it is a great way to save on taxes. Unless you are experienced, you should always hire an accountant who will be familiar with current tax laws.

Payroll Fees

A payroll fee is incurred when you use a payroll service to calculate your payroll (mostly done in higher budget films). If you are doing this, a percentage of a person's pay will be deducted to cover the cost of the payroll service doing the payroll. The average percentage is anywhere from 5/10ths to 2 percent, but always check with your payroll service before doing your budget.

Employee Benefits

There are certain unions that require you to pay a percentage of employees' benefits. These benefits include vacation and holiday pay. The unions that require this are the DGA, SAG, WGA, NABET, and **IATSE**. Always check with the specific union for the latest rates.

UNION VERSUS NONUNION

Whether your shoot is or becomes union depends on a number of factors. There are many ways to have a union shoot. There are five major unions that would be involved in your shoot: IATSE, NABET, DGA, SAG, and the WGA. IATSE is a union for almost all below-the-line personnel. DGA is for directors, assistant directors, production managers, and the **DGA trainee**. SAG is the union for actors and stunt people. The WGA is the union for writers. Your director, production manager, and assistant directors may belong to the DGA, yet the rest of your crew does not necessarily have to be union. You may have an entire IATSE crew, yet your actors may not belong to SAG.

If your shoot is nonunion, it is likely to be lower budget. Although you do avoid the larger costs of union shoots, you also may end up with a less experienced crew. The decision to go union or nonunion may be dictated also by where you shoot. If you are shooting in a major city such as Los Angeles and have a decent budget, you will most likely need to have a union shoot. If you are shooting with a small budget in a small town in Nebraska, you can easily shoot with a nonunion crew. In addition, many states are called **work-for-hire** states. These are states where citizens are guaranteed the right not to lose work because of a union. In other words, you can use a nonunion crew in these states.

BECOMING SIGNATORY

If you do a union shoot, you will need to become **signatory** to that union for the duration of your shoot. Becoming signatory means that you contract with a union to hire a union cast or crew for your shoot. You also agree to abide by that union's pay and working conditions. For instance, if your shoot becomes signatory with SAG, you will be paying your actors scale, or the minimum SAG rate. You also will agree to a number of conditions such as how many hours children of certain ages can work and how long adults can work. You also will agree to pay certain **penalties** if you happen to infringe on any union rules. You should become very familiar with all the unions rules if you become signatory.

LOCAL VERSUS DISTANT

There are two different definitions of local and distant: there are local or distant crew and cast, and local or distant locations. If you are shooting your film in the same area where your production company is located, most of your crew and cast would be considered local. This means that the employees live and work within 60 miles of your locations. However, you may also, for instance, hire a crew member, such as a **director of photography** (DP), from another state. In this case that DP will be considered distant and you might have to pay for her travel, hotel, and per diem. As far as locations are concerned, if you use a set within 60 miles of your main production company, that location is considered local. If you use a location farther than 60 miles, it is considered distant.

Keep in mind that you may have a combination of a local and distant crew and local and distant locations. For instance, you may have a production company that is located in Texas but when you shoot a show in New Jersey, you may choose to bring your heads of departments from Texas. These crew members and your locations will be considered distant. You can also then hire other crew members, such as **production assistants** (PAs), from New Jersey. The PAs would be hired as locals, and you would not need to pay them for any travel, hotel, or per diem. It is also not unheard of to hire a person from another state with the agreement that she work as a local. Some crew members agree to this arrangement because they want or need the work, even though it means they will have to take care of their own travel, housing, and food.

If you are shooting in an unfamiliar area, the first place to look for crew is the area's film office. Each state has a film office, and many states have more than one. These offices often have their own directories, which list people in the area who can fill various crew positions.

Another place to look for local crew is in local production companies. Occasionally these companies may have downtime when their employees are available for other work. They usually also know most of the local crew people, whom they hire as **freelancers**.

Finally, one last place to look for local crew to fill entry-level positions is at local universities or film schools. Contact the director or chair of their film department; he will most likely be happy to put up a flyer advertising for resumes.

BUDGET DISBURSEMENT AND TRACKING

Writing a budget is only the first step of the process of budgeting. The next steps include actually disbursing the funds and budget tracking, or managing the budget as you shoot. This job in higher-budget shoots may be taken care of by your **accounting department**. On lower-budget shoots, you may need to do it yourself. You can also invest in software such as Show Biz, where you can write your budget and then keep track of spending as the shoot progresses. If you are doing it yourself, here's more of what you will need to do.

Disbursing Funds

Funds for any project may be allocated to the production in a number of ways. You may have the entire production budget up-front, or you may receive funds in partial disbursements. One standard way is to receive a third of your funds up-front in order to pay for pre-production. Then you will receive the second third at the beginning of production to cover the costs of shooting the project. You will receive the final third at the beginning of post-production to cover those costs. Either way, you will need to keep track of how money will be disbursed. You can do this with a cash flow worksheet. This worksheet, as shown in Figure 3.4, illustrates how each line item in the budget will be paid for. For instance, in the example worksheet you would pay for **craft services** with a check on a certain date. You could also pay for the rental of your **generator** with a purchase order. Alternatively, you could pay for craft service items with a **cash advance**. The **cash flow worksheet** allows you to organize how and when you will disburse funds for every line item and have control of spending.

Disbursement Forms

There are four main forms for disbursing money on a film shoot. These are a purchase order, **check request**, credit card, and cash advance. A purchase order is a form (see online forms) that promises a vendor—for instance, a generator company—that you agree to rent the generator for a specific amount of time and for a certain rate. The vendor then agrees to bill you for the goods or services. Essentially, it is a promise to pay. Not just anyone can write up a purchase order. You will need to set up an account with the vendor. To do so, you will need to provide credit references. The vendor will check on these and then either approve or not, based on your company's credit.

Once services are rendered the vendor will then send you a bill in the form of an invoice (which will reference a number on your purchase order). Most of these types of vendors are on a thirty-day agreement, meaning you have thirty days to pay the bill. Some services such as certain **catering** companies may require payment the moment the services are rendered. Be sure to check with vendors on their payment practices.

A check request is a form that you fill out for a specific amount of goods and services. For instance, you may need to pay $200 for a wig. Since you know the final cost of the wig, you write a check request for $200, which is then used to pay for the wig.

A cash advance is used when you have many items to purchase and no particular dollar amount. For instance, in your budget you have an allowance for craft

Cash Flow Worksheet

Prepared by: Date

Acct #	ITEM	DATE NEEDED	Amount	WHAT FORM	DISBURSED TO	RECEIPTS IN
2005	VISAS-UPM, Actor, Snd	21-Apr	350.00	cash	Wales, Green, Bow	yes
	Dir, Boom, Actor, DP	21-Apr			Jackson, Din, Johns, Smith	yes
1353	Director-Meals	22-May	175.00	cash	Jackson	yes
1352	Director-Hotel	22-May	200.00	card	Jackson	yes
1353	Director-Shots	20-Apr	100.00	cash	Jackson	no
1452	Actor1-Hotel	22-May	200.00	card	Green	yes
1452	Actor2-Hotel	22-May	200.00	card	Bow	no
1453	Actor1-Shots	20-Apr	100.00	cash	Green	yes
1453	Actor2-Shots	20-Apr	100.00	cash	Bow	no
1454	Actor1-Meals	22-May	175.00	cash	Green	no
1454	Actor2-Meals	22-May	175.00	cash	Bow	
2001	UPM-Fee	01-Feb	1000.00	check	Din	no
2003	UPM-Hotel	22-May	200.00	card	Din	no
2004	UPM-Meals	22-May	175.00	cash	Din	no
2009	Petty Cash	19-May	500.00	cash	Din	yes
3304	DP-Hotel	22-May	200.00	card	Johns	yes
3305	DP-Meals	22-May	175.00	cash	Johns	yes
3333	DP-Shots	20-Apr	100.00	cash	Johns	yes
3404	SND-Hotel	22-May	200.00	card	Smith	no
3404	Boom-Hotel	22-May	200.00	card	Wales	yes
3405	SND-Meals	22-May	175.00	cash	Smith	no
3405	Boom-Meals	22-May	175.00	cash	Wales	yes
3406	SND-Shots	21-Apr	100.00	cash	Smith	yes
3406	Boom-Shots	21-Apr	100.00	cash	Wales	no
3309	Cartage	19-May	544.00	cash	Din	yes
3416	DAT tape	16-May	20.00	check	Din	yes
3520	Vehicles-TA	11-May	1000.00	card	Din	no
3609	Courtesy Payments	22-May	500.00	cash	Din	
3614	Customs	20-May	500.00	cash	Johns	no
1416	Cast Purchases	20-May	50.00	cash	Din	yes
3702	DV Stock	16-May	80.00	check	Johns	no
		TOTAL	7769.00			

FIGURE 3.4

Cash Flow Worksheet.

services, say $5,000. You write a cash advance in the name of the **craft service person** for $5,000. A check is then issued in the craft person's name for $5,000. To account for what is purchased, the craft service person turns in receipts for the whole $5,000. These receipts are then accounted for on a **cost report**.

MANAGING THE BUDGET

As you begin to spend your budget you will need a way to keep track of how much is actually being spent. You may frequently spend less in one area than you have budgeted or spend more than you had anticipated in another. While this is not preferable, it is inevitable. As long as you are tracking these costs you will be less likely to run the risk of going over your budget total. The way of tracking these costs is with a cost report and a **budget report**. A cost report shows an item, how much was originally budgeted for that item, and then how much was actually paid for it. A very necessary understanding of the cost report is knowing what line item in the budget the cost is being attached to. For instance, in the example cost report shown in Figure 3.5, $1,000 was budgeted for camera **expendables**. The cost report shows that there was actually $1,260.00 spent on expendables. Therefore, this line item is $260.00 over budget. Furthermore, the cost report shows that this expense will be reflected in 5000-01, the line item account number for expendables.

The budget report as shown in Figure 3.6 looks very much like the original budget. The difference is between the **Actual** and **Encumbered** columns. The "Actual" column shows exactly what has been spent so far in that line item. The "Encumbered" column shows a cost that may have been incurred, such as a rental, but has not actually been paid yet. An item will leave the "Encumbered" column and enter the "Actual" column when it has been paid.

GOOD BUDGETING VERSUS BAD BUDGETING

Good budgeting means that you have included in your budget all of the items necessary to shoot your project. It also means that you have allowed for unforeseen problems. For instance, if your **shooting schedule** is tight, it is a good idea to allow for overtime in case the crew falls behind and needs to shoot longer days. Good budgeting means that you have allowed for more than just the standard 10 percent contingency. The production of a film or digital show always has difficulties. Locations fall through, equipment breaks down, and crew may be fired. I once worked on a feature film where the DP was fired. Not only did he leave the show, but the entire **grip** and electric departments, out of loyalty, also left the show. We had to fly out the old crew—and in a new crew—within a 24-hour period. The costs for travel were significant.

When you find that you have to start spending out of your contingency during pre-production, you have an insufficient budget. Bad budgeting means that you have not allowed for the items necessary to shoot your project. Furthermore, it means that as the production progresses you will not have the funds that may be needed to take care of unexpected problems. Troubleshooting in the industry should be a necessary skill, not a reaction. You must have the ability to look ahead and see potential problems before they happen. This skill is also required to prevent bad budgeting.

PRODUCTION COST REPORT   Date:

TITLE   "Regina of Icelandia"   Prepared by: L. Wales
TYPE   Expendables   Producer: L. Wales
ACCT   5000   Director: J. Darin Wales

ACCT #	REF #	DESCRIPTION	BUDGETED	ACTUAL	OVER	UNDER	DATE
5000-01	R3452	Expendable package	$1,000	$1,260	$260	0	7/13/2002
		TOTALS	$1,000	$1,260	$260	0	

FIGURE 3.5
Production Cost Report.

Budget Detail

Acct.	Description	Amt.	Unit	x	Rate	Budgeted	Actual	Encumb.	Over	Under
1100	**STORY, RIGHTS & CONTINUITY**						Actual	Encumb.	Over	Under
1101	Writer	1	Flat		50000.00	50000.00	50000.00	0.00	0.00	0.00
1102	Research	4	Weeks		800.00	800.00	800.00	0.00	0.00	0.00
1103	Title		Allow		3000.00	3000.00	2300.00	600.00	0.00	700.00
1105	Script Timing	1	Flat		500.00	500.00	500.00	0.00	0.00	0.00
1106	Xeroxing	200	Scripts		7.00	1400.00	1600.00	50.00	200.00	0.00
1110	Screenplay	1	Flat		25000.00	25000.00	25000.00	0.00	0.00	0.00
	TOTAL FOR 1100					80700.00	80200.00	650.00	200.00	700.00

Acct.	Description	Amt.	Unit	x	Rate	Budgeted	Actual	Encumb.	Over	Under
1200	**PRODUCER'S UNIT**						Actual	Encumb.	Over	Under
1203	Producer	1	Flat		80000.00	80000.00	80000.00	2000.00	0.00	0.00
1204	Associate Producer	1	Flat		20000.00	20000.00	20000.00	0.00	0.00	0.00
1205	Secretary	20	Weeks		600.00	12000.00	14000.00	0.00	2000.00	0.00
1206	Gratuities		Allow		2000.00	2000.00	1800.00	0.00	0.00	200.00
1207	Entertainment		Allow		2000.00	2000.00	1300.00	0.00	0.00	700.00
1208	Airfares	4	RT		1900.00	7600.00	7600.00	0.00	0.00	0.00
1209	Hotels	42	Days		350.00	14700.00	14700.00	66.00	0.00	0.00
1210	Per Deim	42	Days		62.00	2604.00	2604.00	4365.00	0.00	0.00
1211	Miscellaneous	1	Allow		4600.00	4600.00	4500.00	23.00	0.00	100.00
	TOTAL FOR 1200					145504.00	146504.00	6454.00	2000.00	1000.00

Acct.	Description	Amt.	Unit	x	Rate	Budgeted	Actual	Encumb.	Over	Under
1300	**DIRECTOR**						Actual	Encumb.	Over	Under
1301	Director	1	Flat		80000.00	80000.00	80000.00	0.00	0.00	0.00
1351	Secretary	8	Weeks		600.00	4800.00	4800.00	264.00	0.00	0.00
1352	Storyboard Artist	4	Weeks		800.00	3200.00	4000.00	9785.00	800.00	0.00
1353	Dialogue Coach	4	Weeks		2300.00	9200.00	9200.00	53.00	0.00	0.00
1354	Airfares	3	RT		1800.00	5400.00	5400.00	34.00	0.00	0.00
1355	Hotels	42	Days	1	250.00	10500.00	10500.00	0.00	0.00	0.00
1356	Per Deim	42	Days	1	62.00	2604.00	2604.00	435.00	0.00	0.00
1357	Miscellaneous		Allow		2000.00	2000.00	1500.00	0.00	0.00	500.00
	TOTAL FOR 1300					117704.00	118004.00	10571.00	800.00	500.00

Acct.	Description	Amt.	Unit	x	Rate	Budgeted	Actual	Encumb.	Over	Under
1400	**CAST**						Actual	Encumb.	Over	Under
1401	Stars/Leads	2	People		50000.00	100000.00	125000.00	0.00	25000.00	0.00
1402	Supporting Cast									
1405	Paolo	6	Weeks		5000.00	30000.00	30000.00	0.00	0.00	0.00
1406	Tesha	6	Weeks		5000.00	30000.00	30000.00	432.00	0.00	0.00
1407	Brad	4	Weeks		2000.00	8000.00	8000.00	0.00	0.00	0.00
1408	Lucille	4	Weeks		2000.00	8000.00	8000.00	867.00	0.00	0.00
1409	Miram	1	Weeks		2000.00	2000.00	2000.00	45.00	0.00	0.00
1410	Brad's Wife	2	Weeks		2000.00	4000.00	4000.00	0.00	0.00	0.00
1411	Day Players									
1412	Soldier #1	3	Days		600.00	1800.00	1800.00	56.00	0.00	0.00
1413	Soldier #2	4	Days		600.00	2400.00	2400.00	0.00	0.00	0.00
1415	Soldier #3	6	Days		600.00	3600.00	3600.00	0.00	0.00	0.00
1416	Soldier #4	5	Days		600.00	3000.00	3000.00	0.00	0.00	0.00
1417	Grace	1	Days		600.00	600.00	600.00	0.00	0.00	0.00
1418	Elizabeth	1	Days		600.00	600.00	600.00	65.00	0.00	0.00
1419	Cpt. Mawazo	1	Days		600.00	600.00	600.00	654.00	0.00	0.00
1420	Casting Director	4	Weeks		2500.00	10000.00	10000.00	54.00	0.00	0.00
1421	Stunt Coordinator	6	Weeks		3000.00	18000.00	18000.00	0.00	0.00	0.00
1422	Utility Stunts	6	Weeks	6	2000.00	72000.00	72000.00	456.00	0.00	0.00

FIGURE 3.6

Sample Final Budget Report.

Crew	Student Film	Low Budget	Medium Budget	High Budget
STORY				
Writer	Yes	Yes	Yes	Yes
Research	No	No	if needed	if needed
Title	No	No	Yes	Yes
Script Timing	No	No	Yes	Yes
PRODUCER'S UNIT				
Producer	Yes	Yes	Yes	Yes
Associate Producer	No	No	Yes	Yes
Secretary	No	No	Yes	Yes
DIRECTOR				
Director	Yes	Yes	Yes	Yes
Secretary	No	No	Maybe	Yes
Storyboard Artist	No	No	Yes	Yes
Dialogue Coach	No	No	Maybe	Yes
PRODUCTION STAFF				
UPM	Yes	Yes	Yes	Yes
Production Coordinator	No	Maybe	Yes	Yes
Asst. Production Coordinator	No	No	Yes	Yes
Office PAs	No	No	Maybe	Yes
Script Supervisor	Yes	Yes	Yes	Yes
1st AD	Yes	Yes	Yes	Yes
2nd AD	Yes	Maybe	Yes	Yes
2nd 2nd AD	No	No	Maybe	Yes
Set PAs	No	No	Yes	Yes
Production Accountant	No	No	Yes	Yes
1st Asst. Production Acct.	No	No	Yes	Yes
2nd Asst. Production Acct.	No	No	Maybe	Yes
SET DESIGN				
Production Designer	Yes	Combined w/Art Dir	Yes	Yes
Art Director	Combined w/PD	Combined w/PD	Yes	Yes
Assistant to Art Director	No	No	Maybe	Yes
Art Department Coordinator	No	No	Maybe	Yes
Art Department PAs	No	No	Yes	Yes
EXTRAS				
Stand-Ins	No	No	Yes	Yes
Extras	Yes, unpaid	Yes, unpaid	Yes	Yes

FIGURE 3.7

Differences in Crew—Low to High Budget.

BUDGET LINE ITEMS

As stated earlier, one of the major differences between low, medium, and high budgets may lie in the length of your shoot and the amount of crew you can afford. There are certain crew positions that are absolutely necessary. Then there are certain positions that are a "luxury" on medium budgets. Finally, there are certain positions on a low-budget shoot that are not only a luxury but may also be combined. That is, one person may end up doing the job of two, simply because of budgetary limitations. Different types of media productions have different needs, and the line items will reflect that. Shooting interviews for a docudrama may require more travel but only for a crew of two or three. Live events typically require

SET OPERATIONS

Key Grip (KG)	Yes	Yes	Yes	Yes
Best Boy Grip	No	Yes	Yes	Yes
Company Grips	Some	Yes, but few	Yes	Yes
Standby Painter	No	No	Maybe	Yes
Standby Greens	No	No	Maybe	Yes
Security	No	No	Yes	Yes
First Aid	No	Yes	Yes	Yes
Craft Services Person	Maybe	Maybe	Yes	Yes
Catering	Maybe	Maybe	Yes	Yes

PROPERTY

Prop master	Maybe	Yes	Yes	Yes
Asst. Prop master	No	No	Yes	Yes

WARDROBE

Costume Designer	Yes	Yes	Yes	Yes
Asst. to Costume Designer	No	No	Maybe	Yes
Wardrobe Supervisor	No	No	Yes	Yes
Men's Costumer	No	No	No	Yes
Women's Costumer	No	No	No	Yes
Seamstress	No	No	No	Yes

MAKEUP AND HAIR

Key Makeup Artist	Combined w/Hair	Combined w/Hair	Yes	Yes
Asst. Makeup Artist	No	Maybe	Yes	Yes
Key Hair	No	Combined w/Makeup	Yes	Yes
Asst. Hair	No	No	Yes	Yes
Additional Hair	No	No	No	Yes
Additional Makeup	No	No	No	Yes
Body Makeup	No	No	Maybe	Yes

LIGHTING

Gaffer	Combined w/KG	Yes	Yes	Yes
Best Boy	No	Maybe	Yes	Yes
Electrics	Some	Yes, but few	Yes	Yes
Rigging Crew	No	No	Maybe	Yes
Generator Operator	No	Maybe	Yes	Yes

FIGURE 3.7

Continued

many more cameras than you would find on a low-budget webisode. Figure 3.7 presents a chart of these differences. Keep in mind that this chart presents only a guideline. The rule is that there is no rule. You hire who you can afford and who you need to get your project done.

SUMMARY

You need to know the scope of your project before you can create its budget. Know what format you will use, what size crew you would like, how long the final product will be, and what format is required for delivery. Once you have answered these questions you can create a budget either on budgeting software or on your own spreadsheet program. Don't forget to allow in your budget for items such as a 10 percent contingency, fringe benefits, and padding. Once the budget is written, you track your spending with disbursement forms and cost reports. Keep in mind that the goal is to come in at, or under, budget.

The Production Team and Staff

This chapter examines the many personnel on a production team (see Figure 4.1 for their hierarchy), explaining their duties from low- to high-budget films. The people discussed here are the heart of the production process, the support team that works mainly out of the production office. Their place in the process is discussed in Chapter 5.

UNIT PRODUCTION MANAGER

The unit production manager (UPM) works directly under the producer. This person oversees more of the day-to-day running of the crew and set. The UPM is the first person the crew may come to with problems. In fact, much of the day-to-day business of the UPM is solving problems. A good UPM will accept these problems without stressing out and work to solve them. The UPM begins work on a project shortly after the producer begins and works through some of post-production. You will definitely find UPMs on medium-and higher-budget shoots. Many low-budget projects also have UPMs. The main difference from high to low budget in regard to the **production staff** is in the existence of coordinators. A very-low-budget project may not have any coordinators at all, leaving all the coordinating duties to the UPM. Following are the duties and responsibilities of the UPM when there are coordinators in place.

Pre-Production

- Answers directly to the producer and director, although he will work mostly with the producer.
- Contacts and works with the film commission in the city or state of shooting to get assistance in locating local housing, crew, and filming locations.
- Hires the **production office coordinator** (POC) and other crew members, which may include the rest of the production team, the **location manager**, and **script supervisor**.

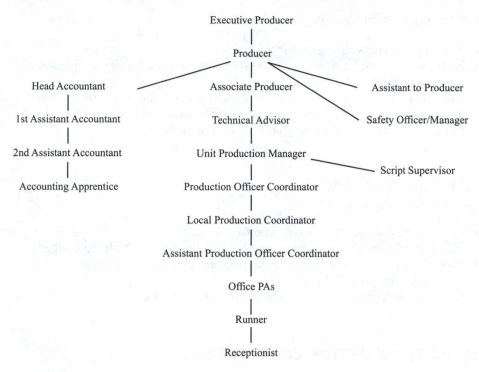

FIGURE 4.1
Production Team Hierarchy.

- Based on recommendations and bids from certain departments, contacts vendors and secures equipment packages. These packages may include but are not limited to the sound, camera, lighting, and **grip packages**.
- Makes deals with crew members. Often, different department heads come with their own crews. It is still the job of the UPM to give final approval to their rates and hiring.
- Goes on location scouts.
- Manages the budget (this continues through post-production). The UPM is expected, as part of his responsibility to the producer, to keep the project from going over budget. Whereas the producer may be looking only at the bottom line, the UPM is supervising all line-item spending.

Production

- Approves all call sheets and production reports.
- Continues to oversee all departmental budgets and spending.
- Spends time on set to handle crew problems.
- Approves purchase orders, check requests, and cash advances for crew members.
- Fires crew if necessary.
- May attend dailies.

Post-Production and Wrap

- Sometimes secures crew gifts for the producer.
- Returns to the studio (if it is a studio shoot) to arrange for the completion of post-production.
- Approves the list of credits, which will then be handed over to the producer.
- Usually spends approximately one to two months in post-production, continuing to monitor the budget and post-production crew.

Qualities of a Good UPM

A good UPM is one who:

- Can handle thousands of details at once.
- Has a great memory for numbers (which helps in dealing with the budget).
- Has no difficulty troubleshooting the constant problems that arise.
- Can anticipate potential problems.
- Can deal with problem personalities and their conflicts.

PRODUCTION OFFICE COORDINATOR

The POC is usually the liaison between the studio and set and oversees the running of the production office. He answers directly to the UPM. The jobs of the POC and assistant production coordinator sometimes overlap. For instance, when I worked as an assistant, I coordinated travel for the cast and crew. Some other POCs may prefer to do travel themselves. It is usually at the discretion of the POC which duties will be covered by the assistant. The POC will start work on a show when a location (meaning city, not set) is secured and will continue through wrapping out the production office. Typically, the POC will finish at this point. However, in some cases, a production company may have a POC permanently on staff who will continue to work from show to show as they arise.

Pre-Production

- Hires the **assistant production office coordinator** (APOC) and office assistants.
- Oversees cast physicals, if needed, and **cast insurance**.
- Sets up the production office. This involves various duties covered in Chapter 5.
- Coordinates production meetings for crew.
- Sets up production files (also in Chapter 5).
- Finishes **deal memos** and tax paperwork with crew after they are hired by the UPM.
- Sometimes procures **product placement**. In low budget this is accomplished by the POC. In higher-budget productions a product placement company may be hired to procure product placement for the project.
- May research equipment packages for the UPM.

- Oversees creation, updates, and distribution of the cast, contact, and crew lists.
- Oversees all paperwork distribution to the crew.
- Sometimes coordinates cast and crew travel.

Production

- Coordinates sending and receiving dailies to and from the film lab.
- Manages **petty cash** for the production office.
- Oversees script pages (changes) and their distribution.
- Opens or closes the production office in conjunction with the assistant coordinator.
- Troubleshoots everything having to do with coordination of the production office.

Wrap

- Wraps out the production office. See Chapter 5.

Qualities of a Good POC

- Is extremely organized.
- Loves and can handle a lot of detail work.
- Has a service-oriented personality.
- Can handle stress well.
- Is able to lead a team of assistants.
- Has excellent sense of follow-through.

LOCAL PRODUCTION COORDINATOR

A **local production coordinator** is a type of coordinator who lives in the area where you are shooting. This coordinator has the advantage of knowing the area and can more easily secure local services. You would find this position only on higher-budget projects. In these higher-budget projects, the production coordinator will run the production office at the current location. When the time is appropriate, approximately two weeks before the crew is to move, the production coordinator or UPM will hire a local production coordinator to set up the production office in the new location. The local production coordinator will continue to work in the office during the time the crew is there and will then wrap out the office after the crew leaves. In some cases when a local production coordinator is not hired, the assistant production coordinator may be given the task of setting up the new office. He will then hire office assistants to help find and secure local services.

ASSISTANT PRODUCTION OFFICE COORDINATOR

The APOC assists the POC in running the production office, answers directly to the POC, and fills in for the POC in her absence. Many of the duties of the POC and APOC overlap or are interchangeable at the discretion of the POC. Many APOCs are hired locally, as they will have better knowledge of local services. Still, some POCs prefer to work with the same APOCs and travel them to the location. The APOC will begin work shortly after the POC starts and continue through wrapping out the production office.

Pre-Production

- May handle cast and crew travel. This job would continue through the production and wrap time. Part of coordinating travel also includes distribution of the movement form (see Chapter 5).
- Handles hotel reservations for the cast and crew as they arrive and leave the location.
- Handles housing for lead actors in high-budget projects.
- Sets up laundry service for cast and crew while on location.
- Locates and secures local services such as beauty salons, restaurants, entertainment, and medical facilities.

Production

- May type call sheets and production reports (sometimes done by the DGA trainee) and is responsible for their distribution.
- Assists in or may be responsible for distributing most of the paperwork for the crew in conjunction with the APOC.
- Coordinates the pre-production party, also called the meet-and-greet.
- Secures **emergency forms** for all crew and cast.
- If required by the studio, completes weekly reports. A weekly report is a compilation of the information found in a week of production reports (see Chapter 5 for a detailed description of the production report).
- Opens or closes the production office in conjunction with the POC.
- Keeps a running **hotel log** of cast and crew.
- Receives the production calls: first shot, lunch, and wrap.
- Continues working on travel.
- Oversees duties of the office assistants.

Wrap

- May compile and type credits for the UPM.
- Coordinates the wrap party.
- Assists the POC in wrapping out the production office.
- May assist in procuring crew gifts.

Qualities of a Good APOC

- Is extremely organized.
- Loves and can handle a lot of detail work.
- Has a service-oriented personality.
- Can handle stress well.

TRAVEL/MOVEMENT

In low budget, travel is often kept to a minimum. Handling **travel/movement** on medium- to high-budget productions can be a demanding job. On a daily basis, anywhere from a few to a dozen or more cast and crew may be traveling to and from the location. The POC or APOC will manage this job. The job begins in pre-production and continues until the last crew and cast have returned home. Following is a general list of travel-related duties and responsibilities:

- Works with travel agency to secure air travel.
- Works with transportation department to provide airport pickups and returns.
- Completes a daily travel log (see Figure 4.2) showing who is traveling where and when.
- Informs hotel of cast and crew arrivals and departures.
- Works with cast agents to provide for specific travel needs of stars.
- Works with AD team to confirm cast arrivals and departures.
- Works with UPM to confirm crew arrivals and departures.
- Works with the accounting department to process reimbursements to cast and crew who may not wish to use their **travel allotment**.
- Keeps a list of ingoing and outgoing flights to and from the location on certain airlines that fly direct.

The process of providing travel on a typical basis is as follows:

1. Use the day-out-of-days to find out when cast needs to travel.
2. Confirm cast travel with ADs.
3. Receive crew travel dates from the UPM or POC.
4. Contact the crew, cast person, or cast person's agent and confirm travel arrangements, such as: Does the person want a window or aisle seat? Does the person need a special meal? Will the person need an allowance for extra baggage? As a rule, all SAG actors and DGA members fly first class.
5. Contact the travel agent to secure the flight booking.
6. Have tickets either issued and sent to the person or held via an e-ticket at the airport.
7. If needed, inform the transportation department of any ground transportation needs via a transportation request form.
8. Inform the hotel of any arrivals or departures.
9. Greet the cast or crew at the hotel once they arrive.

Travel/Movement   **"DATE"**

Name	C	Date	FLT	Date	FLT	TH	TR	Notes
Wales	1st	4/16	UA2148	4/16	UA 345	Y	Y	Transpo p/up
Wales	1st	4/16	UA2148	4/17	UA 345	N	Y	Transpo p/up
Parker	1st	4/16	UA2148	4/16	UA2148	N	Y	Transpo p/up
Lane	1st	4/12	USAIR 59	4/12	USAIR 346	N	Y	Transpo p/up
Johnson	1st	4/11	DELTA 44	4/11	DELTA 1378	Y	N	Transpo p/up
Duran	E	4/14	UA2148	4/16	UA 345	Y	N	Own transpo
Guerrera	E	4/14	UA2148	4/16	UA 345	N	Y	Mu lti-p/up
Piper	E	4/16	UA2148	4/16	UA 345	Y	N	Multi-p/up
Stahl	E	4/10	USAIR 55	4/12	USAIR 34	N	N	Own transpo
Werner	E	4/11	DELTA 44	4/11	DELTA 1378	Y	Y	Mu lti-p/up
Coates	E	4/11	DELTA 44	4/11	DELTA 1378	Y	Y	Mu lti-p/up
Wright	E	4/14	UA2148	4/16	UA 345	Y	N	Own transpo
Quicke	E	4/16	UA2148	4/16	UA 345	N	N	Transpo p/up
Mintle	E	4/10	USAIR 55	4/12	USAIR 34	N	Y	Transpo p/up
Bounds	E	4/11	DELTA 44	4/11	DELTA 1378	Y	Y	Transpo p/up
Schihl	1st	4/11	DELTA 44	4/11	DELTA 1378	N	Y	Transpo p/up
Morton	1st	4/14	UA2148	4/16	UA 345	Y	N	Transpo p/up
Clarke	E	4/14	UA2148	4/16	UA 345	Y	Y	Own transpo
Elvgren	E	4/11	DELTA 44	4/11	DELTA 1378	N	N	Own transpo

FIGURE 4.2

Travel Log.

OFFICE PRODUCTION ASSISTANTS

Office production assistants (PAs) are assistants for the UPM, POC, and APOC. They may begin work shortly after the APOC begins, or may be brought in earlier, depending on budget. They will be used for a short period to help wrap out the production office. A PA holds various duties in the production office during pre-production, production, and wrap:

- May keep **shipment logs** (see the online forms for an example).
- Gets lunch for all office personnel. This duty may seem easy, but it is very difficult. The PA has to get lunch for anywhere from ten to twenty people who all want something different, from a different restaurant. Furthermore, he has to give appropriate change back to each person. I have seen office PAs take up to 3 hours to accomplish this.
- Completes general office duties such as making copies, making coffee, faxing documents, answering telephones (if there is no receptionist to do so), screening calls, running errands, distributing mail, dividing resumes and putting them in a notebook, distributing call sheets in the production office, copying call sheets for the crew, and assisting the POC and APOC in wrapping out the office.

RECEPTIONIST

A receptionist in a production office does what a traditional receptionist in any office would do. She mainly answers telephones, screens calls, greets guests, and takes up any duties of the office PAs as needed. The receptionist can start anytime in pre-production, budget permitting, and would finish work shortly into the wrap period. You basically want a receptionist working by the time your incoming phone calls increase to the point that they interfere with the duties of the office PAs. This frees up the PAs to do other work.

Qualities of Good PAs and Receptionists

- Can handle stress well.
- Has excellent typing skills.
- Is organized, dependable, and can follow orders well.
- Knows how to work office machines such as the fax and copier.
- Can handle a multiline telephone with a large volume of incoming calls.
- Knows enough about production to properly screen phone calls and guests.

HEAD ACCOUNTANT

The **head accountant**, also known as the production accountant, is the person who handles the actual disbursement of funds to vendors, cast, and crew. He may also handle the crew payroll if a payroll service has not been hired. The accountant is the source for all actual currency traffic on a daily basis. Because you start to spend money early on in pre-production, the accountant will start work anywhere from a month or more before principal photography and continue through the end of post-production. In low-budget projects the producer or UPM may cover the duties of the accountant, which can be very time-consuming. Even if you do not have a full accounting team, having someone else handle the finances is wise. The duties of a head accountant include the following:

- Answers to the UPM and producer.
- Examines **expense reports**.
- Produces cost reports.
- Issues petty cash when needed.
- Tracks the budget.
- Makes sure all vendors are paid.
- May issue paychecks.
- May issue payroll reports.
- Submits credit reports to vendors as needed (to establish an account).
- Wraps out all vendor accounts at the end of post-production.

FIRST ASSISTANT ACCOUNTANT, SECOND ASSISTANT ACCOUNTANT, AND ACCOUNTING APPRENTICE

The accounting assistants have various duties under the head accountant. Most assistants are working their way up to head accountant. These assistants will start work that is then finished by the head accountant. How much responsibility is given to this crew usually depends on that person's level of experience. Therefore, their duties are listed together as follows:

- Checks expense reports for errors.
- Delivers paychecks to crew.
- Screens calls for head accountant.
- Processes various paperwork for head accountant.
- Completes general office duties such as copying, typing, and faxing.

Qualities of a Good Accounting Staff

- Knowledgeable with experience in general accounting procedures.
- Knowledgeable in the running of a production.
- Able to deal with the fast pace of a production.
- Excels in dealing with numbers and paperwork all day.

TECHNICAL ADVISOR

A **technical advisor** is a person who comes from a specialized field. This person is hired by the production because she has expertise in one particular area. For instance, if the film is about a military operation, the production will hire a military person to be on set and advise the filmmakers. Or, if the film is a medical drama, the production may hire a doctor to advise. The advisor may also be more scholar-ly. If the film is about the Civil War, the production may hire a Civil War historian to advise. The technical advisor may be needed for advising on the script only or may be hired to be on set for the duration of the shoot. Following is a general list of technical advisor duties and responsibilities:

- Reads the script and advises the writer of technical inaccuracies.
- Meets with the director and/or producer to discuss level of involvement.
- May stand by on set to answer technical questions.
- May stand by on set to give constructive criticism of technique.
- May examine sets for technical accuracy.
- Is expected to speak up if the director or actors are being inaccurate.

SCRIPT SUPERVISOR

The script supervisor is an essential position from the lowest-to the highest-budget project. This person is in charge of the continuity of the film and of ensuring that everything that needs to be shot gets shot. She keeps track of changes actors may make in the dialogue while shooting. If the schedule changes, she knows what can be shot. The script supervisor is the one person on set who must be watching eve-rything in front of the camera, catching all continuity and logging it. Essentially, the script supervisor times all rehearsals and takes and watches the continuity of the actors, while also making notations on each take. This job requires a lot of skill and attention to detail.

One of the most important of the script supervisor's duties is to make sure the **axis** is not crossed. The axis can be an imaginary line extending between two actors, facing each other in a scene. If you shoot one actor from one side of the line, and another actor from the same side of the line, you can cut the two shots together and they will look like they are looking at each other. If you shoot one actor from one side of the line and the other actor from the opposite side of the line, when you cut the shots together it will look like they are looking in the same direction, and not at each other. While continuity is also the responsibility of the director, the director is expected to be able to rely on the script supervisor for support in this area. The script supervisor will start usually one week before principal photography and fin-ish one or two days after principal photography is complete.

Pre-Production

- **Times the script.** This is a process where the script is read aloud and timed with a stopwatch. The supervisor mimics all the movements of the actors and records the times for each scene. The times for each scene are then added to-gether to achieve an estimate of the final film's length in minutes and seconds.
- Completes a form called a **day breakdown** (see Figure 4.3). The day breakdown is useful to the script supervisor and other crew such as the director and DP. In the example breakdown, the column "Day" refers to the day of the story. Scene one takes place on the first day of the story.

"Regina of Icelandia"
Day Breakdown

Prepared by: (Script Supervisor)

Scene #	Day	INT/EXT		Scene #	Day	INT/EXT
1	1	INT		34	14	EXT
2	1	INT		35	14	EXT
3	1	INT		36	14	EXT
4	1	INT		37	14	EXT
5	2	INT		38	14	EXT
6	2	INT		39	14	EXT
7	2	EXT		40	15	EXT
8	3	EXT		41	16	EXT
9	3	EXT		42	16	EXT
10	4	EXT		43	16	EXT
11	5	EXT		44	17	EXT
12	6	INT		45	18	INT
13	6	INT		46	18	EXT
14	6	INT		47	18	INT
15	6	INT		48	18	INT
16	6	INT		49	18	INT
17	6	INT		50	18	EXT
18	6	INT		51	18	EXT
19	6	INT		52	19	EXT
20	7	EXT		53	19	EXT
21	7	EXT		54	19	EXT
22	8	EXT		55	19	EXT
23	8	INT		56	19	EXT
24	8	INT		57	19	EXT
25	9	INT		58	19	EXT
26	9	INT		59	19	EXT
27	9	INT		60	19	EXT
28	9	EXT		61	19	EXT
29	10	EXT		62	19	EXT
30	10	EXT		63	19	EXT
31	11	INT		64	19	EXT
32	12	INT		65	19	EXT
33	13	EXT		66	20	EXT

FIGURE 4.3

Example Day Breakdown.

Scenes two, three, and four also take place on the first day of the story. Scene five takes place on the second day of the story. This breakdown helps people see at a glance on what day of the story a scene occurs. Since scenes are usually shot out of order, this form is very helpful for continuity.

- Completes her own breakdown of the script, checking for any references to future details, as well as overt actions such as running, jumping, and skipping (any action that might require close scrutiny for continuity).

Production

- Stays on set close to the director and camera.
- Never leaves camera. Unlike the positions with assistants who can take their place while they, for instance, use the lavatory, the script supervisor must stay at camera at all times, leaving only during lighting or setup changes.
- Sometimes reads off-camera dialogue to the actors and, if needed, prompts actors with dialogue.
- Times rehearsals and each take with a stopwatch.
- Lines the script according to shot coverage (see Figure 4.4). **Lining the script** is the process of keeping track of what part of the script a shot covers. For instance, in the example script the line that extends from the beginning of scene twenty to the end of scene twenty represents shot number 20A. The shot is called 20A because it was the first shot taken of that scene. The next shot will be called 20B, and so on. Shot 20A's coverage is the entire scene. Shot 20B starts at the beginning of scene 20 and ends right after Dr. Slayvnak's first line. Lining the script allows the script supervisor to have a visual representation of how the scene has been covered. This is important to make sure that all dialogue and every part of a scene is shot.
- Keeps the **scene log**. See Figure 4.5.
- Numbers all the shots as shooting progresses.
- Completes a **daily progress report** for the 2nd AD. See Figure 4.6. This information is then transferred to the production report.
- Takes snapshots at the beginning and end of appropriate scenes. These snapshots can be useful for continuity. For instance, if in a scene an actor falls to the ground, the script supervisor may take a shot of the actor, which captures the actor's exact positioning of arms, legs, etc. This photograph may be needed later if the scene is reshot or covered from another angle at another time.
- Watches for **back matching**. This is when an action or piece of dialogue in a scene references an action or dialogue in another scene. For instance, an actor in scene ten may say, "Hey, that was great pizza we had last night." The script supervisor must then make sure that in the previous scene the actors did eat pizza.
- At the end of the day copies all paperwork and gives it to the **editor**.

20   EXT. FOREST—DAY

Regina and the Wochera stand in the forest with Donato and the doctor.

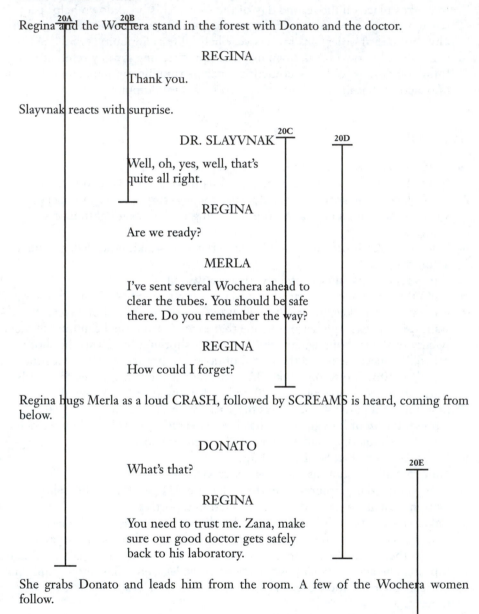

REGINA

Thank you.

Slayvnak reacts with surprise.

DR. SLAYVNAK

Well, oh, yes, well, that's quite all right.

REGINA

Are we ready?

MERLA

I've sent several Wochera ahead to clear the tubes. You should be safe there. Do you remember the way?

REGINA

How could I forget?

Regina hugs Merla as a loud CRASH, followed by SCREAMS is heard, coming from below.

DONATO

What's that?

REGINA

You need to trust me. Zana, make sure our good doctor gets safely back to his laboratory.

She grabs Donato and leads him from the room. A few of the Wochera women follow.

FIGURE 4.4

Sample of Shot Coverage.

SCRIPT SUPERVISOR'S DAILY FORM (FILM)

PAGE   1 OF 25

TITLE: "Regina of Icelandia"   PROD: Wales
CAM: Hanson   DIR: Wales
SCRIPT: Jordan   A.D: Scottson
DATE: 4/25/02   SND: Grather

SCENE	TAKE	SND ROLL	TIME	LENS	FOOTAGE	ACTION
1A	1	1	:30	28	45'	Regina searches.
	2	1	:45	28	50'	NG
	3	1	:36	28	47'	NG
	4	1	:38	28	40'	Regina searches.
1B	1	1	1:00	16	100'	Regina finds home.
	2	1	1:03	16	104'	Regina finds home.
1C	1	1	:58	16	88'	Margee sees Regina.
	2	1	:59	16	86'	Margee sees Regina.
	3	1	:52	16	85'	Margee sees Regina.
	4	1	:49	16	86'	Margee sees Regina.
	5	1	:50	16	87'	Margee sees Regina.
	6	1	:52	16	88'	Margee sees Regina.
1D	1	1	2:01	55	151'	Alb leaves.
	2	1	1:59	55	152'	Alb leaves.
2A	1	1	:10	28	20'	Wochera consel Regina.
	2	1	:12	28	21'	Wochera consel Regina.
	3	1	:11	28	22'	Wochera consel Regina.
2B	1	2	2:30	120	166'	Regina sneaks out.
	2	2	2:34	120	164'	Regina sneaks out.
	3	2	2:36	120	165'	Regina sneaks out.
	4	2	2:22	120	168'	Regina sneaks out.
	5	2	2:31	120	162'	Regina sneaks out.
	6	2	2:32	120	163'	Regina sneaks out.
	7	2	2:45	120	170'	Regina sneaks out.
2C	1	2	:22	16	39'	Regina falls out of tree.
	2	2	:24	16	40'	Regina falls out of tree.
	3	2	:23	16	41'	Regina falls out of tree.
2D	1	2	:09	90	21'	Donato finds Regina.
	2	2	:10	90	19'	Donato finds Regina.
	3	2	:07	90	19'	Donato finds Regina.
	4	2	:06	90	17'	Donato finds Regina.
	5	2	:11	90	19'	Donato finds Regina.
2E	1	3	1:45	28	120'	Donato & Regina—love scene.
	2	3	1:34	28	115'	Donato & Regina—love scene.
	3	3	1:40	16	117'	Donato & Regina—love scene.
	4	3	1:42	16	119'	Donato & Regina—love scene.
2F	1	3	:55	52	86'	Regina walks away.
	2	3	:56	52	88'	Regina walks away.
2G	1	3	:34	52	66'	Donato returns.
	2	3	:35	52	64'	Donato returns.

FIGURE 4.5

Script Supervisor's Daily Form (Film).

SCRIPT SUPERVISOR'S DAILY REPORT

DATE: 3/7/02
DAY: 2 of 42
TITLE: "Regina of Icelandia"
DIRECTOR: Darin Wales
PRODUCER: Lorene Wales

	SCENES	PAGES	MINUTES	SETUPS
TOTAL SCRIPT	120	115 7/8	120:00	
ADDED	0	0	0.00	
DELETED	1	2/8	:23	
NEW TOTAL	119	115 5/8	119:37	
PREVIOUSLY	2	4 1/8	4:30	5
TODAY	3	1 1/8	1:18	7
TOTAL TO DATE	5	5 2/8	5:48	12
TO BE TAKEN	114	110 3/8	113:49	

Lindsey Snyder

SCRIPT/CONTINUITY SUPERVISOR

FIGURE 4.6
Script Supervisor's Daily Report.

Wrap

- Has one day of wrap time where she cleans up the script and notes and turns them over to the editors.

Qualities of a Good Script Supervisor

- Is extremely detailed.
- Can multitask for 10–12 hours per day.
- Has excellent concentration skills.
- Has excellent memory of events.

SAFETY OFFICER/MANAGER

Safety on sets became an important issue years ago when actor Vic Morrow and two children were killed on the set of *The Twilight Zone*. Union shows use a set of established safety guidelines called the **Industry-Wide Labor Management Safety Committee Safety Bulletins**. This document also includes an **Industry Code of Conduct**. Nonunion and lower-budget projects are not bound by these guidelines but would be wise to use them. They are extremely comprehensive in covering all aspects of a production that may require safety monitoring.

The safety officer, also called the **safety manager,** is a person who is responsible for all safety conditions on the set. The safety manager may be under contract with a studio and oversees safety for all the studio's productions. Alternatively, this person may be an independent safety manager and hired on an independent basis. The safety manager may be employed for a certain amount of time or for run of show, depending on the needs of the production. If your stunts and special-effects people were run of show, the safety manager would most likely be also. If not, the safety manager may be needed only for certain situations. The safety manager's duties and responsibilities are as follows:

- May answer directly to a studio.
- May answer directly to the producer and director.
- Reads the script and marks all actions that may indicate an unsafe or hazardous situation.
- Meets with the producer, director, stunt coordinator, or visual effects supervisor to discuss safety issues.
- May advise stunt or special-effects department on set.
- If needed, shows up on set to supervise the safety of any situation deemed necessary.

Qualities of a Good Safety Manager

- Knows the Industry-Wide Labor Management Safety Committee Safety Bulletins.
- Is knowledgeable in various safety practices for stunts and special effects.
- Has a strong enough personality to object to unsafe practices on set.

PRODUCT PLACEMENT

Product placement is placing a brand-name product in a shot so that it is recognizable. A brand-name product could be a simple soda can or a fleet of cars. The amount and use of product placement on your production is determined by the content of your story. In return for a product being placed in a show, the product company will often supply the crew with the product. This situation provides the product company with advertising and the production company with free product, such as soda, which is often used for craft services.

The process of product placement begins with the script. In a low-budget production the POC may do a product placement breakdown and then contact companies directly for use of their product. I once worked a show as a POC and did this. Because our cast needed to smoke cigarettes in a few scenes, I contacted R.J. Reynolds and requested permission to use their cigarettes in our film. R.J. Reynolds read the script, looked at what our distribution was, and agreed. In return for placing their cigarettes in our scene, they provided the production with one hundred cartons of cigarettes!

Another approach is to hire a product placement company, which will go through the script and look for possible product placement opportunities. The company will then contact various brand-name companies and solicit them for placement in the picture. The product placement company then coordinates getting the product to the crew.

Most product companies will require that they receive still photographs of the product in the shot, which you make sure your **still photographer** takes.

SUMMARY

The production team comprises the executive producer, producer, associate producer, UPM, POC, local production coordinator, APOC, and assistants. Assistants work either directly for a producer or UPM or in the production office. Other personnel who work closely with the production team include the accountants, technical advisor, and safety manager. The producer is responsible for the running and final product of a project. The coordinators and assistants lend support by working as liaisons in the day-to-day running of a show. The coordinators and assistants provide the crew with assistance in their daily living, work, and travel. The production team is there to ensure that pre-production adequately prepares the show to run smoothly and that the crew has sufficient support.

The Production Office

Now that you have broken down your script, determined a budget for your production, and started to put your key players together, you need to have a base of operations. That base is the production office. The production office is the hub of communication and operations during pre-production and a source for support during production. Setting up and running a production office may seem daunting with all that needs to be done but, if organized well, can result in a smooth-running show.

THE PRODUCTION OFFICE

There are two kinds of production offices. One may exist wherever your production company is located. If you are shooting in the same vicinity/city as your production company, this office will remain your base of operations. The second office is the one you may need on location. If you are shooting at a distant location from where your production company is, then you need to set up a temporary production office. This chapter will deal with this temporary kind of office; however, each type of office is very similar. Keep in mind that a temporary production office on location is mainly used for feature films. You may still need a small production office area if you are working in documentary or producing life events. These types of productions may not need as many offices or services but the concept is still the same. You need a place to operate from.

Either the producer or UPM determines the location of the office. First, she determines exactly in what location, as in city, the film will be shooting. Once that is decided, the UPM will research different hotels. Hotels are one of the best choices for your production office because you can also house your crew in the hotel, diminishing the need to transport your crew around the city. Not just any hotel will do. Following is a list of services and amenities that are needed in a hotel to house a production coming into town for an extended period of time (anywhere from one month to a year!).

Blocks of Rooms

The hotel must be able to set aside blocks of rooms that will accommodate your crew size. Having blocks means that, at any time, you have access to, for example, seventy-five rooms, even though you are not technically reserving and paying for all seventy-five. Reserving blocks of rooms assures that you'll be able to get a room at any time. Remember, not all of your crew will be arriving at your location at the same time. As crew members and actors arrive in pre-production, and as your other actors arrive during production, you need the ability to secure their hotel rooms.

Ample Office Space

Ample office space is imperative. One standard is that almost all of your key personnel get their own production offices. You can count on an additional five to six offices for other personnel. The point here is to make sure you have enough offices within one office space so that your crew has ample space in which to work.

Proximity to Restaurants and Shops

Because working in a production office, especially in pre-production, leaves little time for taking lunch, most people eat and work at their desks. Having restaurants close by for either delivery or pickup makes sense.

Proximity to Airport

Since you will be transporting cast, crew, some equipment, and possibly dailies to and from the airport, it is better to be close to an airport. This may not always be possible, depending on where you are shooting and where your main sets/locations are, but try not to be too far from the airport.

Room Service

You will find that your shooting days can range from all-day to all-night. Sometimes your crew may finish at four o'clock in the morning. Having 24-hour room service so the crew can get a bite to eat after a long day's shooting is important. It is also important for any days off, when crew members who do not have their own transportation need to eat. Obviously, a good restaurant or two inside the hotel is also preferable.

Nicer Rooms for Stars

Most of your crew is fine staying in a standard hotel room. However, many times actors of a certain caliber or level of fame may require more upscale lodging. Often hotels have larger rooms, suites, or even presidential suites that can accommodate this need. Your director, director of photography, and/or production designer may also require nicer hotel rooms. The determination of who gets what kind of room may be generated by you, by an actor or crew's request, or may even be contractual.

The key is to make sure that the proper type of room for a person is communicated to your APOC, who will be booking the rooms.

Refrigerators

This is a nice item for crew and cast, who'd rather not have to leave their rooms every time they want a drink or snack. If the hotel does not provide these, you can often make a deal with the hotel to bring in small refrigerators from a rental company. It is your decision whether you want to pay for them or have individual crew and cast who want them order and pay for their own.

Parking

On a location shoot you need several kinds of parking. There's parking for **production vehicles** (this is covered in Chapter 16), crew, cast, and visitors. Some of your crew may be hired locally, meaning that they live in the city where you are shooting. These people are called local crew. Local crew, since they most likely have their own transportation, will need a place to park when they come into the office. Some of your distant crew need and should be provided with rental vehicles. They will need parking near the office. Sometimes hotels have ample parking right at the building. However, if your hotel is in a downtown area, you may need to rent spaces in a parking structure.

Proximity to Locations

Ideally, your hotel/production office would be close to your shooting locations. This cuts down on travel time to the set for crew and cast. Again, this may not always be possible when shooting in remote or exotic locations, but it is ideal.

Laundry Service

Just about all hotels have laundry service, and everyone knows how expensive it can be. It is a good idea to hire a local laundry service to come to your office twice a week to pick up and deliver laundry. The laundries can give you bags to disburse to the crew. Usually the crew will turn over their laundry, labeled, to the receptionist, who will later turn it over to the laundry service and then disburse it when it comes back.

SETTING UP THE OFFICE

Once the office is located, the next step is setting it up, making it a workable space specific to film and digital production. The first step is to assign offices to specific departments or crew. The higher the budget, the more offices and personnel you will have. Lower-budget projects may not be able to afford any office space. This is where the producer needs to be creative. Making a film or show without a base of operations will only lead to disorganization, miscommunication, and a lack of cohesiveness for the crew. If expense is a concern, a single hotel room can double as a production office. This is common in field shooting where small crews of two to three people are in a location for only a short time.

Assigning Offices

Certain personnel have the biggest, nicest offices. These are the producer, director, UPM, production supervisor, and **VIPs.** The VIP office is reserved for important visitors such as the executive producer or occasional studio executive. The POC and APOC usually get the biggest space in a central area because they are the hub of coordination and information for the crew.

The following also need offices: locations, the assistant directors, production designer, director of photography, art director, props, wardrobe, accounting (two), editors (two to three), transportation coordinator and captain, grip and electric, and sometimes extras casting. If you are casting extras at the production office, it is wise to place this office outside and away from the other offices. This way you avoid the occasional nosy extra who wants to get his script to the producer.

Other rooms are needed for various situations, such as a viewing room, a room to watch dailies, and a break room with coffee, refrigerator, etc. The main entrance area should be reserved with a space for the receptionist to screen people and answer phones.

Making the Office Operational

Making the office operational involves ordering the following services and equipment:

Telephones. You will definitely need multiline phones, preferably with seven to eight incoming lines. These phones should be set up with extension numbers, conference calling, speaker phones, long-distance service, and automatic redial. The process is to set up an account with a local telephone company: the company can provide the telephones as well as the service. Some hotels already have phones in these spaces and you need only to set up the service. The APOC assigns and keeps a record of extension assignments and makes sure this list is distributed to all offices.

Office equipment. The following standard office equipment is needed in your production office: two copiers (one for general use and one for private use in the accounting office) that can do multiple documents all at once, a fax machine, an answering machine, coffee/cappuccino makers, a refrigerator, a microwave, and a water cooler. You must also outfit the office with the following: office furniture, desks, chairs, and bookcases. You may also need a couple of monitors and DVD players for the viewing room.

Local services. There are many different kinds of local services that need to be available to your crew. These services may be for their personal use or to support their work on the production. These include art supply stores, car rentals, banks, bookstores, cab services, a cake shop for special occasions, a card shop, caterers, a chiropractor, copy places, local hospitals and medical doctors, dry cleaners, florists, grocery stores, health food stores, beauty shops, drug and liquor stores, a notary, police, and a post office.

Couriers. There are many kinds of couriers used on a production because productions tend to have heavy shipping loads. You will be shipping dailies back and forth, sending scripts to cast and crew, and sending equipment back and forth, just to name a sampling. You need to set up an account with an international/national overnight courier service such as FedEx, Airborne Express, or UPS. Most of these companies will give you a discount because of the large volume of shipping that will take place.

You may also need to contact local airlines that will do **counter-to-counter service**. This is very important if you need to ship your dailies to another city for developing. There are also specific **film couriers** who know how to deal with exposed film.

Projection. Depending on how you intend to view dailies, you may need to arrange for a projector to be brought in (not done too much anymore, but still done). If you are watching dailies on 35-mm film, you will need a 35-mm projector. These projectors are large and require at least a day to set up. Certain companies will fly the projector to you, along with a person to set it up. At the end of the shoot, the person will return to tear the projector down and take it back to the company.

If you plan to watch your dailies digitally, you can either have the dailies projected or watch them on a monitor. Check with your director and DP to see which they prefer. Many productions are also watching their dailies online.

Security. Sometimes productions will hire a private firm to provide security for the production office and set. Security may be needed if you have well-known talent and your production has been publicized in the local press.

Crew packets. **Crew packets** are packages of information for arriving cast and crew that contain the following: contact list, crew list, new script pages (if any), hotel information, new memos (if any), film commission information, and brochures and recreational information about the city. Once you create a sample packet, have your PAs put together enough for every distant cast and crew member. When crew or cast comes into town, the drivers from the transportation department should give them a packet. You can also leave it in the person's hotel room.

The wall of envelopes. Because of the large number of people working in a temporary situation, there needs to be an easy way to distribute paperwork to the cast and crew. Generally, all paperwork for cast is given to them individually. Because crews can be quite large, a more efficient form of distribution is used. You can create a **wall of envelopes** for this distribution. There first needs to be a wall in the production office large enough to hold anywhere from fifteen to more than thirty large manila envelopes (the 8.5-by-11 size), depending on the size of your crew. You then cut out the front portion of the envelope so that paperwork can be easily inserted and removed. Next, you need to place labels on all the envelopes, with the name of the person or department. Some crew members get their own envelopes; some envelopes are for an entire department. For instance, the DP will get her own envelope. However, the grip department can have just one envelope. Be sure to know how many people are in a particular department so that enough copies are distributed to everyone.

An alternative to using the wall of envelopes on a production is using email. Some of the people in the production office may prefer email. More than likely, you will need to do a combination of paper and electronic distribution.

RUNNING THE PRODUCTION OFFICE

The POC or APOC opens or closes the office daily. The office should be opened at least a half-hour before call time. Following is a list of various events that will take place throughout the day in the office:

- The APOC types the previous day's production report, gets it approved, and distributes it. The production report is distributed to the 1st AD, UPM, producer, completion bond company, insurance company, and studio executives (if any).
- During pre-production a daily lunch run is conducted for all office crew. Rarely do all office crew have the time to go out to lunch.
- The APOC receives the **first shot call.** This will come from the 2nd AD, on set, when the first shot is achieved. The APOC then notifies the POC, UPM, and producer. The APOC also receives calls when the crew breaks for lunch, when they get the first shot after lunch, and when the crew wraps, which are also passed on to the POC, UPM, and producer.
- The POC troubleshoots. This may involve calls from set; for example, maybe someone forgot to bring along something they need on set (this is common during the first several days of shooting).
- POC and APOC work on revising any paperwork, on travel, and on correspondence to the studio.
- The office receives and makes sure dailies will be ready for viewing. After the shooting day is over the crew will return to the production office for various reasons. You can have the PAs post a sign with the time for dailies. The editors will then prepare the dailies.
- The wrap sheet is completed and distributed to the UPM and producer. See Figure 5.1.

THE MEET-AND-GREET

The **meet-and-greet** is a party given immediately before the beginning of principal photography. The purpose of the party is for crew and cast to meet one another before working together on set. The POC or APOC coordinates this party, arranging for a venue, usually a restaurant. He also informs all cast and crew of the time

DAILY WRAP SHEET

Production Title:	"Regina of Icelandia"
Date:	4/29/2010
Shoot Day:	1 of 42
Scenes Scheduled:	24, 25, 17, 1, 3
Scenes Shot:	24, 25, 17, 1
Call Time:	7:00A
Shooting Call:	8:00A
1st Shot:	8:12A
Lunch:	1:00P
1st Shot After Lunch:	2:19P
Wrap:	6:55P
Notes:	Scene 3 not shot due to rain.

FIGURE 5.1
Example Wrap Sheet.

and location. The meet-and-greet may be paid for by the producer or may be part of the production budget. You will most likely not have a meet-and-greet on lower budget films, merely because you cannot afford it.

THE WRAP PARTY

The wrap party is the event that marks the finishing of principal photography. It is usually held on or immediately after the last day of shooting. In low budget, the party may simply be on set with some light refreshments. On a higher-budget production, the party may be at an expensive restaurant with a full gourmet meal and a band. Sometimes the party will simply be a time when everyone gets together and discusses how tired they are. Sometimes the party has a little more structure. The director or producer may wish to make a short speech, thanking the cast and crew for their hard work. Some wrap parties may feature projection of behind-the-scenes footage for the cast and crew to enjoy. Since there is very little time on a set for socializing, the wrap party also serves as a networking opportunity for crew looking for their next job.

WRAPPING OUT THE PRODUCTION OFFICE

Once principal photography is completed, the production enters a period called wrap. This is when the production office works on getting all cast, crew, and equipment back to their original places. All local accounts are closed out, and a final credit list is prepared. At this time the POC also prepares a final cast and crew list. The **final crew list** is distributed to the entire crew and is valuable to them for networking future work. Finally, the last person in the office, usually the APOC, makes sure the offices are left clean and in order, and that the hotel rooms are all left in good order, "See the online forms for a wrap checklist and example wrap calendar."

PRODUCTION LISTS

A few lists are integral to the smooth running of a production office. The crew, contact, and cast lists provide all personnel with contact information (see Figures 5.2– 5.4). The pre-production calendar provides all personnel with important events and deadlines. These lists are created by the coordinators and distributed by the office PAs (see Figure 5.5).

"Regina of Icelandia"   "Date"
Frame Right Films, Inc.

CAST LIST

ROLE	ACTOR/ADDRESS/PHONE	ASSISTANT	AGENT/MGR		EMAIL
1. Regina	**Kim Lane** 1 PERRY LANE NEW YORK, NY 10960 914/353-3280 914/353-5041 FAX	SUSAN MCTIGUE	TODD SMITH-CAA 9830 WILSHIRE BLVD. BEVERLY HILLS, CA 90212 310/288-4545 310/288-4800 FAX ASST-STUART		Susmct@email.com
2. Donato	**Jeff Johnson** 8440 DELONGPRE #203 LOS ANGELES, CA 90069 213/654-5834 LA. 914/284-1460 ARIZONA	DARYN HOLLAND	STEPHANIE HURKOS-MGR 12214 VIEWCREST RD STUDIO CITY, CA 91604 818/763-6601 818/763-5934 FAX		daryhol@email.com
3. Prono	**Ted Myaopio** 222 UPPER MOUNTAIN AVE UPPER MONTCLAIR, NJ 07043 201/783-5118 201/783-3922 FAX	BONNIE KRAMEN 908/757-3098	SCOTT HENDERSON-TRIAD 10100 SANTA MONICA BLVD 16TH FL LOS ANGELES, CA 90067 310/551-7564		bonnie@email.com
4. Salazar	Sammy Quinn 4 THORNHILL DR RAMSEY,NY 07446 201/327-0084	Steve Stevies	10 SANTA MONICA BLVD #3 LOS ANGELES, CA 90067 310/227-7779		steve@email.net
5. King	**Anthony Guerrera** 439 GOWER ST LOS ANGELES, CA 90004 213/871-1705	Lynn Cannon	DAVID DECAMILLO GERSH AGENCY 232 N CANON DR BEVERLY HILLS, CA 90210 310/274-6611		Lynn@email.net
6. Princess	264 MAGNOLIA PL City, State, VA 999333 412/343-3604 52 MARQUETTE RD. (MOTHER: SARAH)	Brownie Spots	HARTER,MANNING & WOO BEVERLY HILLS, CA 90211 ASST-NICK NEW YORK, NY 10019		brownie@email.com

FIGURE 5.2

Example Cast List.

"Regina of Icelandia"   **4/28/2010**
Frame Right Films, Inc.

CONTACT LIST

TYPE	VENDOR/ADDRESS	WEB/CONTACT	TELEPHONE
Art Supply	**Sally's House of Art** 1 PERRY LANE LOS ANGELES, CA 90345	www.sallyart.com Tim DaVinci	310-424-5873
Car Rental	**Hertz** 8440 DELONGPRE #203 LOS ANGELES, CA 90345	www.hertz.com Mary Car	310-374-4633
Coffee Svc.	**Coffee Coffee** 222 UPPER MOUNTAIN AVE LOS ANGELES, CA 90345	www.coffee.com Jim Starbuck	310-645-2746
Copier	**Copi-Ez** 4 THORNHILL DR LOS ANGELES, CA 90345	www.copiez.com Carole Copy	310-364-9983
Hotel	**William Penn Hotel** 439 GOWER ST LOS ANGELES, CA 90345	www.wmpenn.com Joe Schmo	310-361-8465
Laundry	**Finnegen's Laundry** 264 MAGNOLIA PL LOS ANGELES, CA 90345	www.finnegans.com Sally Laundry	310-463-8836
Office Sup.	**Offices-R-Us** 52 MARQUETTE RD. LOS ANGELES, CA 90345	www.office.com Jeff Jones	310-337-1127
Telephones	**Southwestern Bell** 34 JONES ST. LOS ANGELES, CA 90345	www.southbell.com Marty Spry	310-736-9983

FIGURE 5.3
Example Cast List.

"Regina of Icelandia"   4/28/2010
Frame Right Films, Inc.

CREW LIST - EXAMPLE

TITLE	NAME/ADDRESS	E-MAIL	TELEPHONE
Producer	**Lorene Wales** 1 PERRY LANE NEW YORK, NY 10960	loredur@aol.com	757-424-5873 cell: 757-555-3332
Director	**Darin Wales** 8440 DELONGPRE #203 LOS ANGELES, CA 90069	djrwal@aol.com	610-374-4633 cell: 757-555-2229
UPM	**Kim Wright** 222 UPPER MOUNTAIN AVE UPPER MONTCLAIR, NJ 07043	kwgin@juno.com	610-645-2746 cell: 757-555-9393
1st AD	**Vernon Guinn** 4 THORNHILL DR RAMSEY,NY 07446	vern@aol.com	817-364-9983 cell: 665-555-3939
2nd AD	**Mark Starr** 439 GOWER ST LOS ANGELES, CA 90004	lovey@juno.com	717-361-8465 cell: 444-554-3333
POC	**Kristie Coates** 264 MAGNOLIA PL PITTSBURGH, PA 15228	coat@verizon.net	310-463-8836 cell: 555-555-5555
APOC	**Lynn Cannon** 52 MARQUETTE RD. UPPER MONCLAIR, NJ 07043	lynn@verizon.net	310-337-1127 cell: 332-555-5555
Script	**Deana Deean** 34 JONES ST. VALLEY PINES, MI 09574	deedee@aol.com	915-736-9983 cell: 665-555-7777

FIGURE 5.4
Example Crew List.

EXAMPLE Pre-Production Calendar

March 2004

NOTE: The following is an **EXAMPLE** of one pre-production calendar for a 6-day shoot. Each script and project has its own peculiarities when it come to pre-production. This **EXAMPLE** is meant as a guideline only, and not as a complete list of all duties and deadlines in pre-production.

SUNDAY	MONDAY	TUESDAY	WEDNESDAY	THURSDAY	FRIDAY	SATURDAY
	1	2	3	4	5	6
		LOCK SCRIPT	HAVE WRITER RELEASE SCRIPT		BUDGET DUE	
7	8	9	10	11	12	13
	SCRIPT BREAKDOWN DUE				PRODUCTION STRIPS DUE	
14	15	16	17	18	19	20
	SCOUT LOCATIONS					
21	22	23	24	25	26	27
28	29	30	31			

FIGURE 5.5

Example Pre-Production Calendar.

April 2004

SUNDAY	MONDAY	TUESDAY	WEDNESDAY	THURSDAY	FRIDAY	SATURDAY
				1	2	3
4	5	6	7	8	9	10
	HOLD CASTING SESSIONS				LOCK LOCATIONS	
11	12	13	14	15	16	17
	LOCK CREW	CALLBACKS FOR CASTING	ORDER ALL EQUIPMENT W/EQUIPMENT OFFICE			
18	19	20	21	22	23	24
	LOCK CAST					
25	26	27	28	29	30	
	ORDER FILM & TAPE STOCK	SAFETY MEETING W/SAFETY MANAGER			SUBMIT ALL CHECK REQUESTS & CASH ADVANCES	

FIGURE 5.5

Continued

May 2004

SUNDAY	MONDAY	TUESDAY	WEDNESDAY	THURSDAY	FRIDAY	SATURDAY
						1
						TECH SCOUT
2	3	4	5	6	7	8
	CAST REHEARSALS FINAL PRODUCTION MEETING	CAST REHEARSALS	CAST REHEARSALS	CAST REHEARSALS PICK UP STOCK	CAST REHEARSALS CHECK OUT EQUIPMENT	
9	10	11	12	13	14	15
	SHOOT DAY #1	SHOOT DAY #2	SHOOT DAY #3	SHOOT DAY #4	SHOOT DAY #5	SHOOT DAY #6
16	17	18	19	20	21	22
	RETURN EQUIPMENT					
23	24	25	26	27	28	29
30	31					

FIGURE 5.5

Continued

SUMMARY

Setting up a production office involves first finding the right location with the right amount of space, one that can meet the specific needs of a production. The process is involved, including assigning offices and ordering a variety of furniture, equipment, and services. Production files must be set up. Crew packets need to be prepared for incoming crew. The meet-and-greet must be coordinated. Crew and cast begin to travel to and from the location. The "big" production meeting needs to be scheduled and coordinated. The production office becomes the essential hub of a project, where crew and cast find support and essential information.

The Director's Team & 2nd Unit

The director's team consists mainly of the director, the first assistant director (1st AD), **second assistant director** (2nd AD), **second second assistant director** (2nd 2nd), DGA trainee, and **set production assistants** (set PAs) (Figure 6.1). Other crew that work closely with the director include the **director's assistant, choreographer** (if needed), dialogue coach (if needed), and **storyboard artist.** This chapter covers the duties and responsibilities of each. Because the director and 1st AD work together so closely, some time is spent on their relationship. In addition, since the ADs run the set, this chapter contains a section on set operations. Finally this chapter covers the 2nd unit, what it is, and whether you may need one or not.

DIRECTOR

The full job description of a director, including artistry and aesthetics, would not be appropriate for this type of production book. However, what is listed are certain duties that the director will accomplish in each production period. The difference between low and high budget in terms of the director usually resides in the director's experience. Generally, in low budget you are dealing with inexperienced directors; however, there have been many high-budget films that hired first-time directors. Whatever their experience level, there are many responsibilities the director takes on, beginning in pre-production. Following is a list of general duties of the director.

Pre-Production

- Reads the script and works with the producer to develop a vision for the project.
- Meets with department heads to relate his vision.
- Works with the storyboard artist on **storyboards.**
- Attends casting sessions to hire cast for the project.
- Rehearses the actors.

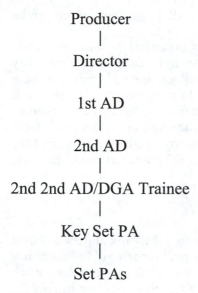

Producer
|
Director
|
1st AD
|
2nd AD
|
2nd 2nd AD/DGA Trainee
|
Key Set PA
|
Set PAs

FIGURE 6.1
Director's Team Hierarchy.

- Meets with the 1st AD to discuss the schedule.
- Goes on location scouts to approve or reject a location.
- Writes shot lists for each scene.

Production

- Works with the DP to execute shots.
- Works with the 1st AD to **make the day.** *Making the day* is the term used for completing the scheduled shots for the day.
- Directs actors.
- Works with the 2nd AD to direct the atmosphere.

Post-Production

- Works with editors to achieve a first cut of the project.
- May have final approval of a finished picture.

FIRST ASSISTANT DIRECTOR

Being an assistant director is not an easy job but it can be extremely rewarding. The following is a guide to the responsibilities of an assistant director. However, it is more than tasks that will make a 1st AD great. It's learning how to handle crew members who are slow. It's learning how to deal with temperamental actors. It's protecting the director from distractions. It's learning how to anticipate problems before they arise on the set. It's knowing how to be tactful, forceful, and patient.

Most of all, it's learning how to get twenty people, all doing different jobs, to be ready for the shot at the same time.

A 1st AD needs to have a strong personality. By the end of the show most crew members will be tired of your screaming in their ears to be quiet all the time. They will try to convince you not to remark on the production report that they were late, or to give them a later call time, but if you do your job properly, they will respect you for working hard to get the day shot on time so that they can get home and get more sleep. As an assistant director, you're the boss on the set (aside from the producer and director). While the producer is worrying about money, and the director is worrying about the shot, the 1st AD has to be worried about this shot, and the next shot, and the next one.

Pre-Production

Most of the work in pre-production involves preparing paperwork and the schedule that will be invaluable once shooting starts. This is also the time to establish a trusting relationship with the director. The director needs to trust that, when shooting, you will have respect for her vision, so that when shooting begins, the director can entrust to you the details that she has no time to oversee. Read the script closely, and know each scene. The 1st AD's duties are as follows:

- Usually starts a month before shooting begins, sometimes earlier.
- Does a **character breakdown** by each scene. Knows exactly how many extras are required in each scene. It's important on set to know exactly what each scene entails.
- Becomes familiar with cast members.
- Goes over storyboards with the director.
- Goes over atmosphere needs for each scene.
- Once the shooting schedule is complete, makes sure that actors know where and when they need to shoot. In low-budget shoots this can be accomplished by the 2nd AD. In higher-budget shoots either the casting agent or the actor's agent covers this.
- Prepares the day-out-of-days according to the shooting schedule and gives it to the POC to distribute.
- Attends and helps coordinate cast rehearsals.
- Works with the director, DP, and producer to organize and orchestrate difficult shots.
- Runs the final production meeting.
- Attends all location scouts.
- Determines the first days call times.
- Gets shot list from the director and places it in the order of shooting for the first day. The 1st AD will continue to do this on a daily basis.

Production

- Gathers all crew together for a safety meeting (if needed).
- Stays with the camera while preparations are made for the first shot.

- Works with the 2nd AD to get actors ready.
- Spends the day running the set and moving the crew along.
- Is responsible for making the day.
- Approves the call sheet and production report. The call sheet (see Figure 6.2) is a document that shows what location, actors, crew, and scenes are shooting the next day. It is traditionally distributed to cast when they are wrapped throughout the day and to crew at the end of the day. The production report (see Figure 6.3) is a document that shows what happened the previous day in terms of footage, actors, scenes, crew, hours worked, and production status.
- Makes a determination of when to break for lunch and when to wrap the crew.

Qualities of a Good 1st AD

- Authoritative demeanor.
- Excellent with detail.
- Quick thinking and resourceful.
- Able to handle multiple items at once.
- Able to deal calmly with temperamental cast and crew.

THE FIRST ASSISTANT DIRECTOR–DIRECTOR RELATIONSHIP

One of the most important working relationships on set is between the 1st AD and the director. A good relationship helps the day go smoothly, while a bad relationship can undermine the success of your day. Following are some of the director's expectations of the 1st AD:

- To keep unnecessary people away from the director.
- To keep track of where the production is in the shot list so that no shot is overlooked.
- To make sure the 2nd AD directs the **background** in a manner consistent with the director's vision.
- To keep the rest of the crew working efficiently.
- To keep the energy going on set and to keep the set quiet so the director can concentrate on his work.

What the 1st AD Wants from the Director

- Accurate storyboards. The 1st AD needs to know exactly what each shot is framing, its composition, what actors are in it, and what background is seen. This allows the 1st AD to communicate needs to the crew and get the next actors ready.
- Trust from the director to run the show. For example, when it is time to get the shot, the director depends on the 1st AD to have everything in place. So, the 1st AD also expects the director to know what he wants, and to be ready.

PRODUCTION MEETINGS

Throughout the process many production meetings are held. The director meets with heads of various departments to impart her vision. The production designer meets with his staff to discuss the progress of set construction and dressing. Each department meets for as many times as it takes to get ready for shooting. There are also two production meetings attended by all crew (not cast traditionally), in pre-production, which the 1st AD runs. These are the concept meeting and the "big" production meeting.

The Concept Meeting

The concept meeting is held early in the pre-production process. Most heads of departments attend this meeting, such as the producer, director, 1st AD, UPM, DP, costume designer, production designer, art director, transportation coordinator, location manager, **casting director, key makeup artist,** stunt and **special effects coordinator,** and the visual effects supervisor (if applicable). The POC coordinates the meeting, informing everyone of the time and place and making sure all have received the latest script or revised script pages. The 1st AD runs the meeting and reads through each scene. Some directors prefer that all dialogue be read word for word; others prefer to have the dialogue summarized or skipped all together. As the 1st AD reads each scene, any concerns regarding shooting are discussed. This is a great time for all crew to ask questions, discuss issues, and solve problems.

The Big Production Meeting

The **big production meeting** is a meeting held any time from 1 to 2 weeks before the first day of shooting. This meeting is attended by all crew, but not the cast. As with the concept meeting, the purpose of this meeting is to go through the script scene by scene and discuss any unresolved issues, questions, or concerns. This meeting can take anywhere from 4 to 8 hours. Therefore, the production coordinators usually arrange for refreshments throughout the meeting.

Whether a production is high or low budget, these meetings are essential. It is a time when everyone can hear and be involved in how the production will proceed. One other important reason for these meetings is that sometimes the director will take a few minutes in one or both of these meetings to discuss the vision of the picture. These comments can help create a sense of shared vision and unity among the crew.

SECOND ASSISTANT DIRECTOR

The 2nd AD assists the 1st AD in running the set. The 2nd AD's duties and responsibilities follow.

Pre-Production

- Usually arrives 2 to 3 weeks before shooting begins.
- Reads the script to know each scene well. Highlights actors in each scene and makes notes on scenes with extras.

- Puts together the **set box.**
- Works with the APOC to determine the travel schedule for cast.
- Goes over the number of extras in each scene with the director and discusses how the scenes will work.
- Prepares the call sheets and production reports with the APOC and POC.
- Determines walkie-talkie channel assignments for all applicable crew.

Production

- Completes the call sheet. This duty will continue daily throughout the shoot.
- Does SAG daily contracts.
- Takes over for the 1st AD if she needs to leave camera.
- Calls "Rolling!" when each shot begins (see the section "Importance of Calling Rolling and Cut").
- Calls in to the production office the first shot of the day, lunch, the first shot after lunch, and wrap.
- Arrives first on set and works with the transportation department to assist cast and crew as they arrive.
- Once they arrive, leads all actors to the **honeywagon** or trailers (if medium to high budget) or into makeup and wardrobe.
- Distributes walkie-talkies. This job may sometimes be given to the 2nd 2nd or DGA trainee.
- Keeps count of how many people go through the lunch line. This number is then put on the production report. This is also sometimes done by the 2nd 2nd.
- Prepares the call sheet, about midway through the day. Once prepared, it gets approved by the 1st AD and UPM. Once approved, it goes to the production office to be copied and attached to the **location map** (if doing paper call sheets).
- Informs the caterer of the next day's count for food.
- Calls actors with call times for the next day. The 2nd AD should be prepared to answer questions about the next day's shooting, scenes, scene order, etc.
- Keeps the set quiet at all times. If the 1st AD has to call quiet, the 2nd AD is not doing her job.
- Takes care of any **Taft–Hartleys.** A Taft–Hartley, used on union shoots, is a contract given to nonunion actors who may be given dialogue. This contract allows them to later become members of the Screen Actor's Guild.
- May be responsible for charging up the walkie-talkies each night so they are fully charged for the next day's shooting.
- Directs the atmosphere, also called the "background," for each scene.

A Note on Directing Extras

The 2nd AD needs to work quickly when directing background. The process begins in pre-production by finding out how extras will be used in each scene. Then, once on set, the 2nd AD helps to ensure that all needed extras are ready, having gone through makeup and wardrobe if necessary. Next, the 2nd AD places the extras in the scene. Either the director or the 2nd AD informs them of what is required in the scene.

Because most extras are inexperienced at being in front of the camera, it is a good idea to give each extra very specific directions. That is, each one needs to be told exactly what to do once the camera starts rolling. This is not always possible. Sometimes scenes with extras may number in the hundreds, which would make it impractical to direct each one. In that case, the 2nd AD becomes a sort of cheerleader, having to motivate a large number of people to perform. I once directed background on a film in which over four hundred extras had to cheer when some fireworks went off. As the 2nd AD, it was my job to motivate the extras. What I ended up doing was running through the crowd, yelling, to get their energy up.

Another issue that comes with this kind of directing is knowing how to choreograph the extras doing **crosses**. Crosses occur when actors walk back and forth on screen, creating the illusion that there are many people in the background. To do this, the 2nd AD must time out cues for each extra. The first cues begin when the extras are told to move. The next cues are timed in a manner that keeps the background active, if that is appropriate. I once directed the background in a newsroom scene. The extras were given rapid cues to move around the office at different times so that the newsroom appeared to be busy.

Qualities of a Good 2nd AD

- Authoritative demeanor.
- Excellent with detail.
- Quick thinking and resourceful.
- Able to handle multiple items at once.
- Able to deal calmly with temperamental cast and crew.
- Able to produce accurate paperwork.

WALKIE-TALKIE ETIQUETTE

Walkie-talkies are an invaluable communication tool on set. Frequently, the crew is spread out over a large area, yet must communicate almost constantly with each other. Walkie-talkies are distributed to the following: 1st AD, 2nd AD, 2nd 2nd and/or DGA trainee, PAs, first **assistant cameraperson**, second **assistant cameraperson**, loader, **set dresser**, and the following departments—grip, electric, wardrobe, makeup, hair, special effects, stunts, props, construction, and transportation.

Usually the 1st AD and director's team occupy channel one at all times. Other personnel and departments are then assigned their own channels. The rule is that everyone stays on channel one to know what is going on, and so that the 1st AD can reach any department head at any time. If anyone needs to speak with someone in his own department, they contact that person and tell them to switch to the department channel. After the conversation is over, both parties return to channel one.

SECOND SECOND ASSISTANT DIRECTOR AND/OR DGA TRAINEE

Many projects with a large cast use the 2nd 2nd AD to help with the cast. If the shoot is a union shoot and signatory to the DGA, then a DGA trainee is assigned to the shoot by the guild. Frequently, the duties of both these personnel overlap and thus are combined in this section.

Pre-Production

- Usually starts 1 week before shooting. May also start the first day of shooting, depending on the budget.
- Assists the 2nd AD with various paperwork, typing of reports, and copying.

Production

- May type the production report for the 2nd AD.
- On a union shoot completes the **exhibit G.** The exhibit G is a form on which SAG actors sign in and out.
- Makes sure all extras' releases are signed. A **background coordinator** may also do this.
- Supports the 1st and 2nd ADs with what is called the **lockup.** A lockup is a situation whereby the area where the camera is pointing is secured. The 1st AD will place other ADs and PAs just outside the perimeter of the frame. When the assistants hear "lock it up," they hold any people or, sometimes, traffic from entering the background of the frame. After the director calls cut, they allow people and traffic to move freely.

SET PRODUCTION ASSISTANTS

PAs, also called "gofers," are there to assist the director's team in any way it needs. This is an excellent starting position for aspiring production people and future ADs. On medium- to high-budget shoots there will be a **key PA,** and then regular PAs beneath him.

Occasionally a production will hire an intern, who may or may not be paid for working on the production. In this case the person signs an intern release guaranteeing **workers' compensation. Production interns** may be people who are just out of film school, looking to break into the business. The producer has the discretion over whether the intern will be paid. Obviously, the interns in low budget are most likely not paid and those in high budget paid a modest salary. Production interns may be assigned to any of the departments on a crew. If an intern wants to someday be a 1st AD, then the intern is placed on set as a set PA.

Pre-Production

- The key PA may or may not start in pre-production, depending on the budget.
- Assists the ADs with copying, getting coffee, and making telephone calls.

Production

- Assists the ADs with lockup.
- May escort actors to and from the set.
- Escorts actors to and from makeup, hair, and wardrobe.
- May escort actors to their trailers.
- May need to sit with the extras in their holding area.
- Gets coffee for the 1st AD.

Qualities of Good 2nd 2nds, DGA Trainees, and Set PAs

- Physically capable of being on her feet for 12 or more hours.
- Great communication skills.
- Attitude of service toward crew and cast.
- Quick thinking and resourceful.
- Understands set protocol.
- Able to handle multiple situations at once.
- Able to deal calmly with temperamental cast and crew.
- Able to produce accurate paperwork.

DIRECTOR'S ASSISTANT

The director's assistant functions much like the producer's assistant. The amount of responsibility in this job can vary from director to director. Again, it is a great job for aspiring directors, who can learn first-hand the tricks of the trade. The following is a list of duties and responsibilities:

- Answers the telephone for the director and screens calls. This is a position that requires discretion.
- May type script pages if the production is not using a script service. A working knowledge of the different screenwriting programs is essential.
- May schedule meetings with a variety of crew members, the producer, and possibly studio executives, if it is a studio shoot.
- May sit in on production meetings, usually so he can take notes and get coffee.
- May become the voice of communication between the director and the studio and/or certain crew.
- May be involved in the director's more personal matters such as picking up the dry cleaning, walking the dog, or scheduling a haircut.
- May be asked to read scripts and complete coverage forms.

CHOREOGRAPHER

A choreographer is needed if there are any dance numbers in a project. She may be employed run of show, or may be needed to choreograph only one or two dance sequences. Perhaps the actors need only to waltz in a dinner party scene, but don't know how. The choreographer would then be needed only for rehearsal and shooting of the scene. If the production has enough musical numbers, as does a musical, the choreographer would also most likely have an assistant or two to help rehearse the cast. I once worked on a show about the rise of a rock-and-roll family. The film had performance numbers spread throughout the schedule. The choreographer worked with the cast in pre-production for a couple of weeks, teaching them the dance numbers. Then, as principal began, the choreographer and his assistants continued to rehearse the cast when they were not needed on set.

Choreographers may be members of the Academy of Dance on Film, which supports members and archives performances, or of Equity, a trade union for performers.

DIALOGUE COACH/DIALECT COACH

A dialogue coach is a person who works with actors on the delivery of their dialogue during pre-production rehearsals. A coach like this is needed if the production is very involved, complicated, or the director wants the assistance. The dialogue coach can also help actors with dialects, or a **dialect coach** can handle the dialect training. The difference between these two is that the dialogue coach not only concentrates on delivery, pronunciation, and inflection but also ensures that the actor is delivering the dialogue as the director intends. The dialect coach works specifically on any accents that may be needed.

STORYBOARD ARTIST

A storyboard artist is a person who works in pre-production to draw storyboards for the director. A storyboard is a small, visual sketch of a shot. The director will describe a shot in terms of angle, framing, and content to the storyboard artist, who then draws it either on paper or in storyboard software. I once worked with a director who liked to paste the storyboards all over the walls of his office as they were completed, so that he could visualize the film better. Once this film's storyboards were complete for each scene, they were copied and distributed to the producer, director of photography, production designer, 1st AD, and 2nd Unit director (there was an aerial unit on this show, which shot scenes involving military helicopters).

SET OPERATIONS

There are many events that must come together in order to get the first shot of the day. The 1st and 2nd ADs are particularly integral to this process. Following is the process.

After arriving on set, the 1st AD informs crew members where the first setup is and keeps the director informed of the progress. Once the lighting is finished, the

1st AD checks with the director to see if he is ready to shoot. At this point actors can be brought in to set for the rehearsal. The 2nd AD or 2nd 2nd escorts actors to the set. When they get near to the camera, the 2nd or 2nd 2nd announces, "First team on set!" This notifies the crew to quiet down and that the shot may be close. When extras are brought to the set, the 2nd AD calls "Background on set!"

After some rehearsal, the director usually informs the 1st AD that she is ready to shoot. The 1st AD will then call for his crew to "lock it up" for the take. Locking it up quiets everyone down and ensures that no one enters the background of the shot. Following is the script of who says what when a shot is called:

> **1st AD:** Sound ready?
> **Sound:** Ready.
> **1st AD:** Camera ready?
> **Camera Operator:** Ready.
> **1st AD:** Roll sound.
> **Sound:** Speed.
> **2nd AD:** Rolling!
> **1st AD:** Roll camera.
> **Camera Operator:** Speed.
> **2nd AD:** Scene 41A, Take 1 (claps the **slate**).
> **1st AD:** Background action (if applicable) or Playback (if applicable).
> **Director:** Action.

When the shot is finished:

> **Director:** Cut.
> **1st AD:** (into the walkie-talkie) Cut.
> ADs and PAs echo "Cut."

Importance of Calling Rolling and Cut

It is extremely important that the director's team call "rolling" when a shot begins *and* "cut" when the shot is over. This way, the crew, who may be some distance from the set or even approaching the set, knows when to be quiet. If the crew members hear "rolling" and hold their conversation but after a while do not hear "cut," they will begin to wonder if the shot is over. It is frustrating to then find out that someone forgot to call "cut" after the director. Maintaining a consistent efficiency in this area is very important to crew communication.

- After the director yells "cut," the 1st AD watches the director. If the director gets up and walks to the actors, he most likely wants another take.
- If another take is warranted, the 1st AD calls, "Take 2 is up."
- If after calling "cut" the director sits there, the 1st AD asks if another take is needed: if yes, the 1st AD calls it; if no, she calls **new deal**. *New deal* is a term used to notify all crew that the shot is changing.
- When the crew breaks for lunch, the 1st AD calls, "Lunch!" The 2nds and PAs echo this announcement for all crew and cast to hear.

At the End of the Day

- The 1st AD calls the last shot, called the **martini.** The 2nd ADs and PAs echo this to the crew.
- Hearing the martini, the crew knows they will wrap soon and begin to wrap out unneeded items.
- The 1st or 2nd AD quiets the set so sound can record **ambience.** Ambience, also called **room tone,** is the natural sound of a room or location.
- When the day is done, the 1st AD calls "wrap" and the 2nd ADs and PAs echo to the crew.
- The 2nd AD and PAs distribute the next day's call sheets.
- The 2nd 2nd or PAs collect walkie-talkies to charge for the next day.
- The 2nd AD keeps track of leave times for all cast and crew and records it on the production report.

CLOSED SET

A **closed set** is called for when there is sensitive material being filmed that could hamper filming in some way. There might be a love scene in which the actors need to be semi- or fully nude. Having a closed set can make the actors more comfortable because on a closed set there are not as many crew standing around. There might be a particularly emotional scene requiring intense concentration by an actor. In this case, the director or actor may request a closed set. The pure definition of a closed set varies according to the situation. In the case of a love scene, often the only people allowed on set would be the director, sound person, makeup, and camera operator. In the second example, the only people allowed may be the director, sound person, and camera operator. Usually the director informs the 1st AD who will be allowed on set, and the 1st AD then clears the set of unnecessary personnel.

Sometimes a closed set will also warrant **closed dailies.** This is when only certain people are allowed to watch certain dailies. In the above examples the dailies most likely would be closed to everyone except the director, producer, script supervisor (who makes notes for the director), and editor (who may run projection).

SET PROTOCOL

There are some characteristics of set protocol that are the same in low-budget as in high-budget productions. There are also some characteristics that are different. Following are some characteristics that are true for most productions:

- The set is to be kept extremely quiet.
- No one touches the camera except the camera team and director.
- All heads of departments must inform the 1st AD when they leave set and when they return.
- All crew are expected to check in and out with the 2nd AD.
- Generally no one converses with the actors, except the director.
- No one is late.

- If there is an accident or injury, no one provides assistance except the first aid person.
- Foul language is kept to a minimum around children on set.
- Locations and their owners are to be treated with respect.
- All cell phones and beepers need to be on vibrate or silent.
- No one orders anyone else's assistant(s) to do anything.
- Wrap is to be completed quickly.
- Distractions to the director should be kept to a minimum.
- Safety precautions are to be observed and practiced by everyone.

The differences between low and high budget occur when there is a union shoot. Under these circumstances the following are also true:

- No one moves set dressing except the set dresser.
- No one moves lights except the lighting department.
- No one moves any equipment that is not in his department.

THE SET BOX

The set box is a box of files that contains all forms that may be needed on the set. In pre-production, gather all the proper forms and make sure they are prepared properly. The files you need should include:

Blank call sheets: If the computer should happen to go down, you need to be prepared with blank sheets to hand write.

Blank production reports: For the same reason as above.

Day-out-of-days: Have some extras in case the actors forget their schedules, so you can quickly see what days they are needed on set.

Shooting schedule: It's amazing how many times crew will lose this and come to you for another.

Extra scripts: It's amazing how many times cast will lose theirs and come to you for another.

Extras releases: Your script will dictate how many you need to keep on hand.

Emergency forms: Safety has become a big issue on film sets. In case of an accident or emergency, this form will tell you any specific medical information that may be important. It will also tell you whom to notify in case of extreme injury. Once all cast and crew fill out these forms, file them in alphabetical order. Also have some blanks on hand for **day players.**

Blank walkie-talkie distribution forms: Every day it will be the job of the 2nd AD to distribute walkie-talkies to crew. A sign-out form ensures that one person is responsible for the return of each walkie-talkie, and it helps in collecting them at the end of the day.

Parent's consent forms: If there are children on set, it's important to have these, especially if a parent intends to leave the set, placing the child in your care.

Cast releases: Even though these should be filled out in pre-production, you never know when a person will be cast at the last second and need a release.

Location agreements: It is wise to have copies of all location agreements and **permits** on set. If the location manager or producer should leave the set, you are solely responsible for proving to any authorities that you have a right to be on that location. These forms also have pertinent information such as whom to contact if there is an accident at the location and the hours that you are permitted to be there.

SAG rules: If you are working on a union shoot with SAG actors, it is a good idea to have their agreement on hand. There are many rules to remember.

AD PAPERWORK

There are two very important pieces of paperwork the AD team deals with: the call sheet and the production report. Each has its purpose and is integral to the smooth running of a shoot. Each is completed every day and must be accurate. Other than a few minor changes in the content of the forms, the need and use of the call sheet and production report are essentially the same from low to high budget.

The Call Sheet

The call sheet (see Figure 6.2) is a report that shows exactly which scenes, cast, and other items are needed for the next day of shooting. It is given to all cast and crew and prepared the day before shooting by the 2nd AD. Approximately halfway through the day, the 2nd AD will start to write the call sheet. It is usually at this point that the 1st AD will know what is being shot the next day; that is, if they are going to shoot what is on the schedule or if any scenes have to be carried over to the next day. The 2nd AD uses the production schedule to transfer information onto the call sheet regarding what is being shot. He then figures out what times the cast need to be called based on when their scenes appear in the day. It is always advisable to have the cast there a little before you need them, but not too far in advance. Actors can get bored easily and do not like to wait around for hours.

On the back of the call sheet are the call times for the crew. Most crew will be called for crew call; others might be called later. For instance, the still photographer usually has a later call because she does not need to be on set while the crew is setting up. The still photographer only needs to be there when shooting is ready to begin. The back also lists crew under "O/C," which means *on call*. Some crew, such as the UPM, POC, and production designer, are on call. This means they come and go from the set as necessary, but are not needed by camera at all times.

The call sheet also shows a shooting call. This is the time at which the crew needs to begin shooting. The difference between crew and shooting call is the amount of time it takes to get set up once most of the crew arrives. This setup could involve lighting or setting up special effects or stunts, so this amount of time is determined by the 1st AD.

After the call sheet is completed by the 2nd AD, he signs it and gives it to the 1st AD for approval and signature. The 1st AD usually will leave the set to the 2nd AD while checking the call sheet. After approving it, the 1st AD sends the call sheet to the UPM for signature. After the UPM approves, the call sheet is copied, usually by PAs in the production office. The office PAs will then attach maps from the location department and send the call sheet back to the set, where copies will be handed out at the end of the day by the 2nd ADs and set PAs. The call sheets become a part of the production files as a record of what the crew intended to shoot each day.

The Production Report

The production report (see Figure 6.3) is a record of what was shot in one day. As the call sheet is prepared the day before shooting, the production report is prepared at the end of the day and distributed the following morning to various personnel such as any studio executives (if applicable), executive producer, production supervisor, the producer, the accountant, and the completion bond company.

The process of preparing the production report actually happens throughout the day. On the back of the report (see Figure 6.4) all crew are listed, but instead of call times, like on the back of the call sheet, the production report shows what hours the crew worked. This is very important for paying crew, especially if there is overtime. At the beginning of each day, it is understood that all crew and cast must check in with the 2nd AD so she can write down their arrival times. At the end of each day, all crew check out with the 2nd AD, so every hour worked is accounted for. The 2nd AD will also keep track throughout the day as cast arrive and leave.

In addition, at the end of the day, the 2nd AC and the script supervisor will turn in the **film stock summary report** and script summary report to the 2nd AD, who then transfers that information to the production report. This information is vital for knowing how shooting is progressing. These reports contain information about how much footage and how many scenes, pages, minutes, and setups were shot that day.

The production report also contains a very important notes section. This is a section in which any problems from the day are noted. For example, if weather caused the crew to shut down for an hour, anyone was injured, or any person or department caused shooting to be delayed, this would be noted. Subsequently, the UPM and producer heavily scrutinize the notes section before the report is distributed. I once worked a show where the UPM had me reorder the notes so that a critical entry about the director was hidden farther down into the notes. The purpose of these notes is to inform anyone who was not on set about any problems that need to be addressed. These notes will usually begin with the 1st AD, who throughout the day will tell the 2nd AD to make notes on the production report as any problems arise.

Once the production report is prepared, the 2nd AD gives it to the 1st AD, who looks it over for signature and approval. The 2nd AD traditionally leaves the report in the production office for the POC. In the morning the POC checks the report for any typos or missing items and cleans it up if necessary, and then shows it to the UPM, who then sends it on to the producer for signature and approval. Once approved, it is copied by the office PAs and distributed, or sent electronically.

Executive Producer:	J. Carter	**CALL SHEET**	DATE: 7/25/2010

Producer: L. Wales
Director: D. Wales
UPM: M. Jones   **"Regina of Icelandia"**
1st AD: F. Smith

DAY 1 OF 45

CREW CALL 6:00A
SHOOTING CALL 7:00A
SUNRISE 5:30A
SUNSET 5:35P

SET DESCRIPTION	SCENES	CAST	D/N	PAGES	LOCATION
EXT. FOREST DAY	21, 45	1, 2	D	1 5/8	2335 Tree Lane
					Virginia Beach, VA 23333
COMPANY MOVE					
INT. CASTLE DAY	103	1, 5, 6, 7	D	2 5/8	789 Castle Drive
					Virginia Beach, VA 23333
		TOTAL PAGES		3 6/8	

CAST/DAY PLAYERS	ST:	PART OF	PICK-UP	IN M/U	ON SET	REMARKS
1. Lorina Wheleen	SW	Regina	6:00A	6:15A	7:00A	
2. Greg Urede	SW	Donato	6:15A	6:30A	↓	
5. Kim Wert	SWF	Worchera	12:30P	12:45P	1:30P	
6. Nancy Feeswra	SW	Wochera #1	↓	↓	↓	
15. Arnie Hunter	SW	King	↓	↓	↓	

SAFETY NOTES

Watch for needles in the forest location (green spikey plant w/yellow leaves).

ATMOSPHERE & STAND-INS	CALL	LOCATION	SPECIAL INSTRUCTIONS
None today.			Rainmaker @ 1:00P

ADVANCED SHOOTING SCHEDULE						
SHOOTING DATE	SET	SCENES	CAST	D/N	PAGES	LOCATION
7/27/2010	INT. LAB	6, 35, 77	1,2,5	D	1/8	Studio
7/27/2010	INT. LAB	3,4,9,10	1,23,45	D	2	Studio
7/28/2010		SUNDAY - DAY OFF				

upm: Martha Jones   1st AD: Frank Smith   2nd AD: Ed Poe

FIGURE 6.2

Call Sheet.

Prod. Co.	Frame Right Films, Inc.	**DAILY PRODUCTION REPORT**		DAY: 1 OF 45
		"Regina of Icelandia"		DATE: 7/24/10

PRODUCER:	L. Wales	EXEC. PROD:		J. Carter		DIRECTOR:	D. Wales
START DATE:	7/254/10	SCHEDULED FINISH DATE:		8/22/2010		ESTIMATED FINISH DATE:	8/22/2010

DAYS	1ST UNIT	2ND UNIT	PRE-PRO	TEST	TRAVEL	HOLIDAY	RETAKES	ADDED SC	TOTAL	SCHEDULE	
SCHEDULED	1	0	0	0	0	0	0	0	1	AHEAD	0
ACTUAL	1	0	0	0	0	0	0	0	1	BEHIND	0

SET	LOCATION	WEATHER 70s SUNNY	
EXT. FOREST DAY	2335 TREE LANE	CREW CALL	6:00A
	VIRGINIA BEAACH, VA 34444	1ST SHOT	8:12A
COMPANY MOVE		LUNCH	12:00P
		1ST SHOT AFTER	2:15P
INT. CASTLE DAY	7890 CASTLE DRIVE	CAMERA WRAP	4:55P
	VIRGINIA BEAACH, VA 34444	LAST PERSON OUT	6:00P

SCRIPT	SCENES	PAGES		MINUTES	SET-UPS	ADD	RETAKES
TOTAL SCENES	120	120	PREV	0	0	0	0
TAKEN PREV	0	0	TODAY	23:00	25	0	0
TAKEN TODAY	3	3 6/8	TOTAL	23:00	25	0	0
TOTAL TO DATE	3	3 6/8					
TO BE TAKEN	117	116 2/8					

SCENE NO.S	21, 45, 103		INVENTORY: STK: 5247		INVENTORY: STK: 5248	INVENTORY: STK: 5297
ADDED SCENES	0		ON HAND	10000'	0	25000'
OMITTED SCENES	0		REC'D	0	0	15000'
RETAKES	0		TODAY	5000"	0	10000'
SCHEDULED BUT NOT SHOT:	0		TOTAL	5000'	0	25000'

FILM	GROSS	PRINT	SOUND
USE	FILM STOCK		CARDS
PREVIOUS	0	0	1
TODAY	15000'	14500'	1
TOTAL	15000'	14500'	1

FILM	N.G.	WASTE	SHORT ENDS
USE			
PREVIOUS	0	0	0
TODAY	0	0	500'
TOTAL	0	0	500'

START-S WORK-W HOLD-H FINISH-F		WH	WORKTIME		MEALS		TRAVEL TIME	
REHEARSE-R TEST-T TRAVEL-TV		SF					ARRIVE	LEAVE
CAST	CHARACTER	RT	CALL	DISMISS	OUT	IN	LOCATION	LOCATION
1. Lorina Wheelen	Regina	SW	6:00a	4:00P	12:00P	1:00P	6:15A	4:15P
2. Greg Urede	Donato	SW	6:15a	3:00P	12:00P	1:00P	6:30A	3:30P
5. Kim Wert	Wochera	SWF	12:30P	4:00P	N/A	N/A	1:00P	4:00P
6. Nancy Feeswra	Wochera #1	SW	↓	↓	↓	↓	↓	↓
15. Steven Hunter	King	SW	↓	↓	↓	↓	↓	↓
PLEASE ADD 15 MINUTES MAKEUP/WARDROBE REMOVAL TIME TO SET DISMISSAL								

STAND-INS & ATMOSPHERE						STAND-INS & ATMOSPHERE					
NO.	RATE	IN	OUT	LUNCH	MPV	NDB	NO.	RATE	IN	OUT	LUNCH	MPV
NONE											

NOTES
1. Joe Thegrip tripped over C-stand, was administered first aid, returned to work.

ASST. DIRECTOR:	*Eunice Asdir*	PRODUCER:	*Lorene Wales*

FIGURE 6.3

Production Report.

PRODUCTION: **DATE:**

	NO	ITEM	NAME	IN	OUT
P	1	UPM	SMITH	O/C	O/C
R	1	DIRECTOR	YAVNEH	6:00A	4:00P
O	1	1ST ASST DIRECTOR	WALES	6:00A	4:00P
D		2ND AD	JORDAN	5:30A	5:00P
U	1	2ND 2ND AD	WYNNE	5:30A	5:00P
C	1	SCRIPT SUPER	COATES	6:00A	4:00P
T	1	POC	STAHL	O/C	O/C
I	1	APOC	DURAN	O/C	O/C
O	1	KEY SET P.A.	THOMAS	5:30A	4:30P
N	2	SET P.A.'S	SNYDER	6:00P	4:30P
			WILEY	6:00P	4:30P
C	1	DIRECTOR OF PHOTO.	BERND	6:00A	4:00P
A	1	CAM OPERATOR	JOHNSON	6:00A	4:30P
M	1	1ST AC	CALVARY		
E	1	2ND AC	BUTTONS		
R	1	CLAPPER/LOADER	KRAMER		
A	1	CAMERA PA	CEELY	↓	↓
	1	STILL PHOTOGRAPHER	JONES	6:00A	4:00P
A	1	PROD DESIGNER	PETRUCELLI	O/C	O/C
R	1	ART DIRECTOR	BOGART	O/C	O/C
T	1	ART DEPT COORD	HETZEL	O/C	O/C
	2	ART DEPT PA	CORN	6:00A	4:00P
			HUNTER	6:00A	4:00P
S	1	SOUND MIXER	SITTON	6:00A	4:00P
N	1	BOOM OPERATOR	BLACK		
D	1	SOUND PA	SHEERER	↓	↓
G	1	KEY GRIP	SOUTHERLAND	6:00A	4:20P
R	1	BEST BOY GRIP	MINTLE		
I	1	DOLLY GRIP	QUICKE		
P	4	GRIPS	CLARKE		
			MORTON		
			SANDERS		
			ENGEL	↓	↓
F		SPECIAL FX			
X		SPECIAL FX ASST			
P	1	PROPERTY MASTER	RAY	6:00A	4:30P
R	1	ASST PROPS	HUNDERR	6:00A	4:30P
P		PROPS PA			
S	1	SET DECORATOR	BOJOREKEZ	O/C	O/C
E	1	ASST TO SET DEC	MARTINEZ	O/C	O/C
T	1	ON-SET DRESSER	GUMBA	6:00A	4:30P
D					
W	1	COST DESIGNER	GUERRERA	O/C	O/C
D	1	WARD SUPERVISOR	JOSE	6:00A	4:15P

	NO	ITEM	NAME	IN	OUT
M	1	MAKE-UP	INART	6:00A	4:20P
/	1	ASST MAKE-UP	GOPRAM	6:00A	4:20P
U					
H	1	HAIR	HEART	6:00A	4:20P
R		ASST HAIR	LAMPON	6:00A	4:20P
E	1	GAFFER	FRAMER	6:00A	4:30P
L	1	BEST BOY ELEC	ROSE	6:00A	5:00P
E	3	LAMP OPERATORS	VASEEL	6:00A	5:00P
C			LOVE	6:00A	5:00P
			SMIMMER	6:00A	5:00P
S		SECURITY	NONE		
E		CITY POLICE	NONE		
C		FIRST AID	MEDIAN		
		FIRE WARDEN	NONE		
		FIREMEN	NONE		
L	1	LOCATION MGR	JOHNSTON	O/C	O/C
O	1	ASST LOC MGR	NOWLAND	6:00A	5:00P
C	1	LOCATION PA	GUINN	6:00A	4:00P
A		AUDITOR		O/C	O/C
U					
D					
E	1	EDITOR	FORDHAM	O/C	O/C
D	1	ASST EDITOR	BOMBERGER	O/C	O/C
I	1	APPRENTICE EDITOR	BRINKMAN	O/C	O/C
T					
C		BREAKFAST	B-FAST TRUCK	5:30A	6:00A
A		HOT LUNCHES	75 RTS @	12:00P	1:00P
T		EXTRA LUNCHES	NONE		
		2ND MEAL	NONE		
T	1	LIGHTING TRUCK			
R	1	GRIP TRUCK			
A	1	PROP TRUCK	ALL		
N	1	CAMERA TRUCK	CALLS		
S	1	WARDROBE TRLR	PER		
	1	MAKEUP TRLR	DICKERSON		
	2	HONEYWAGON			
	1	SET DRESSING			
	1	GENNY TOW			
	5	MINII-VANS			
		SPECIAL EFFECTS			
	4	RV'S			

NOTES

FIGURE 6.4

Back of Production Report

2ND UNIT

In most cases, the 2nd Unit is a crew that shoots scenes that either cannot be scheduled in the main unit or do not require the main unit director, such as "beauty shots" of sunsets or panoramas. The 2nd Unit may be different on various shoots. This unit may be a specialized unit such as an aerial or underwater unit. The nature of your script and your budget will determine if you need a 2nd Unit. The 2nd Unit usually shoots at the same time as the main unit, so a completely separate crew would need to be hired, which can be expensive. In some cases, though it is rare anymore, the 1st AD from the main unit will leave the main unit to become the director of the 2nd Unit. This is mostly done in low-budget productions because hiring a 2nd Unit director would be too expensive.

In low budget the 2nd Unit may consist of only a 1st AD and an AC. Often low-budget schedules are insane, and there is not enough time to shoot everything. Therefore, the director will send the 1st AD off with a camera and an AC (who now gets to run the camera) to get a few shots. These may include actors, maybe seen only in long shots, or be just for establishing certain locations. In higher-budget shoots the 2nd Unit may be a crew of over a hundred people. This is especially true for special effects units. This unit may consist of a large crew doing physical effects as well as a large number of people creating visual effects.

DIRECTOR

As stated, sometimes the director of a 2nd Unit may be the 1st AD from the main unit. The 1st AD may be used because the footage that needs to be shot would probably not require actors. Therefore, there would be no "directing" per se. If the scene did require actors, it is at the discretion of the main director whether he or she entrusts the 1st AD with directing the actors. Each shoot is different. The decision of whether to use the 1st AD would be based on the 1st AD's experience, the nature of the 2nd Unit footage, and the discretion of the director.

The 2nd Unit director could also be someone who is highly specialized in a certain area. I once worked on a film where there was an aerial unit. That unit was in place to shoot helicopter footage for a film about Apache helicopters. The director for the 2nd Unit was a director who specialized in shooting aerial footage. He knew how to shoot aircraft to achieve the best possible action footage, which was appropriate for the project. This 2nd Unit, made up of approximately seventy-five crew, included camera people, military people, pilots, art direction, and special effects.

UNIT PRODUCTION MANAGER OR PRODUCTION OFFICE COORDINATOR

If the 2nd Unit is large enough, there may be a separate production manager and/or production coordinator hired to work with this crew. If the unit has approximately fifty or more crew, it is a good idea to have a second UPM or POC to support this crew. This 2nd Unit UPM would work under the main unit UPM and report to him or her directly. The UPM's job here is the same as in the main unit: to handle problems and make sure the shoot runs smoothly from day to day.

FIRST ASSISTANT DIRECTOR

The 1st AD on a 2nd Unit operates the same as on the first unit. He or she may do a script breakdown and production strips, or just use the portion of the original production strips that apply to the 2nd Unit, in order to form a production schedule. This 1st AD need not necessarily report to the main unit 1st AD because they are each running a separate set. This 2nd Unit AD would report directly to the 2nd Unit director and 2nd Unit UPM. Depending on whether actors are involved, the 1st AD may or may not have a 2nd AD for assistance.

LOCATIONS

The main unit location manager would still find the locations for the 2nd Unit locations. The exception to this would be when there are units in other, more distant locations (see the section "Other Units"). For instance, if the show is on a tight schedule and an extreme number of locations need to be found, the producers may wish to hire another location manager to expedite the process. If there were just one location manager, he or she would make sure that an assistant or location PA would work for the 2nd Unit to handle support.

CAMERA

The camera team on a 2nd Unit may consist of only a cameraperson or may be a full-fledged camera crew with assistants and loaders. Again, it depends on how involved the 2nd Unit footage is and whether you are shooting film, video, or digital. This 2nd Unit cameraperson works closely with the main unit DP to ensure that the 2nd Unit footage will combine seamlessly with the main unit footage.

SOUND

The sound team on a 2nd Unit may consist of a recorder, boom, and cable person, or may be nonexistent. If you are just getting beauty shots, then no sound may need to be recorded. The decision to include sound or not in the 2nd Unit lies with the producer and director.

OTHER UNITS

Other units may be needed in other locations. For instance, if you are shooting in the United States, and you then need to move the crew to Portugal, you will need crew in place in Portugal to get things ready for the main unit crew before they arrive. This could include a location scout to find locations, an APOC to set up the production office, and PAs to help.

Another kind of unit that is being used more frequently is a **special or visual effects unit**. This unit could be operating at the same time as the main unit is shooting. This unit works on the miniatures or digital work that may be required for a show. This way, the special effects are ready when the main unit footage comes in. This timing is important if main unit footage is going to be combined with special or visual effects.

OPERATIONS

The 2nd Unit operates in the same way as the main unit in terms of paperwork and how a set is run. This unit will report to the UPM of the main unit, staying in contact and submitting call sheets and production reports so their progress can be monitored.

EQUIPMENT

Running a 2nd Unit requires paying not only for extra crew but also for extra equipment. Depending on how involved the 2nd Unit needs to be, you may be renting another camera and some lenses. Or, you could be renting an aerial camera such as a Wescam (a special camera mounted on a helicopter) or an underwater camera with specialized rigs. You may even need grip and lighting packages.

PAPERWORK

The paperwork on a 2nd Unit is the same as on a first unit. Call sheets and production reports are done. Location agreements and permits are all handed in to the production office. Once done, they are labeled "2nd Unit" so as not to be confused with the first unit paperwork.

SUMMARY

The director's team is made up of people who assist the director in various ways. The AD team, which includes the assistant directors and the set PAs, is responsible for running the set smoothly so the director can get all the shots he needs. There can be other support personnel such as a choreographer to coordinate dance sequences, a storyboard artist to help draw shots, and a dialogue or dialect coach to help the actors prepare their scenes. The director works with these personnel to achieve her vision. On set there may be various conditions that affect the day. Press day occurs when press come to interview and observe shooting. Sometimes a closed set is needed in sensitive situations. All of the day's activities are recorded on a call sheet (for the next day) and a production report (for the previous day). The 2nd Unit on a production can be small and simple or large and quite involved. The kind of 2nd Unit you have depends on your budget, your script, and your schedule. Smaller 2nd Units may have only two or three crew members. Larger 2nd Units may have a hundred or more crew. The amount of equipment you need is also determined by your budget and schedule. The 2nd Unit always reports to and is monitored by the main unit.

Casting, Actors, Extras, and Stunt People

This chapter, in addition to describing the duties of casting personnel, discusses the process of casting, from using casting agencies to who reads and who auditions, to how final decisions are made and who makes them. In addition, special circumstances such as working with minors and working with SAG and nonunion actors and extras are examined. Finally, because they are also seen on screen, the stunt department is discussed.

CASTING DEPARTMENT

The casting department consists of the casting director, the **assistant casting director** (there may be many casting assistants), the **extras casting coordinator**, extras casting assistants, and in some cases a background coordinator (Figure 7.1). In high budget you most likely will have all of these positions. In low budget, you may only have one person who handles all aspects of casting, including the extras. In very low budget, you may have to do the casting yourself. Following are the duties and responsibilities of the casting director.

CASTING DIRECTOR

In low budget the casting director works as an independent contractor, meaning he is hired as an individual to cast a show. More than likely, casting directors like this are incorporated and hire themselves out from their own companies. In big budget, casting directors may work exclusively for a casting agency. In this case, the casting director may be working on more than one show at a time. On shows with very large casts, a casting agency may assign more than one casting director and a few assistants. The casting director in high-budget productions usually casts all speaking parts and special ability parts but not the extras. If a script calls for a large number of extras, it is wise to have a separate extras casting person or use an extras casting agency (more about these

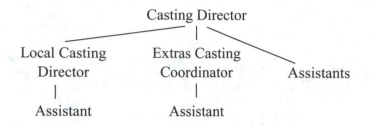

FIGURE 7.1
Casting Department Hierarchy.

later). Casting directors usually start in pre-production, any time from one to three months before principal photography.

Pre-Production

- Meets with the director after receiving a cast breakdown to discuss casting possibilities. A cast breakdown is a list of all speaking cast with a description of physical and personality characteristics (see Figure 7.2). The director or producer, who knows what kind of actors she is looking for, may compile this breakdown.
- Searches her own previous clients for possibilities for each role.
- If it is a union show, searches the academy catalogue for possibilities. The catalogue is a book of actors' **headshots** that is published yearly. The headshots are divided in categories, ingénue female, ingénue male, children, and character actors. In higher budget films, the casting director may put together an **A list** and a **B list**. Yes, the A list is not just a term referring to actors, it is an actual list. The list is sometimes compiled by casting agents who keep track of who is currently "hot" in the business. The B list names actors who may mostly appear in supporting roles or who are no longer as "hot" as they used to be. These lists are changing all the time as actors come into and out of favor with the movie-going public.
- Collects headshots of possibilities for each role and sends these to the director and producer. The director and producer will then look them over and decide which actors they want to read or audition. Whether an actor reads or auditions is determined by their notoriety and experience. A well-known actor could be insulted if asked to audition. Therefore, some well-known actors may be asked only to read. *To read* is to come to a meeting with the director and producer alone and read for the part. They are not considered to be in direct competition with other actors who come to audition. Keep in mind that some actors are well known enough that they are not even asked to read; rather they are only asked to take the part.
- Next, schedules actors for a casting session. In order to do this efficiently, the casting director must know the actors' availability along with the production schedule of the show. There is no sense auditioning someone who is committed to another project during the time when he would be needed.

Regina—Lead Role

Early 20s Caucasian female, petite and muscular. Regina is a beautiful girl, feminine yet strong. She is vulnerable enough to fall in love, yet tough enough to be the leader of the free world. Her stature is demure, yet her spirit makes her a force to be reckoned with.

Uomo

The villain. Mid-40s to 50s, Caucasian male, tall and scrawny. Uomo is a wiry, balding, distasteful, miserly looking man. Evil reigns in his eyes. His plot to take over the kingdom is the mark of a desperate man who exudes malice.

Donato

Uomo's son. Early 20s, no preference of ethnicity. Donato is Regina's love interest.

Fila

A member of the Wochera, the wise women who take care of Regina's training for the kingdom. Fila is small, early 30s, Asian.

Gerie

Kingdom reporter, 30s, no preference of ethnicity. Gerie is the top correspondent to the kingdom, with an anchorman look.

Nick

Regina's sister. Late 20s, Caucasian.

King Raccolto

King of the free world. 70s, African American. Grandfatherly and wise.

FIGURE 6.2   Cast Breakdown for "Regina of Icelandia"

FIGURE 7.2
Cast Breakdown for "Regina of Icelandia".

- Gets **sides** from the director for actors to prepare. A *side* is a copy of a single scene from a script that the actor is expected to use for audition. Having sides for the actors to read ahead of time or not is a matter of preference. Some directors and producers prefer an actor be fully prepared for a scene. Some directors and producers prefer to do what is called a ***cold reading.*** A cold reading is when the actor reads the sides for the first time only immediately before the audition. Some actors do better than others with cold reads. The purpose of a cold read is to see what the actor may bring to a part based on instinct, without thinking too much. This method is more of a spontaneous, let's-see-what-the-actor-can-do-off-the-top-of-his- or-her-head approach.

■ Once the casting session is set up, runs the casting session. As part of his duties, the casting director provides someone to read with the actors, usually an assistant. The casting director may also use the assistant to escort actors into and out of the room, or may bring another assistant to do this. That assistant will also make sure actors are signed in and given sides if necessary. The casting director also provides a camera and shoots each audition.

After the first casting session, the casting director discusses the choices with the director and producer. They then narrow down the list and create a list of actors to call back to audition again. The casting director will then arrange for the **callbacks** and run the callback session. After the callbacks, there may be further callbacks, or the producer and director will decide on who will play each part. Then the casting director calls all the actors (or their agents, if they have any) who have been chosen. Once the actors are cast, the casting director puts the production in touch with the actors or agents directly by providing the first cast list, with contact and agent information (see Chapter 4, Figure 4.2). Sometimes the casting director will also write up deal memos for the cast. Sometimes the unit production manager does this. An actor may be cast and have agreed to do a show, but not all aspects of the contract may have been worked out, such as credit size and placement. I once worked a show where the lead character's contract was still in negotiation even when she arrived in pre-production to begin rehearsals. Once the cast list is turned over to production, the production staff takes care of updating and revising as changes occur. This list is generally not distributed to all crew, as privacy is an issue for well-known actors.

Keep in mind that sometimes the casting director's job continues well into production. There may be one or more parts that are not cast in pre-production, or an actor may become unavailable through sickness or injury. There may also be a need for actors from the local area of shooting. The casting director then works with a local casting director to arrange local casting sessions.

LOCAL CASTING DIRECTOR

The local casting director is a person who lives and works mainly in the area where you are shooting. These people usually have a pool of local talent that they make available for auditions. If the show is a SAG show, the local pool of SAG talent may be quite small, depending on where you are shooting. If you are shooting in New York City, the pool will be huge. If you are shooting in Dallas, Pennsylvania, the pool will be very small. However, if the show is nonunion, the local pool could be quite large. With this quantity may also come many inexperienced actors. In this situation you may have more actors to choose from, but they may not be as high-caliber. Then again, you may get lucky.

The local casting director puts together headshots of local actors, again based on a character breakdown. He then sets up casting sessions with the casting director, director, and producer and runs the casting session much the same way as the casting director. She will also arrange for callbacks.

EXTRAS CASTING

As previously stated, if you have a large number of extras on your shoot, it would be wise to hire an extras casting coordinator or an extras casting agency. An independent contractor in smaller cities can do extras casting. In larger cities, extras casting is usually done by an agency that specializes in extras. In some cases you can get extras from local casting agencies because they know of actors who will work in speaking as well as extras roles, which is why their pool of people can be quite large.

If you use an independent contractor, that person usually can draw from a pool of people who live in the local area. The extras casting coordinator is usually hired for the length of the show, or however long extras are needed. The process generally is as follows:

- The production sends over a list of what kind and number of extras are required, and on which days.
- The extras casting coordinator contacts all available types and secures them for the shooting day. He will tell the extras what to wear (if they are providing their own wardrobe) or, in some cases, help set up wardrobe fittings for the extras (mostly for period shows).
- The coordinator then may come to the set to wrangle the extras. Wrangling means to keep all the extras in one area and quiet. A background coordinator can also do this job. His job is to check in the extras, count them to make sure there is the correct number needed for the scene, and make sure they sign their release forms. This coordinator then works with the 2nd AD or 2nd 2nd to get extras to the set as they are needed.

In large cities there are agencies that cast large numbers of extras. The process for the production is to contract with the agency for the show, and then provide the agency with a script and extras breakdown (see Figure 7.3), which shows the number of extras needed, what types (Caucasian, African American, Asian), and ages. The agency assigns one of its associates to supervise your show and provide extras. Your 2nd AD then provides the agency with a production schedule, showing what dates specific extras are needed. The 2nd AD will then call the agency the day before shooting and inform the contact person of the extras' call times. These kinds of agencies have databases of hundreds to thousands of people available for extra work. Their job is to sift through this database and find exactly what you are looking for.

CASTING ASSISTANTS

Casting assistants have a range of duties. These assistants are usually aspiring casting directors who are developing a keen eye for casting. Following is a general list of responsibilities:

- Answer phones in the casting office (unless they work at a large casting agency, which would have its own receptionist).
- Call actors for audition times.
- Send sides to actors.

"Regina of Icelandia"

Scene	# of Extras	# of Days Needed	Characters	Type
1	50	4	Crowd	All ages
1	6	4	Wochera	Women, 20s, petite stature
2	5/5	1	Court attendees	Men, 20s to 50s; Women, 20s to 50s—Royalty
2	2	1	Guards	Men, 20s, muscle bound
5	7	2	Guards	Men, 20s, muscle bound
5	45	2	Crowd	All ages
6	4	1	Wochera	Women, 20s, petite stature
17	3/3	1	Court attendees	Men, 20s to 50s; Women, 20s to 50s—Royalty
18	100	3	Crowd	All ages
26	16	1	Children	Toddler girls, Asian
77	11	10	Guards	Men, 20s, muscle bound
77	16	10	Children	Toddler girls, Asian
77	6	10	Wochera	Women, 20s, petite stature
102	5	3	Wochera	Women, 20s, petite stature
103	8	6	B-ball players	Boys, ages 12 to 15, athletes
115	100	2	Crowd	All ages

Note: Unless specified, any ethnicity will work.

FIGURE 7.3
Extras Breakdown.

- Assist with running camera, signing in actors, and reading with actors at the auditions.
- Copy, fax, etc.
- Type cast lists.
- May be asked for input on casting possibilities.

HOW TO RUN A CASTING SESSION

There are a few different ways to conduct a casting session. First, you could hire a casting agency. They do all the work: finding actors, calling them, and setting up their audition times. However, in low budget you may need to do the casting session yourself. The following is a checklist of how to set up the casting session:

- Put up flyers in the local area. The flyer should state where the audition is to take place, the time range, a brief character breakdown, and a contact number to call for audition times. The flyer should also state that actors are expected to bring headshots.
- Put advertisements in the following low-cost venues: local newspapers, local cable arts announcements, local trade magazines (if any), local high schools or universities (where applicable for ages), and local casting agencies. Some local casting agencies may allow you to place notices with them, as they are always trying to get work for their actors.
- As actors begin to call you, arrange for sessions of no longer than 15 minutes. Ten minutes is really ideal.
- Make sure the actors know about and are available for the shoot dates before they audition; otherwise, don't let them read.
- Put together sides, one or two scenes from the script. It is wise to choose a scene in which the actors need to display a wide range of emotions. This way you can see if the actors have any range at all. Either email the sides ahead of time or go with cold readings.
- Have someone present to read with the actors. This person should not be the director or producer. The person in charge needs to observe the actors with complete attention.
- Have a sign-in sheet for actors so you can keep track of who auditioned.
- Secure a room somewhere that will accommodate a table for the director and producer, with enough additional chairs to accommodate a few actors.
- Make sure there is an adequate waiting area with chairs for actors.
- Procure a camera to shoot the auditions.
- Make sure the producer and director meet and discuss exactly what they are looking for in each character.

Now that you have prepared, here's how to run the casting session:

- Have someone escort the first actor in.
- Ask the actor if she has any questions regarding the character or the scene. The actor will probably ask what you're looking for, about the particular scene or character, so be prepared to answer.

- You could let the actor know that he is free to move around at will. This is a good idea because the ability to move will show you if an actor has any imagination.
- Have actors slate themselves. Slating in this context means that the actor looks into the camera, gives his name, what part he is reading for, and the name of his agent (if the actor has one). The actor should wait until you tell him you are ready and then read the scene.
- If an actor is really bad, thank him and go to the next person. Most people can tell a bad actor in a few minutes. There is no use wasting time with one.
- If you see *any* talent, ask the actor to read the scene again, giving some direction that sends her in another direction. The next read will show you if the actor has any range and if she knows how to take direction.
- If the second reading is exactly the same as the first, you won't have much to work with. You want to be able to have something with which to work. An actor's ability to act is more important than a particular look you have preconceived.
- Thank the actor for coming.
- Have someone escort the actor out.
- It is a good idea to make notes on the actor before seeing the next one. After a while, you may tend to forget what you did or did not like about the actor.
- If there is time for callbacks, schedule them so you can have certain combinations of actors read together. This is especially important if you are casting a couple. During callbacks you can see if there is any chemistry between certain actors.
- Make sure you confirm with the actors that all of the shooting dates are clear for them.
- Make notes of any conflicts.

Once the casting session is completed, you will need to make some decisions. A good method is to take all the headshots and place them on a big table. This will allow you to see how actors may look together. You can then decide which actors you want for callbacks, if needed, and whom you want to cast. Then call all actors and notify them of your decisions.

SCREEN TESTS

Screen tests are filmed scenes of actors auditioning for a part, usually only done in higher budget productions. In the past they were shot on film, but many productions these days use digital cameras. Screen tests are a more formalized and personal type of audition. The decision to do screen tests rests with the producer and director, based on their knowledge of an actor's abilities. Sometimes screen tests are performed so they can see how a particular actor works with a star. If you want to do screen tests for one or a number of actors, see the following list of procedures:

- Call the actor's agent and book a specific date for the screen test(s).
- Book a room or reserve a space in your production office.
- Book a cameraperson to film or tape the test.
- Review the tests and make your decision.

REHEARSALS AND TRAINING

Once you have finished casting your show, you can begin rehearsals. The amount of time you devote to rehearsing your actors is sometimes based on your budget. Actors in medium- to high-budget films are paid for rehearsals. Actors in low-budget films can be rehearsed without pay. However, if you can afford to pay them, that is okay too. Either way, actors can be rehearsed anywhere from one week to one month, depending on how much the director thinks may be needed. The rehearsals are set up by the production office and run by the 1st AD. Sometimes the director may prefer to work with the actor alone. I once worked a show as an assistant to the director. The director was working on a particularly difficult scene with a well-known actor. The director called me in to read with the actor in his hotel room. The privacy and intimacy of the setting served to increase the quality of the rehearsal. If you plan to do rehearsals, decide based on budget (if applicable) which actors will rehearse and how long they will rehearse.

The 1st AD then will do the following:

- Contact the actors and set up a rehearsal schedule (see Figure 7.4).
- Book a room (usually somewhere in the production office) for all the rehearsals.
- Publish the rehearsal schedule and distribute to the producer, director, and production staff.
- Inform all cast of their rehearsal times and the location.

At the rehearsal the 1st AD is responsible for the following:

- Providing extra copies of the script if needed.
- Making sure no one disturbs the rehearsals.
- Reading with the actors when necessary.

The reason the 1st AD is so involved with the rehearsal is that the 1st ad will deal with these actors on set, so this is a good time to get to know them. In addition, it is good for the 1st AD to see what the director is going for and how much the director makes progress with an actor, which may affect further rehearsals needed on set.

Training actors during pre-production is needed in certain cases. For instance, if your lead actor plays a sword-fighting hero, then your actor will need training with swords. Perhaps some of your cast members play soldiers. You will need to have those actors trained in military practices. Alternatively, your actor may need to be in certain physical shape. You would then hire a personal trainer to get your actor into shape. Again, your choice to provide certain training for your actors will be based on need and budget. Once the trainer is hired, the 1st AD will coordinate a training schedule and inform the production office, director, and producer of the progress.

FITTINGS

Fittings are wardrobe sessions for your cast, during which they try on their wardrobes and the wardrobe personnel make adjustments. If you are shooting a period piece, a few fittings per actor may be needed. Perhaps you are shooting a piece where an actor needs to be in special futuristic armor or some sort of animal suit. Even if you are shooting a contemporary piece, fittings are necessary. Fittings let

June 20, 2002

"Regina of Icelandia" Rehearsal Schedule

DATE	TIME	LOCATION	ACTOR	PART	SCENES
June 24	9A–5P	Rm. 145	Kim Lane	Regina	2,10,13,26,49
June 25	9A–5P	Rm. 145	Kim Lane	Regina	11,34,66,83
			Jeff Johnson	Donato	11,34,66,83
June 26	9A–12P	Rm. 145	Kim Lane	Regina	55,56,57
	1P–5P	Rm. 145	Kim Lane	Regina	92,95,113
			Jeff Johnson	Donato	92,95,113
			Anthony Guerrera	King	92,95,113
June 27	9A–1P	Rm. 140	Kim Lane	Regina	115
	1P–3P	Rm. 140	Anthony Guerrera	King	115
	3P–5P	Rm. 140	Kim Lane	Regina	101,102
June 28	No rehearsals				
June 29	9A–11A	Rm. 140	Kim Lane	Regina	14,16,23
			Scott Porter	Uomo	14,16,23
	11A–12P	Rm. 140	Scott Porter	Uomo	112
	1P–5P	Rm. 140	Kim Lane	Regina	86,99
			Jeff Johnson	Donato	86,99
			Anthony Guerrera	King	86,99

FIGURE 7.4
Example Rehearsal Schedule.

your wardrobe personnel be sure that, once on set, the actor will be ready. In really low budget your actors may be wearing their own wardrobe. In this case fittings may not be necessary, but the wardrobe should still be checked and approved by the director. Following is a checklist for fittings:

- The **wardrobe supervisor** contacts the production staff for a cast list.
- he then contacts each cast member and arranges a time for the fitting. If you are shooting on a distant location, the wardrobe supervisor will work with the 1st AD to set up a fitting schedule, so as not to conflict with rehearsals.
- The wardrobe supervisor then copies the fitting schedule to the AD team.

WORKING WITH MINORS

If you have actors under the age of eighteen, you are working with minors. If such is the case, you will have to make special considerations. First, if your shoot is union, there are specific rules regarding how long minors can work. Even if your shoot is nonunion, it is never a good idea to overwork minors, especially young children. Children often don't last long on set, and you won't end up with good performances if they get overtired. I once worked a nonunion shoot where a small child was needed for a night shooting. We had to make sure that the child's nap schedule was adjusted so that he would be alert and energetic during the hours we needed him. Because we discussed and arranged for this in pre-production, the child's mother appreciated our concern for her son's welfare and was very cooperative with us.

Tutors

If you are shooting during a school year, you will need to hire a teacher to tutor for a certain number of hours each day. There are union teachers in Los Angeles who specialize in tutoring minors on set. You can find them at www.studioteachers.com. They publish on their website their guidelines for working with minors, called **The Blue Book.** Their jurisdiction covers California minors, out-of-state minors who work in California, and California minors who are taken out of state. There are different rules for children of different ages. Their guidelines outline how many hours per day a child may work, have rest time, and have mealtime. They also state how many teachers are required for a certain number of students and if the presence of a nurse is required, as in the case of infants up to six months old. One item of importance to remember—studio teachers are not allowed to extend working hours for children. The only way to accomplish that is to send a written request to the labor commissioner.

Recently, SAG, the American Federation of Television and Radio Artists (AFTRA), and the **Actors Equity Association** (AEA) teamed up to pass a bill called the **Child Performers Education and Trust Act of 2003**. This bill makes it a law that some of a minor's wages (15 percent) must be set aside in a trust, which they can then draw on when they turn eighteen. This new law currently applies to California and New York. The law was inspired by the **Coogan Law**, which came about when child actor Jackie Coogan turned eighteen and found that he had no money in his trust fund. Apparently his father spent his million-plus earnings. At that time, a child's earnings were considered property of the parents.

The Coogan Law provided that a child's earning became community property with the parents and that 15 percent of the earnings had to be set aside in a trust fund for the child until he turned 18. The Coogan Law has been updated. The SAG Young Performers Committee and government relations department initiated the update. The new law, called SB 1162, was revised to protect child performers, musicians, and sports figures, which include actors, dancers, musicians, comedians, singers, stunt persons, voice-overs, songwriters, **composers, conductors,** and designers. In addition, the law covers 100 percent of all minors' contracts, unlike the previous law, which only covered 5 percent of contracts that were court approved. In addition, it separates earnings as property of the child, as opposed to community with parents, and requires producers to make timely deposits.

Another aspect to pay attention to is child welfare law. Each state is different. Some states are extremely strict in enforcing these laws, while others are more lenient. Some states require that you fill out a theatrical permit application and submit it to the welfare office. The office will then send back the permit. Be sure to check the time frame for turnaround with this document. You will want the permits in place before you film the minors. Contact the department of labor in the state where you are shooting for their specific guidelines about working with minors.

Working with Parents

Finally, you need to know how to deal with parents if you are using minors. Some parents can be very hands-off if they trust that you are competent and have their children's health and welfare in mind. Other parents can be very demanding and intrusive. There are no rules here, just diplomacy. You should get a good indication of how easy or difficult a parent will be at the audition. Sometimes it may be worth putting up with a difficult parent because the child is perfect for the role. Sometimes it may not be worth it. The key here is to present yourself as qualified and professional. Make sure the parents are informed of everything the child will be required to do. Make sure they are fully informed as to dates, times, and locations where and when the child will shoot. Second, show concern for the child's well-being. If parents believe that you are taking good care of their child or children, they will be much easier to work with.

WORKING WITH ANIMALS

Working with animals can be a trying experience. However, it can go smoothly if you follow some simple guidelines. First, in medium to high budget you would be able to afford a trainer who works with trained animals. Trained animals perform better on set because they are adept at doing tricks on cue. In low budget you may not be able to afford a professional trainer. Perhaps you are using a friend's dog for a scene. Be prepared in this case to have patience in getting the animal to perform.

Part of working with animals also means contacting the **American Humane Association** (AHA). This association is in the business of protecting animals from abuse. If you are nonunion, you are not required to work with the AHA, but it is a good idea. If you are union, you need to abide by the **Producer–Screen Actors Guild Codified Basic Agreement of 1998.** This agreement states that the producer of a show will notify the AHA if using animals. The AHA then will have the information they need to monitor the situation. If you have treated animals well on your shoot, they will authorize the use of the end-credit disclaimer, which states that no animals were harmed during the making of your project. The AHA cover productions that are shot in the United States, as well as American productions shot overseas, and do not charge for their services. The AHA has specific guidelines regarding the use of animals in the media. You can get more information, including their "Guidelines for the Safe Use of Animals in Filmed Media" on their website www.americanhumane.org.

THE TAFT–HARTLEY

The Taft–Hartley in motion pictures is a process whereby a nonunion actor or extra becomes union eligible. A Taft–Hartley is required only if your shoot is using union actors. It is applicable when an actor who is nonunion has any of the following conditions occur:

- Is given lines on set. Your 2nd AD will take a picture of the actor, which is sent to SAG with a contract.
- Is **bumped** to the position of **stand-in**.
- Is bumped to the special bit, or special ability, category, meaning she has some special skill needed on set (juggling, dancing, skateboarding, etc.).
- Is used to replace a union extra who either does not show up or is fired.

Once an actor is Taft–Hartley'd, he becomes SAG-eligible. This means that the actor has 30 days to join SAG.

CATEGORIES OF ACTORS

On any shoot there are different categories of actors. The category differentiation is variable from shoot to shoot; however, some general guidelines do apply.

Leads

In high budget, you have your stars. These are people who are most likely in a lead role in the film. There are exceptions: perhaps a famous actor does a cameo performance in a minor role. Either way, they are still treated like stars. They are given their own trailers, special food, and special housing accommodations on location. Protocol on set dictates that stars are left alone, not disturbed by crew or civilians wanting autographs. Also, working with stars requires discretion. I once worked a shoot where the local newspaper published an article stating that Michael Jackson was coming to town to observe the shooting of the mini-series about his family. Even though the article was incorrect, we had to install a security system because we had so many people coming to the production office hoping to get a glimpse of him.

Supporting Roles

In low-budget, nonunion land, there are no rules here. A supporting role could be loosely defined as a role where the part is minor to the lead role. Perhaps it is the husband of a woman in the lead role. In medium- to high-budget projects these kinds of roles can also be given to what are called "name" actors, meaning they have reached some notoriety. They may also be actors who are not well known but have a significant role in the story.

Extras

Extras, also known as atmosphere, are actors in the background. They could be an audience in a theater or a crowd at a festival. Alternatively, an extra could be anyone walking down the street. One rule in defining extras is that they have no dialogue. You can have a crowd cheer and make noise, but they will still be extras.

Silent Bits and Special Ability

A silent bit or special ability extra is an actor with a particular skill or physical attribute. Perhaps your script calls for a juggler at a circus. You obviously could not hire just any extra; you need someone with that particular skill. People who work as silent bits usually are paid a little more than a regular extra.

Stand-Ins

A stand-in is a person who is hired to stand in for an actor during lighting setups. This person needs to have similar skin and hair color to the actor for whom they are standing in. This is because the gaffer and lighting team need to see how the lighting looks on the actor's specific hair and skin color. When on set, stand-ins stand by to step in at any time. The 1st AD will call, "**2nd team**," which is the stand-in's cue that he is needed on set. (If the AD calls for "1st team," she is referring to the actors.) Once called, the stand-in takes the position where the actor will be and waits until he is dismissed. Stand-ins on SAG shows are union.

DAY PLAYERS VERSUS WEEKLY PLAYERS

The classification of actors as day players or **weekly players** is found only on medium to higher budget shoots and is based on how they are paid. This has nothing to do with their status of having a lead or supporting role. Day players are actors who work for four or fewer days and are paid a daily rate. If an actor works for five or more days, she is paid on a weekly rate. The actor's shooting schedule determines these categories. In low budget, if the actors are paid at all, they are often paid one flat fee for their services.

STUNTS

Because stunt people appear on camera, they are included in this chapter. To prepare for stunts, you need to determine exactly how many stunts are in your script. A stunt is any action that may result in an actor getting hurt or that requires an actor to perform a dangerous maneuver such as a car crash or a fall off a building.

On a union shoot, all stunt people are SAG. They fly first class and are subject to all SAG rules, benefits, and penalties. They also go on the call sheet along with the other actors. The head of the stunt department is the stunt coordinator.

STUNT COORDINATOR

The stunt coordinator is usually a person who has spent years as a stunt person. Sometimes as stunt people get older, they become stunt coordinators. If you have a large number of stunts, the stunt coordinator is employed for run of show. If there are only a few stunts, you may need to hire one only for a short period of time. If you have scheduled all of your stunts together, you can bring in the stunt crew for that period of time, rather than flying them in and out throughout production. This may not be possible, depending on the availability of your locations. The stunt coordinator is responsible for the stunt budget. He hires stunt people for different stunts, usually working with the same stunt people. The stunt coordinator's main responsibility on set is for the safe execution of the stunt. The following is a list of his duties and responsibilities.

Pre-Production

- Meets with the director and producer to discuss how all stunts will look and how much they may cost.
- Arranges for the proper gear to perform the stunt. This may involve renting or purchasing.
- Hires stunt people to perform the stunts.
- Works with the APOC to travel stunt people to and from the location.
- Meets with and works with the transportation department on car stunts.
- Meets and works with the 1st AD on how long each stunt will take to prepare and shoot.
- Meets with stunt personnel to discuss how each stunt will be performed.

Production

- Maintains authority over the stunt people.
- Coordinates the setup and execution of each stunt.
- Once the stunt is complete, announces "Clear" when it is safe to approach the event.

Wrap

- Makes sure the gear is sent back to the vendor (if applicable).
- Leaves when all stunts are accomplished.

STUNT PERSON

In low-budget or nonunion situations it is wise to make sure your stunt people have experience. I once worked a show where a car was to drive off a ramp, flip, and land. The stunt personnel claimed that they had done this before. The stunt went bad, as the car never flipped and instead ran into a civilian's parked car. As it turned out, the stunt person had never performed this stunt before. The production had to incur the cost of fixing the civilian's car. Thankfully, no one was hurt. One indication that a stunt person has experience and schooled training is membership in the Stuntmen's Association, Stuntwomen's Association, or the International Stunt Association.

Another kind of stunt person is the stunt double. This is a person who specifically doubles on stunts for one particular actor, usually a lead role. There are also utility stunt people and **ND stunt** people. These are stunt people who may be needed in the background of a scene. For instance, say you have a scene where a car is supposed to drive through a crowded market; you could not have regular extras jumping out of the way. The difference between utility and ND is how their contracts are written. Utility stunt people operate under weekly contracts, and ND stunt people operate under daily contracts.

HOW A STUNT COULD WORK: A CAR ROLL

Following is a general description of how a stunt could work. This example is not meant to be an exhaustive list of how to perform this stunt. Again, stunts can be dangerous and should be left to experienced professionals.

- The stunt coordinator visits the location where the car will roll.
- He surveys the area looking for the safest way to do the stunt.
- He discusses with the director where cameras will be placed.
- The coordinator hires a team to build the ramp, and dress it if necessary so it is not seen in the shot.
- The coordinator meets with wardrobe and makeup to disguise the stunt person to match the real actor. Appoints one stunt person to drive the car.
- Once the stunt has been executed, the stunt coordinator is first to approach the vehicle.
- Once he has determined the stunt person is okay, the coordinator calls "Clear," signaling that others may approach.
- Finally, the stunt coordinator has the team tear down the ramp and return the location to proper order.

There have been many terrible accidents on film sets, and many stunts that have gone wrong. If you have stunts happening on set, especially in low budget, you should rent an ambulance to stand by in case of any emergencies.

SUMMARY

The casting department casts the show according to the director's vision and producer's approval. While the casting director will hire distant cast, a local casting director may hire all day players. The casting department sets up and coordinates the auditions until all roles are cast. Cast issues include working with minors, which on a union shoot has special requirements, and working with animals, which has its own challenges. Stunt people also work in front of the camera and are in the same union as actors, SAG.

The Art Department

The art department on a project is one of the most important departments. Like the camera crew, its work is seen completely on the screen. The art department is the team that creates the total look of all the sets and locations. While the camera department, specifically the DP, is responsible for the photographic look of the show, the art department is responsible for everything the camera photographs. As with other departments, your script and the extent of your budget will determine how involved or big your art department is. If the film is very high budget, you will most likely find all of the positions listed in this chapter. If the film is medium budget, you may have approximately 60 percent of the crew in Figure 8.1. If your film is low to very low budget, you may have only a few people to cover this area. In low budget, this means that the few people you have will need to double, sometimes triple, their duties in order to accomplish the production design. Following is a list of the many crew involved in this department, along with their duties and responsibilities.

PRODUCTION DESIGNER

The production designer (PD) is the head of the art department. She is completely responsible for the look of the film. Let's say the film is a futuristic science fiction piece: the PD creates the look of the futuristic world, from what color may dominate the sets to how clean or gritty this futuristic world will look. She is also responsible for the art department budget, which is often a significant part of the overall budget. The PD usually begins working shortly after pre-production has begun.

Pre-Production

- Reads the script and makes artistic decisions, such as what color scheme will be prominent and what style the sets will have. Draws preliminary designs for any sets that are needed.
- Goes to the locations very early to have input into exactly which locations are chosen.
- Meets with the director to collaborate on the look of the film.

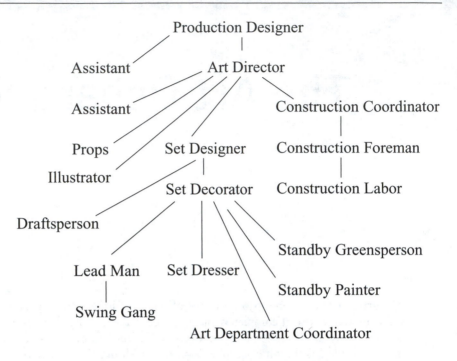

FIGURE 8.1
Art Department Hierarchy.

- Goes over every scene in the script to determine any special needs. Prepares the art department section of the budget for the producer.
- Meets with the producer to approve the budget.
- Hires the art director and possibly the set decorator.
- Delegates the execution of the film's look to the art director.
- Visits the building of various sets periodically to make sure the look is being obtained.
- Holds weekly meetings with the art department crew.
- Continues to meet with the director as needed.
- Continues to work throughout pre-production with the director, DP, and wardrobe to coordinate the look of the show.

Production

- Not on set all the time—may be working on future set designs or wrapping out previously shot sets.
- Approves each set once it is decorated and dressed before shooting begins for that set. Except for the DP and director, the PD has final approval of the set.
- Continues to visit the building of various sets to monitor their progress.
- Continues to monitor the art department budget with the help of the **art department coordinator**.

Wrap

- Wraps up the budget and confirms with the accounting department that all accounts are cleared.
- In the past, the PD's job would be finished at the end of principal photography. However, with the advent and more frequent use of **computer-generated images** (CGI), the PD may be needed in post-production to work with a **visual effects** team to ensure the look of the film is retained. More and more sets are being designed by computer.

ART DIRECTOR

The art director is responsible for executing the look that the PD wants. She also supervises the construction of the sets. The art director comes onto the project shortly after the PD.

Pre-Production

- Draws all the sets.
- Is responsible for special set considerations. These considerations could be anything from finding a medieval throne to designing a futuristic fireplace.
- Delegates the building of sets to the **construction coordinator**.
- Works daily with the PD to implement the look of the film.
- May hire the set decorator and construction coordinator.

Production

- Constantly working one set ahead.
- Troubleshoots for the PD.
- Monitors any sets that are not finished.

Wrap

- After one or two days usually turns over wrap to PD.

SET DECORATOR

The set decorator is responsible for decorating the sets as per direction from the art director and PD. He starts work shortly after the art director is hired.

Pre-Production

- Acquires everything needed for the sets: curtains, furniture, etc.

- May shop for and rent what is needed. The person called the *buyer* may do the shopping. The buyer's sole job is to go out and purchase items as per the set decorator's instructions.
- Meets with the **lead man** and **swing gang** to coordinate getting large items to the set.
- Meets with the set dresser to discuss set items.

Production

- Is always working one set ahead to make sure everything is on the set that needs to be.
- Supervises the lead man and swing gang.
- Supervises the set dresser.

Wrap

- Makes sure everything is returned that needs to be.

LEAD MAN AND SWING GANG

The lead man is the person who arranges for large items to be transported to and from the set. These items could include furniture, drapes, and fixtures. The lead man also supervises the **swing gang**, the people who do all the physical labor of transporting items.

ART DEPARTMENT COORDINATOR

The art department coordinator is responsible for maintaining the art department budget for the PD. He works directly with vendors to process any paperwork needed for sets, such as purchase orders and check requests. The coordinator also helps the department coordinate meetings and communication. He is sometimes hired by the PD, or sometimes by the art director, and begins work shortly after the PD comes on the show. At wrap time the coordinator works one or two days of coordination with the lead man to get set dressing items returned.

SET DESIGNER

The **set designer** works directly under the art director to draw any sets that may need to be constructed from scratch. The set designer's expertise lies in the ability to construct blueprints for the kind of set that is specifically needed for a production. Most set designers have learned this trade from theater experience. The designer begins work shortly after the art director is hired.

SET DRESSER

The set dresser is a full-time on-set art department crew member. He is there to make sure that all set dressing is placed correctly and maintains continuity. It is understood on set that no one except the set dresser is to touch any set dressing. This way the set dresser can keep continuity as accurate as possible. In order to accomplish this, the set dresser generally never leaves camera. The set dresser comes on the show shortly before the start of principal photography.

PROPS

The **props person** is responsible for securing and placing all props on set. A prop can be defined as anything an actor touches. However, just because an actor turns on the television does not make it a prop. The television is still set dressing. The props person can start anywhere from 1 to 3 months before the beginning of principal photography, depending on how "prop heavy" the show is. Following is a list of duties and responsibilities.

Pre-Production

- Takes the preliminary prop list from the ADs and makes revisions and completes.
- Meets with the PD to review props that will be used.
- Acquires or manufactures all props. Acquiring may involve renting or subcontracting for manufacturing.
- Creates a schedule of what props are needed on which days.

Production

- Is responsible for making sure all props are on set when needed.
- Stays close to the camera at all times to retrieve or place props. The props person may also assign the assistant props person to do this.

Wrap

- Is responsible for returning all props and settling all accounts for all rented props. Purchased props go to the studio, are sold, or are given to actors.

ILLUSTRATOR

The graphic artist answers directly to the art director and is the person who draws storyboards of scenes and/or sequences. These are mainly used when a particularly complicated scene or sequence occurs. This position would most likely be filled on medium- to high-budget projects. In low-budget production, the art director or PD would complete this task. The illustrator may work run of show if there are many complicated sequences, or may come in only for a small amount of time as needed.

DRAFTSPERSON

The draftsperson in production is much like the draftsperson for other construction venues. This person is responsible for plan and elevation drawings of any sets that need to be built. Obviously, this person must have the proper training and knowledge of how to deliver these kinds of drawings. The draftsperson will work run of show if there are a lot of sets to draw, or may come in only as needed.

ASSISTANT PROPS

The assistant props person assists the prop master. She could have various duties such as copying prop lists, scouting props, buying props, and retrieving props from the props truck while on set. The assistant props person will start work at the same time as the props person.

ART DEPARTMENT PRODUCTION ASSISTANTS

The art department PAs do everything from getting coffee for the set dresser to returning props or set dressing items. They may begin working on the show at any time. Most often how early in pre-production they begin depends on the budget.

ASSISTANT TO PRODUCTION DESIGNER AND ART DIRECTOR

The assistant to the PD and art director is usually hired only on big-budget films. This person works much like a PA, but exclusively for the PD or art director. Duties include, but are not limited to, getting coffee, communicating with the art department coordinator, making copies, and answering phones. The assistant will begin work at the same time as the PD or art director.

CONSTRUCTION COORDINATOR

The construction coordinator is the head of the construction department and responsible for overseeing the construction of all sets. She reports directly to the art director and will start work on a show as soon as the sets are designed and building is ready to begin. Following is a general list of duties:

- Meets with the art director to discuss what sets need to be built.
- Meets with the set designer to discuss set blueprints.
- Hires the **construction foreman** and **construction laborers**.
- May rent special tools for constructing the set, such as saws, drills, etc.

- Coordinates the building of all sets in conjunction with the production schedule.
- Once a set is wrapped, meaning shooting is fully completed, supervises the striking of the set. The set will not be struck until dailies have returned and the director consents that the set is no longer needed.
- At the end of construction, makes sure all rented equipment is returned.

CONSTRUCTION FOREMAN

The construction foreman deals more with the day-to-day operations of the construction team and the building of the sets. He supervises the construction workers to make sure the sets are making good progress and deals with any problems that may occur along the way. The foreman usually begins working at the same time as the construction coordinator.

CONSTRUCTION LABORERS

The construction laborers, or carpenters, do the actual building of the sets and begin work when the sets are ready to go up.

STANDBY PAINTER

The **standby painter** is a person who paints sets and stays on through the run of the show to paint anything as needed. He works with the set decorator to determine what will need to be painted on any particular sets. The painter usually begins work when the sets are ready to be painted.

STANDBY GREENSPERSON

The **standby greensperson,** who also used to be called the nurseryman, is the person in charge of the maintenance or creation of any foliage on set, including, but not limited to, trees, shrubs, flowers, and bushes. In many cases this person is needed to cover up something with greenery that shouldn't be in the shot. The greensperson begins work anywhere from one week to three months ahead of time, depending on how much greens work is needed. The greensperson may also have a crew of helpers if the work requires it.

OPERATIONS

The operations of the art department are constantly changing. In pre-production the emphasis is on preparing locations and/or building sets. During production, except for the set dresser, the entire department is always working one set ahead to make sure it is ready when the crew needs to shoot. Keep in mind that in order to do this you must secure a location at least one day, and possibly many more, before you actually plan to shoot there. The art department may need time only to dress the set. On the other hand, they may need time to completely transform a location. The art department works with the location department and the director's department to ensure that adequate time is given to prepare a set for shooting. During wrap time the team concentrates on returning locations to their previous state, striking sets and returning equipment.

Following is what a shooting day might look like for the art department:

- The PD, who has already approved the set, may visit set to make sure things are okay.
- The art director may also visit the set or, if applicable, the construction site to check on the progress of the sets.
- The set decorator may continue to acquire set items and will visit sets that are in the process of being decorated, or may decorate the sets with the help of the lead man and swing gang.
- The set dresser, on set, checks to make sure that all set dressing is in its proper place and in proper condition.
- The set dresser stands by camera to ensure that if any set dressing is touched or moved by an actor, it is reset for the next take.
- The lead man and swing gang pick up various set-decorating items and deliver them to set.
- The art department coordinator makes phone calls and processes paperwork.
- Each member of the art department stays in touch with each other to monitor progress, deal with problems, and finish all sets.

SUMMARY

The art department can be one of the largest and most expensive departments on a show, depending on the script. The PD heads up a large team of decorators, artists, painters, dressers, and construction people. The department is large enough on high-budget productions to have its own coordinator to schedule meetings and process funds.

The Camera Department

The camera department, like the art department, is one of the few departments whose entire work is seen on the screen. Camera people are extremely meticulous. Every little focal length and film roll must be tended to with care. This is one department where using only a few people because of the budget could cause you trouble. Furthermore, in this department more than the others, it is important that your crew have experience. With experience also comes a sense of urgency that is very valuable on set. A slow camera team can slow down your shoot like no other department.

Camera teams usually work together on a regular basis. I once worked on a film where the director of photography (DP) was fired. Not only did the camera team leave with him, but the electric and grip departments also quit. These crews have strong loyalty. This chapter outlines the protocol and job descriptions of the camera crew. The operations section covers the all-important decisions this crew must make to ensure that the director's vision is brought to screen. See Figure 9.1 for the camera team hierarchy.

DIRECTOR OF PHOTOGRAPHY

The DP is responsible for three departments. These include the camera department as well as the electric and grip departments. The DP is responsible for the photographic look of the picture, whether you are working in film or the digital world. He works closely with the director to ensure that the photographic vision is in line with the director's overall vision for the project. The DP will start work around the same time as the production designer. Following is a list of duties and responsibilities.

Pre-Production

- Decides on stock.
- Hires the gaffer, key grip, camera operator, and sometimes the first assistant cameraperson (1st AC).
- Determines what the **camera package** will be.

141

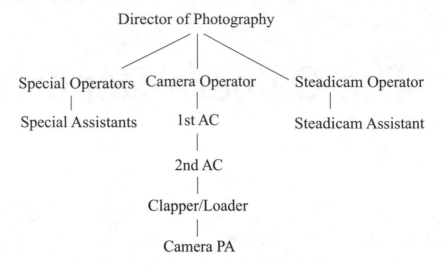

FIGURE 9.1
Camera Team Hierarchy.

- Meets with the director and discusses each scene to see how the photography will match the vision of the film.
- Runs the **hair and makeup tests.**
- May sometimes do stock tests.
- Meets with the gaffer to explain the look of each scene and how each scene will be lit.
- Goes on location scouts. The DP will have significant input into the choice of locations.
- Usually flies first class to the location (except on low-budget shoots).

Production

- Supervises the lighting of the set and the work of the camera.
- Checks the lighting for proper exposure.
- Takes and gives the meter reading to the 1st AC after confirming it with the gaffer. A meter reading is the setting for what the exposure will be.
- Constantly watches the photography to make sure the vision is being achieved.
- Attends dailies.

Wrap

- As with the production designer, in the past there was no reason for the DP to be involved with post-production, that is, until the prints of the film were being made. Now, with the advent of computer-generated images (CGI), DPs are often needed in post-production to ensure the CGI maintains the color scheme and proper photographic style of the film.

CAMERA OPERATOR

The camera operator is the person who runs the camera. She answers directly to the DP and is in charge of the assistant camerapersons. The operator also has special skill in moving the camera steadily and has an aesthetic sense for good framing of the image. The camera operator usually has no pre-production or wrap time. In low budget your DP will most likely double as the camera operator.

Production

- Responsible for the care and condition of the camera.
- Runs the camera.
- Usually has a working knowledge of how to fix a camera.
- May check the height and level on the tripod (**sticks**). The camera operator does this only if there is no 1st AC.

FIRST ASSISTANT CAMERAPERSON

The 1st AC on a shoot assists the camera operator in the operation of the camera. He is the main person in charge of the care and maintenance of the camera. In pre-production, anywhere from a few days to a week before principal, the 1st AC "builds" the camera. This means he gets the camera ready for the first day's shooting. This includes, but is not limited to, cleaning the camera, attaching the lens, and testing that it is working properly. Following is a general list of responsibilities:

- Checks the height and level on the tripod, also called the sticks.
- Sets the exposure on the camera as given by the DP.
- Possibly hires the second assistant cameraperson (2nd AC).
- Measures and **pulls focus.** Measuring for focus is the process of taking a tape measure or electronic measuring device and calculating the distance from the camera lens to the subject. Pulling focus is the process of adjusting the focus knob on the camera so that the actor always stays in focus.
- Assists the camera operator with any needs as necessary.
- Checks the gate after a setup is finished (if using film). **Checking the gate** is the process of opening up the camera lens and checking a mechanical device inside the camera called the gate. The 1st AC checks to make sure no debris such as dirt or a hair has gotten on the gate. If debris is found, the shot is taken over, because these fragments could appear on the filmed image.
- Cleans the camera lens.
- May load the **film magazines** (mags) (if there is no 2nd AC).

SECOND ASSISTANT CAMERAPERSON

The 2nd AC assists the 1st AC. On low-budget shoots there may not be a 2nd AC purely for budgetary reasons. On smaller shoots, you may not need a 2nd AC merely because a video or digital camera can be less technically involved (no mags or stock to handle). Keep in mind that many of the newer digital-format cameras are extremely involved and would require hiring a 2nd AC. The 2nd AC begins on the show a few days before principal photography. Following is a list of general responsibilities:

- Sometimes loads the mags (if shooting film). The mag is the housing device for the film stock. It attaches and detaches from the camera. Usually extra mags are loaded in advance to cut down on the time taken to replace the mag. Loading mags may also be done by the loader.
- Operates the slate or clapper if there is no specific person hired to do so.
- Writes the **camera reports** (see Figure 9.2). These camera reports show how much footage was shot for each take. It is important that a copy is made of these reports before the rolls go to the film lab.
- Fills out the film stock summary report. At the end of the day this report (see Figure 9.3) is given to the 2nd AD, who will notate the information on the production report.
- Sets up, runs, and maintains the monitor for the director.
- Packages the film for shipping.
- Gives the camera reports and film to the 2nd AD at the end of the day.
- Cleans the lenses (if not done by the 1st AC).
- Runs mags from the camera truck to the set and back. This can also be done by a loader or camera PA, if there is one.
- Is responsible for moving the camera boxes around when the camera changes setup.
- Gives the footage of each take to the script supervisor so he can record it on the daily log.

CLAPPER/LOADER

The positions of **clapper** and loader usually exist only on larger budget shoots. If there is no clapper or loader, then these duties are taken up by the 2nd AC. In some cases, the clapper and loader are combined into one position. The clapper operates the clapper, or slate. The loader loads the mags and runs them to and from set. He may also help move the camera boxes when the camera needs to be moved.

CAMERA PRODUCTION ASSISTANT

The camera PA is much like the other PAs on set. Her duties can vary from getting drinks for the camera team to moving camera boxes, to running mags to and from the truck. Sometimes the camera PA guards the camera during lunch. Film and many digital cameras are expensive items, and leaving them on either a hot truck or an unguarded set would not be acceptable. Thus, the PA either sits with the camera or takes the camera with him or her and guards it during lunch.

Date	06/04/02	Page 1 of 1	Project Title	*Regina of Icelandia*
Film Stock		7978	DP	Jane Fitzwater
Emulsion #		4783907	Director	J. Darin Wales

Scene	Take	Remarks	Start Footage	End Footage	Camera Roll
3	1	Okay, possible glare in lens.	15'	115'	4
	(2)	Good.	116'	214'	4
↓	3	N.G. sun came out.	215'	310'	4
18	1	Hair in the gate.	312'	452'	4
	(2)	Good.	455'	600'	4
	(3)	Good.	0'	301'	5
	4	Aborted take.	302'	350'	5
	(5)	Good.	351'	451'	5
↓	(6)	Good.	455'	589'	5
61	(1)	Good, establishing shot.	591'	625'	5
↓	(2)	Good, establishing shot.	627'	667'	5
88	(1)	Good.	669'	768'	5
	2	N.G. sun went in.	770'	812'	5
	3	Okay, glare in lens.	811'	900'	5
↓	(4)	Good.	900'	980'	5

Special Instructions
CRITICAL ENDS

FIGURE 9.2

Camera Report.

Note: The circles that you see in the take column are the printed takes.

Film Stock Summary Report

TITLE: "Regina of Icelandia"
DATE: July 26, 2002   DAY   20   OF 42

Film Inventory	
ON HAND	10,000'
RECEIVED	5,000'
TODAY	3000'
TOTAL	12,000'

Film Use	GROSS	PRINT	WASTE	N.G.	SHORT ENDS
PREVIOUS	25,000'	22,000'	500'	500'	2000'
TODAY	3000'	2200'	0	0	800
TOTAL	28,000'	24,200'	500'	500'	2800'

FIGURE 9.3

Film Stock Summary Report.

This report can be explained as follows. The "Film Inventory" section keeps track of how much film you have left at the end of the day. In this example, you had, at the beginning of this day, 10,000 feet of film. On this day, you received 5,000 more feet of film from the lab and you shot 3,000 feet of film on set. That leaves you with 12,000 feet at the end of the day.

The "Film Use" section warrants some definition of terms. **Previous** is what you shot previously, up until this day. "Today" is what you shot this day. "Total" is the sum of "Previous" and "Today." This total tells you how much footage you have shot up until now.

The columns are the different ways the stock was used. "Gross" is how much film, total, was used. "Print" is how much of that film you actually printed. Keep in mind that in 35mm you do not have to print all the footage you shoot. You can print what is called *selected takes*. The lab will look at the camera report, which indicates which takes you want printed, and print only those. *Short ends* are film that is left over from any certain roll. This is stock that you plan to use again. "Waste" is how much film was or may have been damaged and was thrown away. *N.G.* stands for *no good*, which is any unprinted stock. The rule here is: *Print plus Waste plus N.G. plus Short Ends should equal Gross.*

VIDEO ASSIST

Video assist on a set means having a person whose sole job is to provide a monitor for the director that will show what was just shot. The playback unit is hooked up to the main camera and records footage as the camera is recording film. The director may want to see what was just shot to see if it is acceptable. The playback operator's job is to provide this footage at a moment's notice. For convenience, some video assist companies can provide a database of all footage shot on the production and can record footage for up to four cameras at a time. The video assist operator will start on the first day of shooting. Following is a general list of the operator's responsibilities:

- At the beginning of the day sets up playback close to camera.
- When the director moves, he moves the monitor into position so it is near the director.

- Records everything the camera shoots.
- Turns in all footage at the end of the day so the director has access to it at all times.

STEADICAM OPERATOR

The steadicam operator is a cameraperson who operates a special device called a steadicam. A steadicam is a device that mounts a camera on an operator's body. It is used for moving shots, or to create movement in a static image. Steadicam operators are specially trained to operate this equipment and are usually hired as a package, the operator and the steadicam, for a daily or weekly fee. Some shows (lower budget) will only hire a steadicam operator for the particular days when steadicam is required. Some shows (medium to higher budget) will hire a steadicam operator for run of show so that the director can use the steadicam at any time.

There is also a device called a **Glidecam** that is much like a steadicam but not mounted to the operator's body. It is a much simpler rig, and can be operated by most camera people without special training.

SPECIAL OPERATORS

Sometimes a shoot may require special operators. These operators know how to use specialized cameras and equipment. For instance, if your shoot requires that a scene be filmed under water, you will need an underwater camera and an operator who is experienced shooting under water. These kinds of operators are licensed divers as well as experienced in operating underwater cameras. I have seen in low budget that special boxes or bags can be rigged to go around a regular camera and used underwater. This is much less expensive than a specific underwater camera, but also more dangerous. A homemade device carries with it the risks that water might get into the camera, which can damage it and its contents.

Other specialized operators are used for aerial photography. For instance, there is a unit called a **Wescam,** which is mounted on the outside of an aircraft or ship. This machine allows the camera to tilt and pan by remote control. When you rent this device, you rent the entire rig and usually also have to pay a fuel fee for the helicopter. This fee is based on the distance the helicopter needs to fly. There is a similar item that is a small remote-control airplane with a camera mounted underneath. This camera is operated from the ground as the airplane flies over land that may need to remain undisturbed, such as snow or water, or that may not be passable on the ground, such as a volcano.

THE CAMERA PACKAGE

The camera package is made up of the camera(s), lenses, filters, tripods, and other items. The DP determines exactly what she needs in a film package and gets a rental cost from a camera rental house. Rental houses usually package their systems with different accessories but are open to customizing a package. Camera packages are rented on a three- or four-day basis. This means that, although you are renting the equipment for a full week, you are charged for either three or four days.

There are other types of cameras that you may need to rent, such as a **remote camera system.** These are used when it is not feasible for an AC to reach the camera to turn it on. This system is a unit that holds a camera and can be mounted almost anywhere.

OPERATIONS

The efficiency of the camera department is important to the smooth running of a shooting day. Like no other department, if you are waiting for the camera department to be ready, you cannot continue shooting. Following is a list of how a camera team conducts its day:

- The night before, stock (if shooting film) for the next day is loaded into the mags.
- Crew arrives at the location and unloads the camera and accessories off the camera truck.
- Crew arrives on set and finds out where the first setup of the day is. This information is given to them by the 1st AD. The camera team may need to wait to set up until most of the lighting is finished so as to not get in the way of the lighting team.
- The team stages all the camera boxes so they are close to camera.
- The 1st AC or 2nd AC puts the mag on the camera.
- Once lighting is almost set, the crew moves the camera into place.
- Once stand-ins are in place, the 1st AC measures focus and adjusts the focus knob.
- Once the DP determines the exposure, the 1st AC sets the exposure.
- The camera team stands by for rehearsals and shooting.
- Throughout the day, the team loads new mags onto the camera.
- At the end of the day, the team wraps the camera and returns it to the camera truck.

There are a few special rules that apply to the camera department that are worth noting here. For instance, no one touches the camera except the camera personnel, or by permission of the camera operator. Frequently the director may want to look through the camera lens to check the shot. Or, the script supervisor may want to look through the lens to check the framing of the shot (so she knows what is in frame and what is not). Second, the camera should never be left alone. The camera could be knocked over, damaging expensive parts, or worse, stolen. I once worked a shoot where the camera was not operating well, so it was going to be returned to the rental house for repair. A PA and his girlfriend were assigned to drive the camera 1 hour back to Los Angeles to return it to the rental house. In the middle of the night we got a phone call from the pair claiming that the camera had been stolen out of their car. After a police investigation, it turned out that the PA and girlfriend made the whole story up, stealing the camera themselves and hoping to sell it for a good deal of money. Needless to say, you need to be careful whom you let take care of the camera.

STOCK

Film or video stocks are items that are ordered in pre-production. Be sure to order your stock in plenty of time to allow for shipping delays. Films can be shot on 16mm, usually for low budget or student applications, or 35mm or 70mm, for professional theater distribution. Projects have a variety of digital formats to choose from, and are changing every day, in addition to digital formats. If using film stock, there is a special way it is ordered for a shoot. You can tell the lab that you want all film stock from one bath, meaning all of the stock was created in one process. This ensures uniformity in the stock. The lab will then ship portions of the stock to you throughout the shoot. This way, you do not have to deal with storing many cans of film, which need to be refrigerated until used. The amount of stock received on this basis is recorded on the film stock summary report so that an accurate tally of the stock can be maintained. In low budget the stock is kept in a hotel room. In higher budget shoots it is kept in an air-conditioned camera truck throughout the day. If shooting digitally this may be the time to acquire the proper drives or computers needed for recording and archiving. In some cases stock is no longer needed, as when digital footage is recorded directly onto hard drives. Again, determine which workflow will be appropriate for your shoot in pre-production.

DAILIES

If you are shooting film, you will need to have your film processed. You need to set up an account with a film lab to do your processing. The lab then knows to keep your negative for you until it is needed for the **negative cutters.** Choosing a film lab is a matter of preference or location. Most low-budget shoots will try to use a film lab that is close to them so they can save on shipping costs. Medium to higher budget shoots will choose a lab that the DP is comfortable with and ship the footage to the lab each day. Following is the process for shipping this footage, called dailies. First you get special boxes from your lab special for shipping film. Then, you set up an account with an airline that ships cargo and a courier that transports film. Next, on a daily basis, the following should occur:

- At the end of the day, the 2nd AC packs up the film, attaching camera reports to the cans. Keep in mind that the 2nd AC might break film during your shooting day. **Breaking film** is a process that involves taking all the film that has been shot so far that day and packing it up for shipping. This is done because labs have a certain time by which they must receive film in order to get the dailies back to the production the next day. This timing is determined in pre-production so the 2nd AC will know each day when to break film.
- The 2nd AC turns the film over to the 2nd AD, who will make sure it is transported to the production office.
- The POC or APOC packs the rolls into the special shipping boxes and arranges for someone to take the film to the airport. It is important that this person get the tracking number from the airline or courier in case the shipment should get lost.
- The POC or APOC calls the film courier on the other end (in the city where the lab is) and informs them of the tracking number and flight arrival time.

- The film courier picks up the film at the airport and transports it to the lab for processing.
- The lab processes the film and, when finished, calls the film courier to pick up the dailies and transport them to the airport.
- The film courier then calls the production office with the tracking number and flight arrival time.
- The POC sends someone, either a PA or, if there is a transportation department, a driver, to the airport to pick up the film.
- The dailies are then picked up and turned over to the editors to prepare them for viewing after the end of the shoot day.

Whether to project your dailies on film or digitally is determined by the producer and director. This decision needs to be made in pre-production, since it will affect the budget and some preparations. If you choose to watch your dailies on film, then you will need to pay for printing and processing. Labs charge a certain amount of money per foot for each process. This cost should be reflected in your budget. In addition, you will need to hire a projectionist to project the dailies.

If you choose to watch your dailies digitally, the lab will do a process called **telecine** or **transfer.** The lab will transfer your footage to video or a digital format and send back videotapes or files. You can have them transferred to a number of analog and digital video formats. In addition, many labs will send your footage to a designated Internet site for viewing as well.

BEHIND-THE-SCENES FOR DVD

With the advent of DVD release, all films now shoot behind-the-scenes footage to be used on the DVD. On low-budget shoots, where you probably do not have a unit publicist, the producer hires a cameraperson to go around shooting interviews and footage throughout the shooting period. The producer, the show's editor, or the cameraperson, if qualified, may edit this footage. On higher budget shoots, the publicist hires a cameraperson and behind-the-scenes producer to guide the shooting. Because behind-the-scenes is so popular now, there are companies that specifically shoot behind-the-scenes for media projects. After principal photography is over, the footage is edited together to make **featurettes** that will appear on the DVD. These featurettes are also placed in the **electronic press kit** (EPK).

TESTS

Camera tests are performed in certain cases in which the director and DP want to see how a stock looks and/or how the actors look on film. Tests are usually done only in medium to higher budget shoots because of the costs they incur. However, a simple stock test is not that expensive and could be done for low-budget shoots. There are four kinds of tests: stock, makeup, hair, and wardrobe.

The stock test is done to see how certain stocks look in certain lighting situations. Stock houses are continually coming up with new stocks, and DPs need to test them out before using them, to ensure a quality image while shooting.

Makeup and hair tests are performed to see how a particular actor or actress looks with the new "look" defined by their character. They may also be done if special-effect makeup is required, for instance, on a science fiction project.

Wardrobe tests are shot to see how a particular actor or actress looks in wardrobe. This is usually done on period films and science fiction projects where the wardrobe may be designed from scratch or be very involved.

To complete any of these tests, do the following:

- Hire the DP and rent a camera to shoot the test.
- Secure a room or location to shoot the test.
- If applicable, contact the actors and schedule them for the test.
- Arrange for processing the footage, if shooting film.
- Arrange for a viewing with the producer, director, DP, key makeup artist, **key hair** artist, and costume designer (where applicable).

Once the tests are complete, the people involved discuss any changes that need to be made.

SUMMARY

The head of the camera department is the DP, who also is responsible for other departments such as grip and electric. The DP works to achieve photographic excellence in line with the director's vision. The camera crew can consist of an operator and one or two assistants or may include additional operators for complicated shots or shots that need to be covered from many angles, such as stunts or special effects. Camera operators can be highly specialized, such as the steadicam operator and aerial and underwater operators. As technology and formats progress, the camera department works hard to keep up with new processes and digital cameras. Finally, in addition to main unit camera operators, small camera crews also frequent the set, shooting featurettes and behind-the-scenes footage for DVD release.

Grip and Electric

The grip and electric departments work very closely together, which is why they are grouped together in this chapter. Both departments also answer to the DP and work along side the camera department. In this chapter the grip and electric teams are delineated along with descriptions of the many pieces of equipment required to run these departments. Additionally, one important aspect of these crews is their speed of operation. Nothing can slow an entire production down like a sluggish lighting team. Of particular importance is the end-of-the-day wrap. This crew must wrap quickly and efficiently. Therefore, special attention is paid to this procedure. Figure 10.1 shows the lighting hierarchy.

GAFFER

The gaffer is the head of the electric department and thus is in charge of the lighting budget and lighting crew. Her main responsibility is to light the set as per the vision of the DP, using the lighting crew. He uses this crew to set lights in place, point them, turn them on, and focus them. The gaffer starts anywhere from two weeks to two months into pre-production.

Pre-Production

- Has several meetings with the DP to discuss the vision for lighting.
- Goes over **lighting grids** with the DP. A lighting grid is an overhead drawing of a set. The grid shows where lights will be placed, what kinds of lights, and where they are to point. The grid may also make note of any gels that should be placed over the lights.
- Puts together and orders the **lighting package.**
- Hires the lighting team.
- Makes sure the lighting package is in order when it arrives.
- Orders expendables. Expendables are items that are used and then thrown away. Items such as gaffer's tape, camera tape, canned air, lumber, and dulling spray are expendables used by the camera, sound, grip, and electric departments.

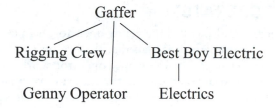

FIGURE 10.1
Lighting Hierarchy.

Production

- At the beginning of the shooting day, coordinates the first lighting set up.
- May need to tie in. **Tying in** is the process of hooking the lights up to the electrical system of the location. This is only required if you are using **house power.** Tying in also refers to hooking up the lights to a generator.
- May keep an "electric" on each light until the lighting is set.
- Takes meter readings and confers with the DP.
- Continues to oversee the lighting team.

Wrap

- Makes sure the lighting package is returned in good working order.

BEST BOY ELECTRIC

The **best boy electric** is the person who works directly under and assists the gaffer. He is also in charge of the lighting truck and is responsible for the lighting inventory. The best boy is also in charge of the care and maintenance of the lighting equipment. To do this he completes frequent inventories of all the lights and lighting equipment to ensure nothing is lost or, if something is damaged, that it is returned. The best boy usually has a working knowledge of lights, can fix them, and replaces blown bulbs on lights when necessary. Finally, the best boy is in charge of loading the truck at the end of the day. The best boy can start work as soon as the lighting truck arrives at the location.

ELECTRICIANS

Electricians, also sometimes called electrics or lamp operators, are the people who place the lights. They also lay a cable called **banded.** Banded is the cable that connects the lights to the generator or house power. It is important that electrics are continually standing by to adjust the lights as necessary. At the beginning of the day they pull lights off the truck, take them to the set, and set them in place as directed by the best boy or gaffer. At the end of the day, they strike the lights and banded and load them on the truck.

GENERATOR OPERATOR

The generator operator, also called the **genny operator,** is in charge of the generator. She makes sure the generator is placed at the beginning of the day, gassed up and ready for the gaffer to tie in. The genny operator works when the generator is needed. You may need a generator for the duration of a shoot. Or, you may use a location's house power and not need a generator at all. On the other hand, you may use a generator only at specific locations. The determination for using a generator is based on the type of location in which you are shooting, whether you have permission to use house power, and your budget. For instance, if you are shooting in the woods at night, certainly you will need a generator to provide power to light the scene. However, if you are shooting in a hospital, you may have permission to use their electricity, and thus not need the generator while at that location.

RIGGING CREW

The **rigging crew** is a lighting crew that works one set ahead of the main unit, prelighting a set. They also strike the lighting the day after the main unit shoots. Rigging crews are mostly seen on larger budget shoots because of the extra cost of the crew. A rigging crew might be considered a luxury, but can greatly speed the pace of your shoot, since you will not need to light sets from scratch on the day of shooting. They are employed sometimes on a daily basis and sometimes on a weekly basis, depending on the budget and needs of the production. If the budget can allow, the rigging crew will work run of show.

KEY GRIP

The key grip is in charge of the grips and the grip budget. He is in charge of acquiring the grip package and works closely with the gaffer to make sure everything is ready for the camera to shoot. Figure 10.2 shows the grip hierarchy.

Following is a list of general responsibilities.

Pre-Production

- Puts together and orders the grip package.
- Coordinates getting the grip truck to the location.
- Hires the **best boy grip** and **company grips.**

Production

- Sets **flags,** nets, and **silks.**
- Blocks out windows with black material, called **black wrap,** when needed.
- Gets rid of **flares** for the camera by placing flags in the way of the glare source.
- Never leaves the camera without another grip standing by to assist.

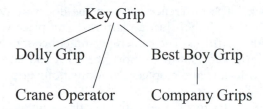

FIGURE 10.2
Grip Hierarchy.

- Supervises laying the **dolly track.**
- May be needed to help set up a **jib** or a crane.

Wrap

- Makes sure all grip equipment is accounted for and in good working order.
- Makes sure the grip truck is returned to the grip company.

BEST BOY GRIP

As in the electric department, the best boy is in charge of the truck. He performs frequent inventories of all grip equipment and is responsible for all equipment being in good order. On the first day of shooting or in pre-production, the best boy will inventory the grip truck, making sure that each item ordered is there and in good working order. The best boy spends most of the time on the truck managing the equipment. Finally, he is responsible for having the truck loaded properly at the end of the day. At the end of the shoot the best boy will submit a final equipment report to the key grip, noting any equipment that is missing or damaged.

COMPANY GRIPS

Company grips work directly under the key grip and have a myriad of duties. They haul grip equipment to and from the truck as needed. They set flags, nets, and silks and load the truck at the end of the day.

DOLLY GRIP

The **dolly grip** is a grip with special skill in operating a **dolly.** A dolly is a platform that travels on tracks. You place your camera on the dolly, which also has a hydraulic lift so you can change the camera height. The dolly also has seats for the camera operator and director. There is also a **doorway dolly,** which is a platform that travels on tracks. The difference between the doorway dolly and a regular dolly is that the doorway dolly is just a platform. You place your camera, which goes on sticks, on the platform. The cameraperson either stands or sits on an **apple box.** The dolly grip knows how to move the dolly so that the ride is smooth, without jerks, and will start and stop gently. Many dolly grips also know how to smoothly operate a jib.

A jib is a device similar to a crane, with the camera on one end and the operator on the other end of a long pole. Jibs can range from 2 to 7 feet in height, and have a 5- to 8-foot reach. Most dolly grips in medium- and high-budget projects work run of show. If working this way, the dolly grip will start a few days ahead of principal photography to make sure the dolly is in good working order. In low budget, since dollies are not included in a standard grip package, they have to be rented at an additional cost. Therefore, the dolly grip would work only for the time that a dolly is being rented.

CRANE OPERATOR

The crane operator is a person with skill in operating a large crane. Cranes are used to get the camera high in the air (see more in the section "The Grip Package"). The use of a crane operator works the same as a dolly grip. In high budget, cranes are often used run of show, so the crane operator will come in a few days early to test the crane. In low budget, the crane would be rented only for certain days because of the additional cost.

OPERATIONS FOR GRIP AND ELECTRIC

At the beginning of the day, the lighting team unloads the lighting truck of lights and cables that are needed for the first setup. The gaffer knows the first lighting setup and thus directs the best boy and electricians where to place the lights. If organized, the gaffer will have certain electrics laying cable and certain electrics setting up the lights. Then, if She has enough crew, the gaffer may have electrics stand by at each light, ready to adjust until the lighting setup is complete. Meanwhile, the gaffer has asked the 1st AD to get the stand-ins to the set. As the scene progresses, if possible, the gaffer will have electrics prelight the next area, so that when the camera moves there, it will be almost ready to go.

Before the end of the day, the gaffer will decide what equipment may be wrapped to the lighting truck, items that will no longer be needed that day. When the martini is called (the last shot of the day), the gaffer directs electrics to begin returning items to the truck and start loading the truck. Once wrap is called, the electrics return all items to the truck, and one electric performs an idiot check. An idiot check is the process of someone examining the location closely to make sure no equipment is left behind.

At the beginning of the day, the grips unload the grip truck with frequently used items and put them in a predetermined **staging area.** If dolly is first up, they begin laying dolly track. They also put flags and nets on **c-stands** so they are ready at a moment's notice. A c-stand is a stand on which you can position flags and nets that allows them to be moved in different directions. These items are frequently used to block flares or placed in front of a light to reduce its power. The grips may also begin to set up a 12-by-12, or other size, silk. A silk is a large frame covered in material. It is used to reduce or soften light shining on the actors. If shooting exteriors, grips also will set up a flag contraption that is used to provide shade for the director. There are hundreds of pieces of equipment at the grips' disposal, such as C-clamps, alligator clamps, **sandbags,** and more items than could be mentioned here. It is beyond the scope of this book to mention them all. However, it is important that a producer understand the scope of this equipment. If you have rented a grip package, spend time on the truck getting to know the equipment and review the paperwork for the package. Once their initial equipment is set up, the grip team stands by to make adjustments as needed.

Before the end of the day, the key grip assesses the need for grip equipment. She may instruct the grip team to wrap certain items (take them back to the truck) that are no longer needed that day. Once the martini is called, more items are returned to the truck. At this point, or before if possible, the key grip may send some grips to begin loading the truck. Once wrap is called, all items are returned to and loaded on the truck. The key grip will also assign someone to do an idiot check.

THE GRIP PACKAGE

The grip package is typically a truck loaded with grip equipment, rented from a grip and lighting company. Grip packages come in different sizes, all containing more or less equipment. These sizes are measured in tons. For instance, you can rent a 2-ton grip package, which is usually sufficient on low-budget shoots. Alternatively, you can rent up to a 10-ton package for high-budget shoots. Most grip packages are rented on a three- or four-day week. Keep in mind that if you are shooting in a city that does not have a rental house, the truck will need to be driven to your location. This applies to the lighting package as well. You need to plan for travel time to allow the trucks to get to your location in time to inventory them before shooting.

There is another specialized item that does not come as part of a standard grip package. It is a **camera car.** A camera car is a truck with mounting surrounding it on which a small crew can walk and place a camera. This vehicle allows you to shoot actors inside the vehicle or travel ahead or behind another vehicle while shooting. When renting this type of device, you pay for the car rental as well as a driver. Companies that rent camera cars employ drivers who are experienced in driving their vehicles safely.

THE LIGHTING PACKAGE

The lighting package is a truck loaded with lighting equipment. On low-budget shoots the grip and lighting packages are combined on one truck. On medium to higher budgets each department has its own truck. Sometimes, if needed, a shoot may have more than one lighting truck. Because lighting needs for a shoot are so specific, a lighting package can be custom ordered. The gaffer will look at the lights available and make a complete list for the rental house. The rental house then sends back a cost for the package. Most lighting packages are rented on a three- or four-day week.

LAYING DOLLY TRACK

There is an organized and efficient way to lay dolly track. Depending on how much track needs to be laid, the process should take no longer than one-half hour to an hour. The key to efficiency is crew assignments. The key grip will direct the grips as to their specific assignments. First, certain grips are assigned to bring track from the truck or staging area (when the key grip knows that dolly is required for a scene, she will make sure enough track is placed in the staging area, space permitting). Next, certain grips are assigned to get the **wedges.** Wedges are little pieces of wood that are placed under the dolly track to provide a level surface. Next, the grips lay the dolly track end to end, hooking them together. As they do this, a grip on each side of the track places wedges under the track, not worrying yet about being precise. Then, either the key grip or another grip walks up the track placing a level at various points. He or she then directs two other grips, one on either side of the track to insert the wedges more accurately, leveling the track. When the key grip or grip gets to the end of the track, this job is almost done. Meanwhile, other grips have been assigned to bring the dolly to the track. The grips place the dolly on the track and move it up along the track, testing for smoothness. Sometimes powder or furniture polish is put on the track to lubricate it, making the ride smoother. Once the dolly has a smooth ride, it is ready for the camera, which is placed on the dolly by the camera team.

TRUCK WRAP

When the camera wraps, there still needs to be the same sense of urgency that keeps the crew moving while shooting. Loading a small- to medium-sized grip truck should not take more than 45 minutes to 1 hour. Now, this time varies greatly depending on the size of the crew and how involved the shooting is.

There is one method of loading the grip truck that works well from low to high budget. It is called the **two-point system.** The key to a quick truck wrap is to assign grips or electrics specific jobs. For instance, say one or two electrics are assigned to wrapping cable. Then, one or more electrics take lights down and bring them to the truck. Sometimes hot lights are all placed in the same area to cool down before being loaded onto the truck. Light stands are all placed in the same area. Other items such as cables and sandbags are placed in their own areas. Someone is located on the ground telling crew where to put all the items. This person may then hand pieces of equipment to the people on the truck. On the truck there are two or more people, one in back and one in front, placing the equipment in their proper places. The front person will hand the equipment to the back person or put it away. The front person then determines what comes next. If the next piece of equipment is something that is to be loaded in the back of the truck, he then calls for it and hands it to the back person. The front person then calls for another item (a front item) and places the item in her area.

SUMMARY

The grip and electric departments support the camera team and DP by providing rigging and lighting for the scene. The gaffer and key grip work directly under the DP to lead their teams in this support. The speed of these crews is very important. These departments use various methods to make sure lighting and grip support is quick and efficient. Grip and lighting equipment is rented in packages, and while there are some standards, each package is different based on the needs of the shoot.

The Sound Department

The sound department is one of the smallest, yet most important crew on a film shoot. Unfortunately (mostly in low budget), it is sometimes treated as an afterthought when putting together a crew. Thus, this chapter approaches the subject of the sound department as essential to a successful film and smooth audio post-production. The importance of getting good sound on location is discussed in addition to job descriptions and operations.

Most first-time directors may not understand the importance of good sound when on set. The director might think that he is in a hurry and so shoots without sound. He may think, "Oh, there's no dialogue in this scene, let's just shoot **MOS** (without sound)." The trouble comes when you get into the sound edit and suddenly you need to create an entire world of sound for one scene because you decided to shoot it MOS. This creates more work for your sound editing team, and could therefore cost more for your sound editing equipment rental. See Chapter 17 for the process of **sound editing.**

SOUND MIXER

The sound mixer is responsible for recording sound on set. She records each take, as well as **wild sound** and room ambience. Wild sound is sound not synchronized to picture. For instance, a shot calls for a car to pull up and the actor to get out and go into a house. In addition to recording this shot, the sound mixer will also try to get the sounds of the car turning off, the keys coming out of the ignition, and the car door opening and closing. It is difficult to get much wild sound on location because the pace of the day is so fast. However, it is good for the sound mixer to get what she can.

Ambience, or room tone, is the sound in a room when no one is speaking or creating sound. It is the background sound of a room or location. Sometimes room tone is very quiet, as in a room inside a house. Sometimes ambience is full of sounds that create an atmosphere, such as a field in the country. These recordings are very important to the sound editing process (see Chapter 17).

The sound mixer will start work on the first day of shooting. Following are the duties and responsibilities of the sound mixer.

Pre-Production

- Reads the script to determine special sound requirements.
- Hires a **boom operator.** Most sound mixers work with one or two boom operators on a regular basis.
- May hire a **cable person** and sound PA if the budget allows.
- Goes on the technical scout to determine any special sound problems such as planes overhead, nearby construction, or noisy traffic.

Production

- Once on set, sets up the sound equipment in a designated staging area.
- Reviews the shot list and location of the first setup.
- Confers on microphone placement with the boom operator.
- Operates the recording machine during rehearsals to get levels.
- May adjust placement of the boom if necessary.
- Records a slate for each roll/tape/DVD that states the number of the roll, the date of shooting, and the name and type of recorder being used.
- Records approximately 30 seconds of reference tone on the tape.
- Records the take.
- Fills out the **sound report** (see Figure 11.1).
- Before wrap is called, records ambience, or room tone.
- At the end of the day labels all sound tapes and turns them over to the 2nd AD.

BOOM OPERATOR

The boom operator is the person who holds the boom in a position that will result in the best possible sound. Boom operators must be physically fit: it takes a lot of strength to hold up a boom pole all day. Most boom operators are people aspiring to become sound mixers. It is important that a boom operator know and understand good microphone placement. She should know where to put the boom for optimal sound recording. Otherwise the sound mixer would have to worry about it. The sound mixer needs the freedom to concentrate on getting good levels. The boom operator has no pre-production. Following is a list of general responsibilities:

- Builds the microphone each morning. **Building the microphone** is the process of putting the proper microphone on the boom pole and choosing the right amount of cable.
- Hooks up to the audio machine (1/4-inch reel-to-reel, **digital audio tape [DAT]**, disk, or DVD).
- Holds the boom in place for rehearsals and takes.
- Helps wrap out equipment at the end of the day.

Sound Report

Date: _____
Production: _____
Director: _____
Snd Mixer: _____
Format: _____

Recorder: _____
Media: _____
Boom: _____
File Type: _____

SLATE# SCENE #	SHOT #	TAKE	SNC/WLD	TC/File #	COMMENTS
1	A	1	S	01:20:00:00	Good levels, running thru woods
		2	S	01:22:05:09	Good levels , best take.
		3	S	01:24:00:00	Bad take, airplane
		4	S	01:26:05:10	Bad take, airplane
	B	1	S	01:28:56:00	N.G. background noise
		2	S	01:32:55:00	Good. Regina & Donato talk.
		3	S	01:36:00:18	Okay levels. Regina soft.
		4	S	01:40:15:10	Good.
		5	S	01:44:00:00	Best take.
		6	S	01:48:31:06	N.G. bad levels.
		7	S	01:52:00:00	Good.
		8	S	01:56:21:12	Good.
14	A	1	S	01:56:00:00	Good. Regina finds rock.
		2	S	01:56:05:09	Good.
	B	1	S	01:57:00:00	Okay, background noise.
		2	S	01:58:05:10	N.G. bad levels.
		3	S	01:59:56:00	N.G. airplane
		4	S	02:02:55:00	Best take.
			W	02:05:00:18	Running thru woods.
			W	02:07:55:00	Stumbling over rock.
	C	1	S	02:10:00:18	Good. Regina climbs tree.
		2	S	02:11:55:00	Good.
		3	S	02:12:00:18	Okay levels, scratching on tree.
		4	S	02:13:55:00	Okay levels. Regina soft.
		5	S	02:14:00:18	Good.
		6	S	02:15:55:00	Best take.
		7	S	02:16:00:18	Good.
		8	S	02:17:55:00	N.G. bad levels.
		9	S	02:18:00:18	N.G. aborted take.
		10	S	02:19:55:00	Good.
		11	S	02:20:00:18	N.G. Plane

FIGURE 11.1
Sound Report.

The relationship between the sound mixer and boom operator is very important. I once worked a show with a husband-and-wife sound team. They knew sign language and would sign back and forth between takes, adjusting the boom placement. Clearly this team knew how to communicate. The fast pace of shooting requires that the mixer and boom be able to communicate clearly and quickly.

CABLE PULLER OR CABLE PERSON

This position, formerly called the **third man,** is the person who keeps track of the cables that go from the boom operator to the sound mixer. In some cases the boom operator may need to be some distance from the mixer. With all kinds of crew walking around, someone is needed to protect these delicate cables. Also, the boom operator may need to move with the camera; the cable puller is then needed to pull cable. For instance, the shot calls for two actors to walk down a sidewalk, having a conversation. The camera will cover the actors by moving with the actors on a long dolly track. The boom operator must then walk alongside the camera, with the boom pointed at the actors. The cable puller follows behind the boom operator either picking up or handing out the cable as needed. This process is needed so that no one trips over the cable and so that the boom operator has sufficient cable to move with the camera.

SOUND PRODUCTION ASSISTANT

The sound PA is much like other PA positions. He is there to assist the sound team in many ways. The sound PA might get coffee for the sound mixer or boom operator. Or, perhaps he will be needed to retrieve stock for the sound mixer. Many sound PAs double as cable pullers.

THE SOUND PACKAGE

The **sound package** for a production consists of the audio recorder, microphones, boom poles, cables, sound cart, and, oftentimes, walkie-talkies. The package is sometimes rented from an audio rental facility. However, many sound people own their own equipment. You would then pay for the sound mixer and her package together. The recording format can be a sound person's decision or the preference of the director. Historically there was 1/4-inch reel-to-reel audiotape, an analog format that is used with a **Nagra.** Then there was DAT tape, which is recorded on a digital machine but uses tape. There is now also disk, which is used on a hard-disk recorder. There is also DVD-R, which is recording on a DVD recorder. Be sure to keep up on current formats that may be used on your next show.

OPERATIONS

Once on set, the sound mixer goes over the shot list and determines where the boom will be placed for the shot. She then discusses this with the boom operator, including any movement that may be required. The sound mixer will be sure to watch the 1st AD and camera team as they prepare for the shot. When the actors are brought to set, the sound team gets ready for the rehearsal. During the rehearsal the mixer will get levels, making sure the boom placement is the best it can be for the shot. The rehearsal is the only time the sound mixer may have to get these levels.

Immediately before the shot, the 1st AD will ask the sound mixer if she is ready, to which the sound mixer replies, "Ready." The 1st AD will then check with the camera team and director to make sure they are ready. When everyone is ready, the 1st AD will call, "Roll Sound." The sound mixer turns on the recording machine. When the machine is at full running speed, the sound mixer calls, **Speed.** Then as the shot commences, the sound mixer records the take.

When the shot is finished, the 1st AD may ask the sound mixer if the take was good or not. Some 1st ADs may not do this. It is up to the sound mixer to say something if the take was not good for sound. Perhaps a crew member made noise in the background over an actor's dialogue. That would be a bad sound take.

The sound mixer then makes the proper notes on the sound report (see Figure 11.1). In between takes the sound mixer may make adjustments to boom placement to improve the sound as much as possible.

At the end of the day, the sound mixer tells the 2nd AD which sound reel or tape he is on or, if the roll is completed, turns it over.

PLAYBACK

Sometimes sound playback is needed on set. There are many situations where this may be the case. Perhaps it is a music video shoot. On these shoots, the music is prerecorded and then played back on set as the artist performs and lip-syncs to the song. Alternatively, the situation may be that a dance scene is being shot and music needs to play for the dancers to dance to. Maybe the scene requires a band to play in a bar scene. In this example, the song the band plays will most likely be prerecorded. Then, on set, playback is used.

The process for playback requires some preparation. Cues are predetermined so that at any time the director can call for the playback to begin at any certain point. The process of setting up these cues should happen before getting on set. On low- to medium-budget shoots, the sound mixer can double as the playback operator. On some medium-budget and most high-budget shoots, a separate playback operator may be hired, depending on how much playback is needed. For instance, if you are shooting a musical, it is a good idea to hire someone different since there will be a lot of playback.

SUMMARY

The sound department, while quite small, is one of the most important departments in terms of its final product. The sound team records all dialogue and on-set sound effects. When possible, the sound recordist also records wild sounds of various actions that the actors take. Some situations call for the recordist to operate playback, such as for a music video or if there are singers or musicians on set.

Special Effects and Visual Effects

This chapter approaches the subject of special effects as an ever-changing department that finds its growth in ever-changing technology. Entire books have been written on special effects, so it is not the intention here to write with that degree or scope. What this chapter will do is delineate the major kinds of special effects and the primary personnel that work on them. This chapter will also give a general overview of the personnel and process of visual effects. Visual effects can be differentiated from special effects. Special effects are effects created on set and sometimes in post-production. Visual effects are effects that are created digitally on set or in post-production.

SPECIAL EFFECTS

There are two kinds of special effects, **physical effects** and **mechanical** effects. The team that accomplishes these may be individuals who do special effects or a company that specializes in these effects. Some of the many different kinds of effects that can be achieved this way are as follows.

Creature Design

Creature design can be a physical effect that combines the special-effect and makeup departments. Creatures are first designed on paper and then constructed with various materials. This kind of effect usually has a person inside: an actor, a stunt person, or a person who either dances or fits the stature of the costume. Creatures of this type are also sometimes combined with visual effects to do such things as fly, jump, or perform actions impossible for a normal person. Creature design can also be done digitally. Whether you do creatures physically or digitally is usually determined by the preference of the director, producer, or the budget.

Creature Manufacturer

The **creature manufacturer** is a person who is in the business of creating physical creatures for motion pictures. This person usually works for a special effects house and is hired out by the company to create creatures.

Modelers

Modelers are the craftsmen who construct physical models of creatures with wire frames, latex, and paint.

Miniatures

Miniatures can be small physical models of aircraft, sets, and creatures—almost anything. The miniatures are constructed and then filmed at exterior locations or on a sound stage. This footage is either used alone or combined with visual effects.

Remote Vehicles

Remote vehicles can be aircraft or ground vehicles, usually in miniature, that need to be filmed away from the camera. Therefore, they are operated by remote control.

Miniature Pyrotechnics

Miniature pyrotechnics is a form of special effects where miniatures are in some way destroyed. I once worked a show where helicopters had to be blown up. The special-effects team constructed some miniature helicopters and shot them against the sky from a low angle, while blowing them up. The proper amount of pyrotechnics made the effect appear as if a full-size helicopter had been destroyed.

Matte Painting

A **matte painting** is a hand-painted background that could not be found in the real world or is not located conveniently for shooting. The painting can be combined with live action footage or visual effects. Most matte paintings today have been replaced with digital images.

Full-Scale Physical Effects

Full-scale physical effects are effects that are created on set by the special-effects team. These kinds of effects happen in real time and on an actual, life-size scale. Some examples of full-scale effects follow. Keep in mind any of these can also be created digitally.

Pyrotechnics Pyrotechnics include the use of explosions and fire. Explosions are created with mortars, black powder bombs, or det cords, which can be used to blow up almost anything. Fire effects can be created using propane torches, gas burners, or fire bars. You should also always have fire extinguishers standing by on set in case of an emergency. Make sure the **Bureau of Alcohol, Tobacco, and Firearms** (BATF) licenses your pyrotechnics people. Many states also require a local license with the fire marshal.

Squibs   Squibs are small explosive charges that are attached to an actor to give the illusion that he has been shot. I once worked on a low-budget show where many of the crew doubled as extras in the film (not uncommon in low budget). I played the part of a forest woman who is shot. I was dressed in a toga (the story takes place post-Armageddon, and of course the only wardrobe left would be togas!). In order to move into the shot, I had to jump up onto a rock. I was so nervous about not disturbing the squib on my stomach that I stepped on the toga on the way up the rock. All I heard next was someone yelling, "Wardrobe!" as I stood there with the toga around my waist, exposing myself to the entire crew!

Ground Squibs   Ground squibs are squibs used to give the illusion that a bullet has hit the ground, a wall, or some other such surface.

Weather Effects

Weather effects are a type of physical effect that recreates a certain weather situation.

Floods and Rain   Water effects are created by using **rain towers** or stands that shoot water over the shot. These stands can be mounted on the ground, over a car, or even hung across large distances, using cables to create the rain. Sometimes you can also hook up to a fire hydrant with permission from the local fire department and use special valves to create rain effects. It is important when using rain effects that your wardrobe and makeup team are standing by with dry clothes and towels for your actors.

Wind   Wind effects are created using fans of various sizes to recreate anything from a gentle breeze to hurricane force winds up to 100 miles/hour. Safety is an important issue with wind machines, as they can also pick up debris and create dangerous projectiles.

Snow   Snow effects are created using various methods. You can use plastic flakes, shaved ice, salt, shaving cream, or foam machines. The advantage of using foam machines is that the foam lasts longer than salt or shaved ice and is less messy to clean up than plastic flakes.

Smoke   Smoke effects are created using various **foggers,** with liquid nitrogen, oil, kerosene, or dry ice. It is important that, when creating smoke effects, especially on a large scale, you inform the local authorities about what you are doing, so as not to create alarm that a real fire may be burning.

SPECIAL EFFECTS COORDINATOR

The special effects coordinator is in charge of the special effects budget. He works with the director to discuss each effect and determine how each effect will look.

The coordinator then hires various teams to create the effects. He may also work with the visual effects coordinator if any of the effects will be combined with CGI. The coordinator could begin work months into pre-production if the show has many effects, or may be hired for only the period of time that a certain effect is required. Following is a general list of duties:

- Breaks down the script and approximate cost of each special effect.
- Meets with the director to discuss how each effect should look.
- Works with the 1st AD to schedule effects, ensuring that enough prep time is given to accomplish the effects safely.
- May assign a special effects supervisor to supervise different effects if needed. This is done on projects where a large number of effects are required.
- May meet with the safety manager to discuss safety considerations.
- On set, supervises the safety of each effect.

OPERATIONS ON SET

The special effects coordinator and her team may arrive on set a day or more before shooting to pre-rig devices as needed. On the day of shooting the team continues to prepare the effect for shooting. This may involve moving a rain machine into place or placing explosives for a car to blow up. The coordinator keeps the 1st AD informed of the preparations so that the 1st AD can judge when to move to the effects shot.

Increasingly, for safety reasons crews will complete a dry run-through. A dry run-through is a kind of rehearsal of the effect. The 1st AD quiets the set and calls the run-through. During this time, the special effects coordinator walks everyone on set through what will happen, step by step. This dry run is important for safety. It not only allows everyone to see what will happen but also gives them the ability to know if something has gone wrong.

Once the effect is executed, the special effects people notify the 1st AD when the set is clear. The 1st AD will then pass this information on to the rest of the crew.

VISUAL EFFECTS

Visual effects are created in computers. These effects can be created completely by the computer or may use footage from the main unit. If main unit footage is part of the shot, sometimes a **motion control camera** will be used on set. A motion control camera allows computerized positioning of the camera. The camera has the ability to move in exactly the same position or direction, either panning or tilting, take after take. This accuracy allows the footage to be easily combined with CGI later.

Visual effects can be used in a number of different ways. They can be used to clean up a shot: For instance, an actor may need to fly through the air and thus will be hooked to a safety line to do so. In post-production, the visual effects people will remove the safety line from the shot using visual effects.

Visual effects can be used to create set design. In many cases, more often than the average person can recognize, the background you are seeing may not be completely real. An establishing shot of a medieval city may consist of some sets constructed by the art department. Then the visual effects team may add more buildings with CGI, a certain cloud-filled sky, or mountains in the background.

Visual effects can also be used to provide more cast. Frequently, when shooting large crowds or armies, a minimum number of actual people are placed on set and photographed. Then in post-production, a larger number of CGI extras are added. This helps to fill a baseball stadium or battlefield with more people without having to hire them.

Finally visual effects can even be precreated and then used on set in combination with live actors to complete a scene. This is usually done with science fiction or fantasy films where the entire world may be digital. This way the director can see exactly how the effects will work as the live action goes on in front of it. Also keep in mind practically anything can be created as a visual effect. All physical and mechanical effects including creatures and miniatures are frequently done digitally.

VISUAL EFFECTS PRODUCER

A **visual effects producer,** also called the visual effects supervisor, is a person who works either independently or for a visual effects house. Her job description is much like that of a special effects coordinator. A general list of duties follows:

- Completes a breakdown of all possible visual effects in the script.
- Meets with the director to discuss the look of the effects.
- Oversees the budget costs of various projects.
- Monitors the visual effects budget.
- Makes sure all deadlines for the effects are met.
- Works with the special effects house or houses to ensure delivery of the effect on time.
- Works with the 1st AD to schedule shots that require a motion control camera.
- Sometimes supervises shooting on set to ensure the shot will work well when it goes to the visual effects house.

There is a whole team of people that works under the visual effects producer. This team works on different aspects to achieve the total effect. In 2D animation these can include a computer graphics supervisor, a compositing supervisor, compositing lead, compositors, an animation supervisor or director, animators, shaders, and 2D animators. In addition, when a film utilizes CGI or 3D technology, there are dozens of personnel involved in the process (too many to name!). Just look at the credits of the latest big-budget sci-fi or fantasy film and you will see why these credits take so long.

OPERATIONS

If you have special effects in your film, hire a special effects house. The key to hiring a good house is finding one that has done a lot of work with the kinds of effects you need or that fit your style. To begin with, contact a few effects houses and look at their reels. When you find one or two that you like, send each one a script and preliminary storyboards of the shots that need effects. Next, meet with each house and discuss whether it has had experience creating the effects you need, or if the effect has to be created with new technology. If your effect has to be created with new technology, check to see if the company has done this before. Some effects houses are more interested in turning out effects than spending the time to create something that has not been done before.

The special effects house will send you a bid for the cost of the effects. Choose the house and sign a contract with it. In the contract be sure to specify the cost, the time frame for delivery, and what kind of credit the house requires on your project. You may also need to hire more than one special effects house, depending on the type of effects you need. One house may not be able to handle a specific kind of effect you need or produce all the effects all in the time frame you need.

Once you've hired the house, the house's supervisor assigned to your project meets with the director and producer to finalize the vision, costs, and time frame. At this point the director should provide more detailed storyboards so that the supervisor has a more specific idea of what is needed. The supervisor then returns to the house and either waits for footage, if original footage is to be used, or begins creating the effect. During the process, the supervisor will send over preliminary looks at the effect for input from the director. Once the effect is finished, it will go to the director for approval. Once approval is reached, the effect is either recorded onto film, if film is the final format, or sent over digitally, to be edited into the project.

SUMMARY

Special effects and CGI constantly change during projects. While there are some standard physical effects such as pyrotechnics and squibs, writers and directors are frequently coming up with new ideas that require the special effects team to be flexible and creative. The advent of CGI in the 1980s and its abundant growth in the 1990s has led to more and more traditional effects being created digitally. Entire cities and their populations can now be created digitally using a vast visual effects team. When it comes to effects, there are no rules. If a full-scale visual effect fits the shot the best, then it will be shot on set. If the effect could be created and result in a more effective shot with a computer, then, budget permitting, it is done.

The Wardrobe Department

From beautiful gowns on a princess to outrageous armor on a forest creature to a pair of boots for a streetwalker, these are the creations of the wardrobe department. Their work is sometimes obvious, sometimes subtle. Arguably, when a wardrobe department is recognized for its work via an academy award, it is usually on a period film, which brings along with it particular challenges. However, all wardrobe is created with a sense of a particular character in mind. How a person dresses reflects that person's character. The same concept applies for a character in a project. Even in contemporary projects where the wardrobe may not need to be designed, great care is taken to ensure that each actor's look is specific, purposeful, and in line with the director's vision for the project as a whole.

In low budget you may only have one person handling the entire wardrobe for all the actors. In higher budgets you probably would have all the positions described below. Figure 13.1 shows the wardrobe hierarchy.

COSTUME DESIGNER

The costume designer is the head of the wardrobe department. She is responsible for the overall look of the wardrobe for all actors in conjunction with the director's vision. She supervises the running of the wardrobe department and makes sure throughout the project that the director's vision is being served by the wardrobe. Sometimes the wardrobe needed for a project will already exist and may only need to be purchased or rented. If the wardrobe does not exist, then the costume designer will design the pieces, which will then be sewn by her staff specifically for the project. As the head of the department, the costume designer is also responsible for the wardrobe crew and the wardrobe portion of a project's budget. The costume designer can start on a show for anywhere from one month to more than three months of pre-production, depending on how involved the wardrobe needs to be.

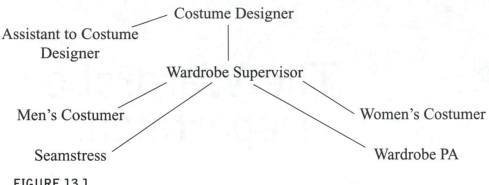

FIGURE 13.1
Wardrobe Hierarchy.

Pre-Production

- Meets with the director and discusses the general vision of the wardrobe and the looks of particular characters.
- Depending on the type of show, may conduct research. Research could be required if the show is a period piece. The costume designer may need to research medieval wardrobe and accessories or the particular wardrobe look of another ethnicity.
- Completes a **wardrobe breakdown** by scene, showing what wardrobe occurs for each actor on each story day.
- Hires the wardrobe supervisor.
- May begin designing wardrobe as needed.
- May meet with the production designer to discuss the wardrobe look.
- Gets measurements of all the actors.
- Supervises all wardrobe fittings.
- Meets regularly with crew to monitor progress.

Production

- Always on call, may not necessarily be on set. The designer may still be monitoring fittings and continuing to design pieces of wardrobe.
- If on set, continues to monitor all wardrobe operations.

Wrap

- Makes sure all rented wardrobe is returned and all purchased wardrobe is sold or returned to the production company.

WARDROBE SUPERVISOR

The wardrobe supervisor answers directly to the costume designer. This person is on set all day, making sure each actor is dressed properly. In lower-budget projects this person may also dress the actors. In higher budgets this is usually taken care of by the costumers. The wardrobe supervisor begins work shortly after the costume designer is on the show.

Pre-Production

- Does a wardrobe breakdown per scene and confers with the costume designer (see Figure 13.2).
- Goes over wardrobe requirements for each actor with the costume designer.
- Discusses any time-intensive wardrobe pieces with the costume designer.
- Discusses any major time-intensive wardrobe changes with the 1st AD. This is done so that if an actor is shooting and requires a long period of time to get into the wardrobe, then the 1st AD can allow for this.
- Discusses any wardrobe that needs to be doubled or tripled. Wardrobe may need to be doubled, for instance, in a scene in which an actor is hit in the face with a pie. There could be many takes to get the shot right, so the wardrobe department must make sure there are extra pieces of the same wardrobe for the actor to have for each take.
- Makes sure all actors' measurements are accurate for design.
- Acquires all rented costumes. These costumes could come from wardrobe rental houses, or specific items such as a fur coat may be rented, for example, from a furrier.
- Oversees the sewing of originally designed costumes.
- Creates wardrobe list by scene.
- Distresses any wardrobe as necessary. Distressing wardrobe is the process of making it appear to be well worn. This could involve repeated washings to fade the color or applying certain chemicals that make the wardrobe look older.

Production

- Responsible for the continuity of the wardrobe while actors are shooting. This responsibility involves watching each actor as they perform and remembering their actions. For instance, if an actor comes into a room, takes off his coat, and pulls his tie so it hangs loosely, the wardrobe person has to remember at what point the coat comes off and at what point the tie is loosened. This is important because the action may be covered by another camera angle and the wardrobe has to match each time so the scene can cut together.
- Supervises or dresses each actor in proper order for the first scene.
- Supervises the dressing of each actor throughout the day.
- Stands by on set to repair or adjust wardrobe as needed.

Wrap

- Returns all rented wardrobe to vendors.
- Makes sure all designed wardrobe is sold or returned to the production company as per its policy.

Scene	Character	Wardrobe	Accessories	Notes
1	Regina	Loin cloths	none	distressed for desert
1	Alb	Blue robe, orange pants	earring	none
1	Margee	Red robe, white sheath	earrings, ring	none
1	Gerie	Black pants, white shirt	tie, hat	none
1	King Raccolto	Royal robe	crown	none
2	Regina	Loin cloths	none	distressed for desert
2	Donato	Black pants, orange shirt	tie, eyeglasses	none
2	Doctor	Doctor's robe over street clothes	stethoscope	doubles needed
2	Uomo	Black pants, black shirt	beret, monocle	none
2	Margee	Red robe, white sheath	earrings, ring	none
3	Regina	Pink wochera robe	none	4 copies needed
3	Donato	Black pants, orange shirt	tie, eyeglasses	none
4	Regina	Pink wochera robe	eye mask	none
4	Fila	Pink wochera robe	none	none
5	Regina	Pink wochera robe	none	none
5	Donato	Black pants, chartreuse shirt	tie, eyeglasses	none
5	King Raccolto	Royal robe	crown	none
5	Guard #1	Full armor	headpiece	distressed for wear
5	Guard #2	Full armor	headpiece	distressed for wear
5	Guard #3	Full armor	headpiece	distressed for wear
6	Regina	Pink wochera robe	none	distressed for desert
7	Regina	Pink wochera robe	royal headdress	none
8	Donato	Black pants, black shirt	eyeglasses	none
8	Uomo	Black pants, black shirt	beret, monocle	doubles needed
9	Regina	Fuchsia robe, white sheath	royal headdress	none
9	King Raccolto	Nightgown	none	none
9	Guard #1	Full armor	headpiece	distressed for wear
9	Guard #2	Full armor	headpiece	distressed for wear

FIGURE 13.2
Wardrobe Breakdown.

MEN'S COSTUMER/WOMEN'S COSTUMER

In the "olden" days, there used to be one costumer who would dress any and all actors. However, in our age of sexual harassment suits, we now have **men's**

and women's costumers. Obviously, the men's costumers dress the men and the women's costumers dress the women. The costumers usually only work during production; however, if needed, they might be hired to work pre-production. This can occur if some of the wardrobe is very involved and some instruction on how to dress the actor is needed.

SEAMSTRESS

A seamstress is one of those positions that may exist in higher-budget productions but usually is not found in lower-budget films. In lower-budget films, any sewing would be done by the wardrobe supervisor or sometimes even the costume designer. If this position does exist, most of the special sewing is usually done in pre-production. In period films, there may be a whole team of seamstresses to sew massive amounts of extras wardrobe. Some seamstresses are hired for run of show if much of the wardrobe is being made from scratch. Other times, the seamstress may be hired on a daily or weekly basis to complete only certain pieces.

WARDROBE PRODUCTION ASSISTANT

The wardrobe PA is someone who is just starting out in the business and probably aspires to be a costume designer someday. This person becomes the wardrobe gopher, doing everything from sewing to picking up wardrobe pieces to getting coffee. Sometimes this person also serves as the **assistant to the costume designer,** if there is not already one. The wardrobe PA could start on a show immediately after the wardrobe supervisor begins. Sometimes for budgetary reasons this PA may be hired only shortly before principal photography.

ASSISTANT TO THE COSTUME DESIGNER

The assistant to the costume designer is like a personal assistant. He is usually found only on larger-budget shoots. Specific duties vary depending on the style of the costume designer. Some assistants may field phone calls, copy sketches, get coffee, and coordinate schedules with other departments. The assistant begins work as soon as the costume designer starts.

OPERATIONS

During pre-production the wardrobe team organizes the wardrobe and labels each piece according to the production schedule. Each piece will have a tag that states when the particular piece is needed and which actor it is for. The night before each shoot the wardrobe is double-checked to ensure that everything needed for the next day is ready.

On the morning of the shoot, the wardrobe team pulls each piece of wardrobe according to the call sheet. The call sheet shows actors' on-set arrival times, as well as what time each actor will report to wardrobe. As actors are brought to the wardrobe trailer, male and female costumers hand them their wardrobe and direct them to their assigned dressing rooms. After an actor dresses, the costumer checks the actor to make sure the wardrobe is properly fitted and all accessories are present. The costumer or wardrobe supervisor then informs the set PA or 2nd AD—whoever is standing by—that the actor is ready and may then proceed to the set.

The wardrobe supervisor may stay in the trailer until the first actor goes to set. After the first actor is on set, the wardrobe supervisor makes sure that a representative from wardrobe is always on set to handle the wardrobe or make any necessary adjustments.

When an actor is wrapped at camera, meaning done for the day, the actor is escorted back to the wardrobe trailer to remove the wardrobe. The wardrobe is then removed with the help of the costumer and set aside for washing if it will be needed again.

At the end of the day or sometimes, if necessary, throughout the day, the wardrobe PA may need to wash the day's wardrobe in preparation for the next day.

OTHER ISSUES

During a shoot, each actor's wardrobe is washed at the end of each day. In low budget this is usually accomplished by sending someone from the wardrobe department to a local laundromat. In medium- to higher-budget films the production may rent a washer and dryer and have them installed somewhere in the production office.

Once a piece of wardrobe is wrapped, meaning it is not needed anymore for shooting, there are a number of things that may happen to it. In some cases, for instance, there may be suits that have been tailored to fit one actor specifically. The actor may then have the option of purchasing the items for himself or herself. Some producers may give these actors the wardrobe as a gift. If wardrobe was rented from a wardrobe rental house, it is returned. It is important that the wardrobe is returned in the same condition in which it was received; otherwise the production may incur costs to repair or replace the piece.

In some cases, at the end of a shoot the production has a **garage sale.** Various departments will take items that are no longer needed or wanted by the production company and have a sale to the public. Many times wardrobe is a large part of these sales. The sale is held shortly after principal photography is finished and is open to the public.

It is important that no item be sold or returned until all dailies have been reviewed. If by chance a reshoot is needed, the appropriate wardrobe must be available.

Oftentimes in a certain film a large number of extras are needed. In some cases, extras provide their own wardrobe, usually if the project is a contemporary piece. If the project is a period piece, having a large number of extras presents a special challenge for the wardrobe team. For instance, if a large army from medieval times is needed for a scene, these large amounts of people must be dressed in a short amount of time. On these occasions extra wardrobe personnel are brought in to handle the added workload. The production may also hire extra wardrobe PAs to dole out massive pieces of armor. Extra costumers may be hired to help check that each extra is wearing the armor properly.

SUMMARY

The wardrobe department works to dress actors as appropriate to their characters and in line with the director's vision. Wardrobe may be originally designed by the costume designer or rented from wardrobe houses. The wardrobe team on set must work quickly to get actors to set and use costumers to help the actors dress. Sometimes, when there are large numbers of extras, additional crew members are needed. This is especially true for period productions, where actors or extras may not know the proper way to wear period costumes.

Makeup and Hair

As discussed in Chapter 13, the wardrobe and makeup and hair teams are often recognized in either period films or films with outrageous looks that require special looks, such as science fiction. However, it should be noted that all makeup is an art, even on shows where no special makeup is required. The makeup team on a project varies greatly depending on the budget and scope of the project. In low budget, you will most likely have one makeup artist who handles all makeup, hair, body, and special effects makeup for the entire cast. On a medium-size budget, you will most likely hire a key makeup artist, key hair, and a couple of assistants. On higher-budget shoots you could have all the personnel listed in this chapter and more. Many stars prefer to use their own hair and makeup people. These people are brought in and specifically do only the hair and makeup of the person they serve. I once worked a show where there were three leading women. Each one had her personal hair person flown in for the duration of the shoot. This chapter discusses the role of each person in the hair and makeup team. Figure 14.1 shows the makeup and hair hierarchy.

KEY MAKEUP

As head of the makeup and hair department, the key makeup artist is in charge of the makeup and hair budget. Usually the key makeup artist will do makeup for the stars on a shoot. The assistants may then do actors in the supporting roles. The makeup person can start work for anywhere from one week, for simple shoots, to three months of pre-production, for more complex shoots requiring special effects. Following are the duties and responsibilities of the key makeup artist.

Pre-Production

- Writes and submits the makeup and hair budget.
- Meets with the director to discuss the makeup requirements of each actor in each scene.

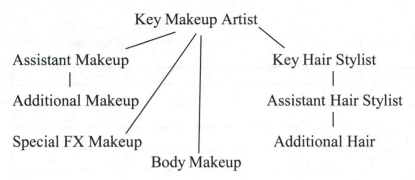

FIGURE 14.1
Makeup and Hair Hierarchy.

- Completes a **makeup breakdown** per character and scene. This breakdown changes as each actor is hired. For instance, the first breakdown notes any special makeup considerations. As each actor is hired, the breakdown gets more specific. This is because once the makeup artist knows who the actor is, she can decide on which makeup to use. Once all actors are cast and each makeup choice is made, the makeup artist will construct a makeup breakdown for each actor, according to scene (see Figure 14.2).
- Contacts actors and reviews color photographs to determine proper makeup for each actor.
- Orders makeup for each actor.
- May supervise makeup tests, if needed.
- Hires makeup assistants.
- Meets with the key hair person to discuss each actor's look.
- Determines additional makeup personnel needs for large cast days.

Production

- May complete makeup on stars.
- Never leaves set, or makes sure a makeup representative is always on set.
- Supervises all makeup continuity on set.

Wrap

- Makes sure all rentals are returned to their vendors.
- Wraps out the budget with the accounting office.

OTHER MAKEUP PERSONNEL

The **assistant makeup** artist answers directly to the key makeup artist. He will also do makeup for some supporting actors and day players. In addition, the assistant makeup person may need to stand by on set if the key makeup artist has

"Regina of Icelandia"

Scene	Character	Base	Notes
1	Regina	Tan #24	sunburned
1	Alb	TBD	none
1	Margee	TBD	none
1	Gerie	TBD	none
1	King Raccolto	TBD	none
2	Regina	TBD	sunburned
2	Donato	TBD	black eye
2	Doctor	TBD	mustache
2	Uomo	TBD	goatee
2	Margee	TBD	none
3	Regina	TBD	sunburned
3	Donato	TBD	black eye
4	Regina	TBD	none
4	Fila	TBD	none
5	Regina	TBD	faded sunburn
5	Donato	TBD	black eye
5	King Raccolto	TBD	full beard
5	Guard #1	TBD	none
5	Guard #2	TBD	none
5	Guard #3	TBD	none
6	Regina	TBD	tan
7	Regina	TBD	none
8	Donato	TBD	black eye
8	Uomo	TBD	goatee
9	Regina	TBD	tan
9	King Raccolto	TBD	full beard
9	Guard #1	TBD	none
9	Guard #2	TBD	none

FIGURE 14.2

Actor Makeup Breakdown.

to work on another actor. This assistant may have some pre-production work, depending on how involved the makeup for the show is, or may begin work on the first day of principal photography.

Additional makeup artists, also known as extra makeup, are used when there is a large cast on set. This situation may take place for only one or two days, or may continue for weeks. In pre-production the key makeup artist will look at the production schedule and determine when additional makeup artists are needed. These additional artists are then hired only for the duration of the time when the large cast is shooting.

Body makeup is used when a scene requires an actor to be partially or fully nude. In other words, the key makeup artists handle the face, neck, and hands of an actor, and a body makeup artist handles the rest. There are a few exceptions to this. Let us say an actor has to wear a bikini in one scene, but that is the only time the actor will be seen this way. It is more cost-efficient to have an assistant handle the body makeup than pay to fly a body makeup artist in for one scene. Body makeup is also a position in which an actor may prefer one certain artist. The choice to use that person is usually outlined in an actor's contract.

The special effects makeup artist is used when an actor needs to have bullet wounds, bleeding, sores, growths, or **prosthetics.** Prosthetics in films can be items such as a larger nose, an aged look, or an entire facial mask (e.g., if the character is an alien, a werewolf, or some other creature). Sometimes, minor special effects makeup is taken care of by the key makeup artist. However, if the shoot requires extensive special effect makeup, a separate person is hired, either for run of show or for the duration the special effects are needed. If the special effects person is for run of show, he would most likely have enough effects to warrant a team of assistants and would begin work with anywhere from one to four months in pre-production.

- Meets in pre-production with the key makeup artist and director to discuss effects.
- Orders any fake blood or prosthetics as needed.
- May manufacture prosthetics as needed.
- May meet with actors to fit them for prosthetics, if applicable.
- Works with the 1st AD to discuss how much time each makeup effect will require to prepare.
- In pre-production, may practice new techniques if there are any unusual effects.
- Stands by on set to supervise each effect.
- May hire assistants as needed.

KEY HAIR

Doing hair for actors can be as simple as putting someone's hair into a ponytail or as involved as applying a prosthetic that makes someone look bald. The key hair stylist, sometimes called the key hair artist, is responsible for all hair on all actors of a project. She works directly with the key makeup artist to keep hair and makeup costs on budget. The key hair person will begin work with anywhere from a week to a month or more of pre-production, depending on whether or not there are a lot of wigs or special appliances that need to be manufactured or rented in pre-production.

Pre-Production

- Meets with director to discuss looks as people are cast.
- Never leaves set.
- May supervise hair tests.
- Constructs a **hair breakdown.**
- May order wigs or hairpieces as needed.
- Contacts actors and reviews color photographs to determine the look for each actor.
- Hires hair assistants.
- Meets with the key makeup person to discuss each actor's look.
- Determines additional hair personnel needs for large cast days.

Production

- Completes hair on stars.
- Never leaves set, or makes sure a hair representative is always on set.
- Supervises all hair continuity on set.

Wrap

- Makes sure all wigs or hair weaves are returned.
- Makes sure all accounting for the hair budget is complete.

ASSISTANT HAIR/ADDITIONAL HAIR/EXTRA HAIR

As with the assistant makeup personnel, the assistant hair people assist the key hair person and will usually begin work on the first day of principal photography. The exception to this, for example, would be if there are a large number of wigs or tests in pre-production. In this case the key hair person may need assistance to get ready for the first day of shooting. Any additional hair people are used only on days when a large cast is required.

OPERATIONS

During pre-production the makeup and hair team prepares all wigs, hairpieces, and special effects that will be required for the shoot. Makeup and hair artists have their own organizational strategy but each will follow the production schedule in order to have the proper makeup or hair needs ready for the appropriate actor at the right time. On the day of the shoot the makeup team pulls out the proper makeup for the first actors of the day. The actor or actors are brought to makeup by either a set PA or the 2nd AD. Once the actor's makeup is completed, the actor is turned over to the hair person. Once the hair person is done, the actor is escorted to wardrobe by the set PA or 2nd AD. This process continues throughout the day until all actors have completed initial makeup and hair.

As with the wardrobe department, as soon as the first actor is taken to set, a representative from the team is always standing by on set to do touch-ups between takes. The key makeup or hair person or an assistant, depending on which actor is on set, may do touch-ups. It is the on-set person's responsibility to make sure that makeup and hair continuity is maintained and that the actor looks appropriate. After the director cuts a shot, the director may move in to give further direction. The makeup or hair person has to be sensitive not to interfere with the director's work. After the director is done, the makeup or hair person may have only seconds to jump in and do touch-ups. The touch-up should never hold up shooting. Hair and makeup are expected to get in and out before the next shot is called.

QUALITIES OF A GOOD MAKEUP AND HAIR TEAM

- Extremely creative, able to put the director's vision onscreen.
- Can do its job quickly, without loss of quality.
- Has extensive knowledge of makeup, hair, and the proper hygiene required to work with these items safely. A note on proper hygiene: In low budget, where lack of money dictates a lot on set, the one area that people sometimes skimp on is makeup. I have seen some makeup artists use the same makeup, sponges, and other applicators for many actors. This practice is highly unsanitary. Make sure your makeup people have the funds to do their jobs safely.
- Able to work well with particular actors and their proclivities.

SUMMARY

The makeup and hair team on a show could be made up of one person or many people, depending on your budget and the complexity of your show. Some actors prefer to have their own personal hair and makeup people. If you are working in low budget, you will not be able to afford this luxury, but it is a common situation in high-budget projects. If your project contains a lot of special effects makeup, you may have to hire a separate makeup artist who specializes in effects. Finally, you want to make sure your hair and makeup team know sanitary makeup and hair practices to ensure the health and safety of your cast.

LOCATIONS

Locations is the one department on a project that requires people with very diplomatic personalities. Good location people are diplomats, able to communicate effectively with nonproduction people. This ability is a special quality that is invaluable when working on a show. The location person has to get someone to let a crew of ten to fifty or more people onto his property, carrying in all kinds of equipment, for 10–12 hours per day. A good location person will know how to present this situation and maintain good relations with the owner of a location. A bad location person could lose a location entirely, leaving you to scramble for a place to shoot. In addition, the location team provides support services for a location as needed, such as security, firefighters, police, and lavatory facilities. This chapter discusses the location team's duties and its particular relationship to the community. The two different kinds of scouts are discussed, along with who goes and what they are looking for at each location. Support personnel and services are also discussed in terms of who is needed and when they are needed. Figure 15.1 shows the location hierarchy.

LOCATION MANAGER

The location manager is the head of the location team and thus responsible for the location budget. As discussed, this is a person with great diplomatic acumen. She not only has this personality but is also a creative force. A good location manager can find locations that completely fit with the director's vision and provide interesting production value for the screen. Think of a western with beautiful panoramic views of cascading mountains and wide open prairies. The location manager has found these settings with the vision of the film in mind. In low budget, the location manager may perform all of the duties of the location department, from finding the locations to completing the paperwork. In higher budget, the location manager will use a team of location people to fill in on these jobs. The location manager will usually start work on a project with anywhere from one month to more of pre-production, depending on how many locations are needed. Duties and responsibilities of the location manager follow the location hierarchy.

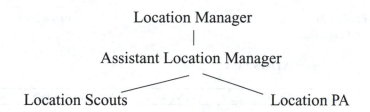

FIGURE 15.1
Location Hierarchy.

Pre-Production

- Discusses the location looks with the director and producer.
- Works with location scouts to find possible locations.
- Compiles pictures or footage of each possibility, puts the pictures in a folder or on a CD or DVD, and presents these shots to the director and producer. If the location looks good, then they will arrange to see it on a formal location scout.
- May have to approach the owner of a site and try to nurture interest in having a film crew come and shoot on her property.
- Supervises location scouts.
- If the location is chosen, will work with the owner to work out possible pay.
- Informs the owner of shoot dates and has the owner sign a **location release agreement.** A location is not locked until this is done. You should never assume a location is locked with a secretary; always make arrangements with the owner.
- Arranges for payment to the location owner.
- Arranges for access to the location.
- Supervises the **tech scout.**

Production

- Lets the crew into the location.
- Makes sure there are no violations of the location. There may be a situation where the owner of a house may want crew only on the first floor and not the second. The location manager makes sure that the location team adequately marks the location with signs prohibiting anyone from going on the second floor. The location team will constantly be watching to make sure the location is being used as agreed upon.
- Follows up with the location owner if there is any damage to the location.
- Makes sure any damages to locations are paid for.

Wrap

- Makes sure all locations are left in good order.
- Publishes a final **location list** (see Figure 15.2).

"Regina of Icelandia"   04/29/2002
Frame Right Films, Inc.

LOCATION LIST

LOCATION	ADDRESS	CONTACT	SHOOT DATES	SCENES
Icelandia Desert	**Route 115 & Carson St.** Kerlina, CA	Harold Jimes 310-345-8756	July 22-24	1,3,67,54 57,58,72
Wochera Tower	**113 Highway 46** Kerlina, CA	Misty Kilner 310-789-7890	July 31-Aug 1	5,14,52,49 10,62,60 61,63,9
Margee & Alb's Home	**763 Humice Lane** Los Angeles, CA	Noreen Johnson 213-789-7652	Aug 10-15	7,8
Castle	**8722 Vernon Drive** Augora Hills, CA	Dan Rodman 310-364-9983	July 25-29	66,16,26 65,68,74
Sport Theater	**LA Forum** 837 Gower St. Los Angeles, CA	Mike Starr 310-361-8465	Aug 2-7	13
Wochera Dining Hall	**9111 Magnolia Place** Los Angeles, CA	Yvette Alnon 310-463-8836	Aug 15-16	15
Research Center	**Universal Stage** 34 Jones St. Los Angeles, CA	Joan Arefton 310-337-1127	July 30	18,22
Majesty Room	**Universal Stage** 34 Jones St. Los Angeles, CA	Joan Arefton 310-337-1127	Aug 8-9	17,19,21

FIGURE 15.2
Location List.

ASSISTANT LOCATION MANAGER

The **assistant location manager** assists the location manager. He may be someone who lives locally in the area and therefore knows where certain locations can be found. Alternatively, he may be someone who works frequently with a location manager. In low budget, the assistant may also work as the location scout. The assistant location manager will usually start work shortly after the location manager begins. Following is a general list of responsibilities:

- Puts together and maintains the location list. The location list is a record of each location along with any pertinent contact information. As locations are locked, this list is updated (see Figure 15.2).
- Informs neighbors that a crew will be in the area. This task is important for good relations, not only with the owner of the property but also with the community. The assistant will either do this in person, knocking on doors, or leave flyers announcing when the crew will be in the area.
- Sees to any details of the location not covered by the location manager.
- Procures security, fire, or police as necessary.
- Orders portable lavatory facilities as needed. Portable lavatories are always needed when shooting exteriors. It is customary, if you can afford it, to have separate lavatories for men and for women.
- Stays on set if the location manager is gone.
- Keeps the location owner happy.
- Provides copies of all location releases and permits to the ADs for the set box. This is important. If for some reason none of the location people are on set with them, the crew must have documentation that allows them to be there.
- May assist the location manager in following up after the shoot is done to make sure the location was left in good order.

LOCATION PRODUCTION ASSISTANT

The location PA, like other assistants, may be responsible for getting coffee or typing (in this case, the location list). In addition, the location PA may be required to do the following:

- Mark the area with signs that lead to the location.
- Mark the location with signs for parking.
- Put out traffic cones as needed. Traffic cones may be needed to block off a certain part of a location that is off-limits to crew, either because it is not safe or because the owner does not want crew in a certain area.
- May be required to stay overnight at a location, if this is not covered by security. This situation arises if, for example, you have at a location a fairly elaborate setup that you do not want disturbed. Staying overnight at a location is usually covered in the budget by security, except on a low-budget shoot, in which case security is too expensive.

LOCATION SCOUT—THE PERSON

The location scout is a person who very early in the pre-production process scouts, or finds, possible locations for a project. He has been given a script and will have some idea of what kinds of locations to look for. For instance, if the script calls for a contemporary restaurant, the scout will glean from the location manager exactly the type of restaurant to look for. Is it an upscale modern place with red carpet and valets in front? On the other hand, is it a family-style franchise-type restaurant? The scout's job is to get as close to the vision of the director as possible. The scout will take pictures and send them to the location manager. In the old days, pictures were done on film and overnighted to the location manager, who might not be in the area yet. Now, pictures are taken digitally with either cameras or picture phones and emailed to the location manager. The location manager will then give the scout feedback to either take more pictures of the same type of location or not.

Location scouts are usually local. They have grown up in the area, or at least have lived in the area long enough to know it well. This is important because they will be able to find possible locations quickly. The scout will work in pre-production as long as locations need to be scouted.

LOCATION SCOUT—THE EVENT

The **location scout (event)** is a preliminary look at various locations before any are chosen. At this point, the location manager has narrowed down the choices, in consultation with the director and producer, from what has been submitted by the location scout. This scout may involve a few or a number of crew. Minimally, the scout, location manager, director, and producer will visit the location. This kind of scout may also involve the director of photography and the production designer. The process for setting up a location scout is as follows:

- The location manager or assistant location manager calls each location and sets up a time for the crew to arrive and inspect the location.
- The assistant location manager or, if there are any, a location PA puts together a cooler with drinks and snacks for the crew, to be put in a van.
- The assistant location manager coordinates with the transportation coordinator to arrange for a van and driver for the day, to transport the crew to each location.
- The location team puts together maps and directions to each location for anyone who may not travel in the van.
- The location manager determines a call time to leave for the scout and informs each person.
- The van then sets out to visit each location.

At each location, there are several considerations. A good location should have certain qualities that not only match the director's vision but also have practical applications for shooting. These considerations may not make or break the decision to shoot there, but are only considered at this point in the process. A list of these considerations follows.

Location Considerations

- What are the creative considerations? Are the colors right? How much may need to be altered?
- Is the location available when you need to shoot? This consideration should be worked out before taking the crew to see it.

- Do you need any permits? If so, which ones?
- How much will the permits cost?
- Is there adequate parking?
- Are there lavatory facilities that would be available to crew, or will the production need to rent port-a-potties?
- Are there any safety considerations?
- Will you need security? Police? Fire?
- Based on what needs to be shot there, what are the restrictions? I once shot in an old theater that had a floor that was not stable in all places. The crew had to promise to restrict their movements within the theater in order to shoot there.
- Are there any sound considerations such as frequent air or ground traffic?
- Are there any time restrictions? In other words, does the owner not want crew there after or before a certain time?
- What is the electrical situation? Will a generator be needed?
- Are there proper staging areas for eating, equipment, and extras holding?
- Is there adequate parking for all the trucks?
- Is there easy access for the trucks?
- Would shooting occur on the first floor? If on the second floor, are there elevators? This is important because of the equipment.
- Is there any normal business that may impede shooting?
- Are there any neighbors (residential or business) close by that will be affected? If so, who will need to be informed about a crew's being in the area?

The location manager will make notes on each location, based on any questions or concerns the producer, director, DP, or production designer might have. For instance, the production designer may want to add more foliage to an outdoor garden scene. The production designer would discuss this with the location manager. The location manager would then check with the location owner to see if this would be possible.

Depending on the availability of the locations, there may be many location scouts before all locations are finally chosen. Once the locations are locked, meaning they have all been selected, the location manager will obtain the proper paperwork to secure the location (see the section "Location Paperwork").

Next, the location team will arrange for a final look at the location before shooting, called the technical scout or tech scout.

THE TECHNICAL SCOUT

The tech scout is a chance for more key personnel to visit the location and determine what needs they might have for that specific location. Key personnel that would attend the scout include the location manager, assistant location manager, director, producer, production manager, director of photography, production designer, art director, set decorator, key grip, gaffer, transportation coordinator, visual effects supervisor, construction coordinator, 1st AD, and possibly the sound mixer. The location manager contacts each location and sets up a schedule to visit each location. Coolers with snacks and drinks are put in a few vans to transport crew to each location. On a tech scout the location manager will send the assistant location manager ahead of the crew to make sure the location is open and ready for the crew to inspect. The key difference between a location scout and the technical scout is that a tech scout happens at a location that has been secured for shooting. Therefore, some of the same considerations apply as in the location scout, but now they become resolved. Different crew members will now need to determine their specific needs.

Location Determinations on a Tech Scout

Director: Determines what areas the camera will and will not see. (This is important information for the rest of the crew members so they know where they can stage equipment.)

Producer: Makes sure all personnel are working to determine their needs.

Director of photography: Takes light readings and discusses general lighting setups with the gaffer.

1st AD: Makes notes on any safety considerations, such as dangerous or off-limit areas. Works with the location manager, key grip, and gaffer to determine specific staging areas. These staging areas include areas for extras, eating lunch, and possibly the following: wardrobe, makeup, grip equipment, lighting equipment, and sound equipment. Makes notes on lock-ups that will be needed.

Gaffer: Determines, if needed, access to electricity, or where a generator will be staged so as not to interfere with sound.

Key grip: Works with the 1st AD to determine where the grip equipment will be staged. Works with the transportation coordinator to determine what is the best way to get the equipment from the truck to the set.

Transportation coordinator: Will make a sketch showing where all production vehicles, including trucks, vans, and personal vehicles, will park.

Production designer: Works with the art director and set decorator to finalize art department needs. The production designer may also do this earlier, with just members from the art department.

Sound mixer: Makes notes on where the boom will be placed for various shots. Determines if any special equipment may be required to achieve good sound. Checks for any conditions that may hinder sound, such as air conditioning, construction, etc.

Once the tech scout is completed, each department should know exactly what is needed to arrive at that location and shoot without any delays.

MAPS

One of the key functions of the location department is to make sure that each crew and cast member is able to find each location on the day of shooting. Therefore, the location team is responsible for preparing accurate directions and maps for each day of shooting. These maps and directions will be attached to each call sheet (by either a location PA or an office PA), which is then distributed to all cast and crew. Depending on the situation, these documents may also be emailed to cast and crew. The accuracy of these directions is of utmost importance. One wrong turn on the directions and your crew ends up aggravated and late to the set. Therefore, the location manager will have either an assistant or PA drive the route to the location, making notes of exit names, street name spellings, number of stop lights, miles, special markings, and buildings. Then she will take a copy of a detailed map with streets, white out a section for written directions, and write the directions in the whited-out area (some people also put the directions on the back of the map). Multiple copies are made, and then a PA will highlight each map, outlining the route from the production office to the location. Once the maps are completed and attached to a call sheet, the documents are then given to the 2nd AD to hand out at the end of the day. Note that many crew members do rely on GPS systems to get to set, but as we all know, those are not entirely accurate 100 percent of the time. Knowledgeable directions from the location team is the only way to insure your cast and crew will be less likely to get lost and, therefore, more likely to be on time to set.

LOCATION SERVICES

Certain locations may require that the production hire security, firefighters, or police for various reasons. If the shoot is happening in a neighborhood that would attract a large crowd, security is hired to help control the crowds. If the shoot has a big-name star, security may be hired to protect the star from well-meaning but disturbing fans. Security may be hired to protect the crew if shooting is in a dangerous neighborhood. The decision to hire security is usually made by the producer. There are security firms that specifically handle this type of work.

If you are shooting a scene that requires pyrotechnics, or fire of any kind, you must hire firefighters to be standing by on set in case of an emergency. Sometimes firefighters are also needed to create rain with their water hoses (this is mostly in low budget; in higher budget, a rain tower is rented). It is always a good idea to contact the local fire station and check on their requirements for your area.

Police are hired for a film crew for some of the same reasons security might be hired. Police might be needed for crowd control, although it is understood that it is security's job to handle this first. The main reason police are hired is if you need streets to be blocked off. It is illegal to impede traffic in any way without the authorization of the police. Usually you can hire off-duty police for this job. Just contact the police station in your precinct.

Although police may not need to be hired for your shoot, the location team should always have contact with the local police in certain situations. For instance, if you are filming with weapons that will be either brandished or actually fired, you need to inform the local police. Any passerby could see a man holding a gun to a person's head and not realize it is part of a film shoot. This is especially critical for low-budget shoots, where only a few vehicles are around and may look even less like a film crew is there.

It is the responsibility of the location department to ensure a comfortable working environment for cast and crew. Sometimes a crew may shoot in a building where heat or air conditioning may not be present, or may not be available for use because of sound considerations. In these cases, the location department rents portable heating or cooling units that are designed to be quiet for shooting or that may be easily turned off and on. Perhaps the location is an exterior that will be extremely hot, such as a desert. In this case the location department may rent a water cooling system to provide relief for the crew. Perhaps the location is a cabin high in the mountains with no electricity. The location department may then rent a portable heater to provide warmth for the crew. It is the responsibility of the location manager to inform the producer of any such needs in pre-production so they can be allotted for in the budget.

SHOOTING ON LOCATION VERSUS IN STUDIO FACILITIES

The decision to shoot on location or in studio facilities is not black and white. If a certain location does not exist, then it may need to be created inside a studio facility. For instance, science fiction films that have interiors of spacecrafts are usually shot on sound stages because they obviously are not available in real life. There are advantages and disadvantages of both settings.

Advantages of Shooting on Location

- Authenticity of an environment.
- Often cheaper than renting a studio.

Disadvantages of Shooting on Location

- The location's owner determines your time constraints.
- You have less control over sound infringement.

Advantages of Shooting in a Studio

- You have control of the environment in terms of sound.
- You have a better guarantee of being able to shoot when you want to.

Disadvantages of Shooting in a Studio

- You may lose authenticity of an environment if you do not have enough money to build genuine sets.
- Can be expensive.

LOCATION PAPERWORK

There are three main types of paperwork that deal with location. They are location agreements, permits, and **certificates of insurance.** It is important to have all of these documents on set while shooting, in case any questions or problems arise.

The documents are kept with the location representative, and a copy is placed in the set box in case the location people need to leave set.

Location Agreement

A location agreement is an agreement between the production and the owner of a location. The agreement grants the production legal access to and permission to film at that location. The agreement also guarantees to the owner that if there is any damage to the location, the production will pay for repairs. The location agreement also states what location fee or **site fee** will be paid to the owner for use of the property. In low budget, there may not be enough money to pay **location fees.** In this case the location manager will make sure to choose locations that will not request a fee. However, this may not be easy, depending on where you are shooting. If you try to get a free location in Los Angeles, you will probably run into resistance. Because there has been so much production in that city, it is difficult to find anyone who does not know that they can request a location fee. Sometimes the agreement may also guarantee the owner that any electricity or phone use at that location will be reimbursed by the film. See Figure 15.3 for an example location agreement.

Certificate of Insurance

A certificate of insurance is a document drawn up by your insurance company that guarantees the location owner that you have sufficient funds to pay for any damage or loss to the location. Whereas the location agreement states that you agree to repair any damages, the certificate of insurance actually guarantees that you have the money to pay for damages. Most location owners will require that both the certificate of insurance and the location agreement are signed before anyone sets foot on their property for shooting. See an example certificate in Figure 15.4.

Permits

A film permit is a document given by a city, granting a production permission to film in that city. Many cities require permits if you shoot anywhere in the city. Some cities require permits only if you shoot in public areas. Some smaller, rural areas may not require permits at all. The best choice is to check with the city where you are shooting to determine what its requirements and possible fees are. Some cities handle permits through their film offices (if there is one), convention and visitors' bureaus, or communications offices.

The permit outlines the specific date(s), hours, area, and number of people that will be on the shoot. You are not permitted to film outside of these parameters. Some offices will require a certificate of insurance before even granting a film permit. Again, it is important to check with each office's different requirements.

LOCATION RELEASE AGREEMENT

Location Release Agreement dated_____June 15_____, ___2002___, between Frame Right Films, Inc. and _____Mike Starr_____ (RELEASOR), for the following location(s) __LA Forum, 837 Gower St., Los Angeles, CA 90004__ ("premises").

FRAME RIGHT FILMS, INC. AND RELEASOR AGREE AS FOLLOWS:

1. RELEASOR grants FRAME RIGHT FILMS, INC. access to and from, and use of, the above listed premises for the purposes of (i) erecting and maintaining temporary motion picture sets and structures, (ii) photographing the premises, sets and structures, (iii) recording sound for any scenes FRAME RIGHT FILMS, INC. may desire, and (iv) any other purposes as FRAME RIGHT FILMS, INC. may desire.

2. RELEASOR acknowledges that RELEASOR has received good and valuable consideration in exchange for granting FRAME RIGHT FILMS, INC. the right to use the premises, including but not limited to the opportunity to participate in this project.

3. RELEASOR acknowledges that FRAME RIGHT FILMS, INC. may begin to use the premises on or about __Aug. 2-7, 2002__ (date) and may continue to use the premises until the completions of all photographing and recording for which FRAME RIGHT FILMS, INC. may desire the use of the premises for the proposed scenes, including but not limited to all re-takes, added scenes, changes and process shots.

4. RELEASOR acknowledges that FRAME RIGHT FILMS, INC. shall have the right to remove all of its sets, structures, and other materials and equipment from the premises.

5. RELEASOR acknowledges that FRAME RIGHT FILMS, INC. shall own all rights to all photographs and recordings of any kind made by FRAME RIGHT FILMS, INC. on or about the premises in all media now known or hereafter devised, and in perpetuity throughout the world, and that FRAME RIGHT FILMS, INC., its affiliates and licensees shall have the right to use such photographs and recordings in any manner it may desire without limitation or restriction of any kind.

6. RELEASOR warrants that RELEASOR is the owner, or the authorized agent of the owner, of the premises and is fully authorized to execute this location release, and that the rights granted in this Agreement do not violate the rights of any person or organization.

OWNER/AGENT:	**FRAME RIGHT FILMS, INC.**
Date Signed: _____	Date: _____
Signed: _____	Signed: _____
By: _____	By: _____
Address: _____	Address: _____

FIGURE 15.3
Location Release Agreement.

Acme Insurance   Certificate of Insurance Liability

Insurance Company	Production Company	
Acme Insurance 8799 Cartwright Ave., Suite 1844 Los Angeles, CA 89998 310-789-8765 Fax: 310-789-8766	Frame Right Films, Inc. 1890 Eagle Point Drive Los Angeles, CA 80009 310-664-6282 Fax: 310-664-6883	Date of Issue: June 1, 2002 Its: LW Its: JR Page 1 of 1

Title of Project:	"Regina of Icelandia"

Type of Insurance	Effective Date	Exp. Date	Pol No.	Limits
General Liability				
Commercial General Liability	July 1, 2002	Aug 31, 2002	ABR796	Gen. 3,000,000 Personal Inj 1,000,000 Products 1,000,000 Med Exp 25,000 Fire 50,000
Automobile Liability				
Owned Vehicles	July 1, 2002	Aug 31, 2002	GHW887	Bodily Injury 1,000,000
Rented Vehicles	July 1, 2002	Aug 31, 2002	GHV887	Property 1,000,000
Excess Liability				
Umbrella Form Other than Umbrella Form	July 1, 2002	Aug 31, 2002	SEF789	Each Occ 1,000,000 Aggregate 1,000,000
Worker's Compensation				
Worker's Compensation	July 1, 2002	Aug 31, 2002	JED89798	Each Acc 1,000,000 Policy Limit 1,000,000 Each Emp 1,000,000
Other				
Third Party Prop Damage	July 1, 2002	Aug 31, 2002	SIT82979	Limit 3,000,000 DED $5000
Miscellaneous Equipment	July 1, 2002	Aug 31, 2002	SIT82980	Limit 3,000,000 DED $5000
Negative	July 1, 2002	Aug 31, 2002	SIT82981	Limit 3,000,000 DED $5000
Cast	July 1, 2002	Aug 31, 2002	SIT82982	Limit 3,000,000 DED $5000
Art & Wardrobe	July 1, 2002	Aug 31, 2002	SIT82983	Limit 3,000,000 DED $5000

Description

Holder is an additional insured &/or loss payee, as their interests may appear with respect to all operations of the named insured in connection with the production titled: *Regina of Icelandia*

Coverage

This is to certify that the policies of insurance listed below have been issued to the insured named above for the policy period indicated, notwithstanding any requirement term or condition of any contract or other document with respect to which this certificate may be issued or may pertain, the insurance afforded by the policies describe herein is subject to all the terms exclusions and conditions of such policies, limits shown may have been reduced by paid claims.

ACME Form CIS-45	Auth. Rep.: John Robinson	*Acme Ins. Agency 2002*

FIGURE 15.4
Certificate of Insurance.

SUMMARY

The location department on a shoot must be staffed by people who are diplomatic and creative at the same time. A good location manager makes sure that all locations are treated properly and accurately fit the vision of the director. The location team provides support in the form of perfect maps, security, fire, heating or air conditioning, and police if needed. Shooting on location or in a studio has different advantages and disadvantages. Securing a location requires working with the location owner as well as the city to secure the proper permits.

The Transportation Department

This chapter outlines the one department that is rarely seen on a low-budget film. The transportation department is responsible for all production vehicles and picture vehicles. In low budget, the only production vehicle may be one truck that serves the grip, electric, camera, and even sometimes craft service departments. In high-budget productions, each of these departments has its own vehicle, as do other departments such as art, wardrobe, and makeup. In addition to the transportation personnel, this chapter discusses the many production trucks that exist, what their purposes are, and how many might be needed based on script and budget level. Figure 16.1 illustrates the transportation hierarchy.

TRANSPORTATION COORDINATOR

The **transportation coordinator** is the head of the transportation department (also known as "transpo"). He oversees and is responsible for the transportation budget. The coordinator also oversees the acquiring of all picture vehicles and coordinates airport pickups and deliveries. Following is a description of the transpo coordinator's duties and responsibilities.

Pre-Production

- Arrives early in the pre-production process to set up accounts with local businesses such as limousine services and vehicle maintenance.
- Works with the APOC to pick people up at airport and deliver them to the hotel. The coordinator will receive a movement list, or travel log (see Chapter 4, Figure 4.2, for an example), from the APOC, which outlines airlines, flights, and times of arrival. The transportation coordinator will send out a pickup report with the driver that outlines the pickup time, location, and airline. See Figure 16.2. In the figure, the **pickup report** shows that the driver is taking an actress to the airport and picking up a crew member in the same trip.

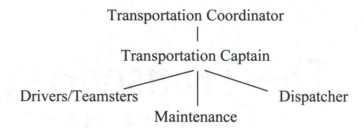

FIGURE 16.1
Transportation Hierarchy.

- Goes on location scouts. The coordinator is always looking to make sure there is ample parking for all production vehicles at locations.
- Designs parking diagrams for each location for all the production vehicles. These parking diagrams show where each truck will be parked. This form ensures quick and efficient placement of the vehicles each morning.
- Arranges for all production trucks to get to the location. Sometimes these vehicles may come from different states. For instance, the production may rent a grip truck from North Carolina, which may need to be driven to Virginia. The coordinator hires the driver and makes sure all arrangements are made so that the vehicle gets to the location safely and on time.
- Hires the **transportation captain** and drivers.
- Schedules drivers for cast and crew pickup at the hotel and transportation to the set every morning of shooting.
- Schedules rental vehicles for appropriate crew members. The transportation budget, as approved by the producer, states which crew members get rental vehicles. Typically, on a medium- to high-budget shoot, the following would get a rental car: director, producer, production designer, prop master, set decorator, visual effects supervisor, production supervisor, and stars.
- Loans rental vehicles on weekends for cast and crew.
- Meets with the director to discuss the look of the picture vehicles.
- Searches for any picture vehicles, photographs them, and presents them to the director. Once the director chooses, the transpo coordinator will then acquire the vehicles.
- May need to coordinate with the stunt coordinator and special effects supervisor if vehicles are needed for stunts or special effects.

Production

- Is first to arrive on set, to place all trucks.
- Coordinates parking as crew and cast arrive.

Transportation Department
Pickup Report

DATE: _____ JULY 19, 2002 _____

(CAST) CREW VIP

NAME: _____ MARY STAR _____

PICKUP LOCATION: ___ PENN HOTEL-LOBBY _____

PICKUP TIME: _____ 6:15A _____

TRANSPORT TO: _____ LAX _____

AIRLINE: _____ DELTA _____

FLIGHT DEPARTURE: _____ 10:15A _____

COMMENTS: _____

CAST (CREW) VIP

NAME: ___ JOE JOHNSON _____

PICKUP LOCATION: ____ LAX _____

AIRLINE: _____ USAIR _____

FLIGHT NUMBER: ____ 8907 _____

FLIGHT ARRIVAL: ____ 1:20P _____

TRANPORT TO: _____ PENN HOTEL _____

COMMENTS: ____ WILL HAVE EXTRA BAGGAGE _____

FIGURE 16.2
Transportation Department Pickup Report.

- Makes sure all cast and crew are transported to and from the set as needed. It is the job of the transpo department to be available for these rides. Also makes sure there is always a driver on set for emergencies.
- If there are scenes with lots of picture cars, helps the ADs on set to coordinate the vehicles' movements for the camera.

Wrap

- Makes sure all accounts are settled.
- Coordinates traveling people to the airport.
- Sells any purchased vehicles.

- Returns any rental vehicles.
- Makes sure all production trucks are returned.

TRANSPORTATION CAPTAIN

The transportation captain assists the coordinator and may perform any of the duties listed in the section "Transportation Coordinator." Which specific duties may be delegated to the captain is determined by the work style and discretion of the coordinator. In some cases, the captain may concentrate only on coordinating and managing the drivers. The captain usually begins work shortly after the transportation coordinator. Other duties that would usually fall to the captain include the following:

- Sets up accounts with local gas stations for production vehicle fuel.
- Locates local garages for maintenance of production vehicles.
- Assists anyone with getting into accidentally locked vehicles. Although this is not a formal part of the job description, the transpo personnel usually help in this respect.
- Arranges for local crew parking. Sometimes local crew members who work in the production office can park in a hotel parking lot. I once worked as a local on a show that had its production office in a hotel in downtown Pittsburgh. Since the hotel was in the middle of the city, there was no hotel parking. The transpo team arranged for local crew to park in the parking garage across from the hotel.

MORE TRANSPORTATION CREW

A **dispatcher** is usually found on larger-budget films. This person works solely to schedule drivers for transporting cast and crew to and from the airport or to and from the set. The dispatcher starts work in pre-production as soon as large numbers of crew begin to travel into the area.

Drivers are just that, drivers. They transport cast and crew to and from the airport and the set. Drivers work the longest hours of anyone on set because they must transport the first people to set and the last people off the set. During times when they are not transporting people, they stand by the vehicles, ready to give a ride at a moment's notice.

Teamsters are drivers that belong to local transportation unions. Whether you are working in a **right-to-work state** or not would determine whether you need to hire teamsters as drivers. Teamsters are also drivers that are trained in operating bigger vehicles such as your production vehicles. Drivers or teamsters would begin work shortly after the dispatcher. The transportation coordinator may start with only a few drivers and add more as they are required.

QUALITIES OF A GOOD TRANSPORTATION TEAM

- Respectful attitude toward crew and cast.
- Knowledgeable about cars and the history of various vehicles.

- Resourceful. Sometimes scripts call for vintage vehicles or vehicles that do not even exist yet. A good transpo person can find or help create any vehicle.
- Knowledge of vehicle maintenance.
- Great scheduling abilities.

OPERATIONS

First up in the morning for the transpo team is to park the production vehicles. Either the transportation coordinator or captain uses a parking diagram so that each vehicle has an assigned spot. After the production vehicles are in place, the drivers usually stand by the vehicles to perform any needed maintenance, move the vehicles, or, as is usually the case, sit around and talk with the drivers of other production vehicles.

At the same time, drivers are picking up crew and cast from the hotel to bring them to set. The drivers are scheduled to do this, according to crew and cast call times. Most crew will have the same call time, but actors are usually given **split calls**. This means that they are all given different call times, based on when in the day they shoot. The transportation team must figure out how to get all the cast to the set just before they are needed so that they are neither sitting around needlessly nor late. Usually, this timing means that the team is running drivers back and forth to the hotel throughout the day. The team must also be ready to transport actors back to the hotel when they are finished, again so they are not sitting around needlessly.

When a production is using stars, there are usually certain drivers assigned to certain stars. A driver picks up the star at the hotel or wherever she is staying and brings him to set. The driver may do other runs throughout the day, but must be available when the star is finished to transport him back "home." The transpo team also makes sure that any local crew or visitors to the set have adequate parking. They will have signs posted for crew parking that is separate from the production vehicles.

Throughout the day, the transpo team has to make sure that all vehicles are gassed up and running properly. The transportation coordinator or captain will make sure that vehicles are getting gas as needed during runs. In pre-production the coordinator will set up an account with a local gas station that is conveniently located to most of the locations. Then, when a vehicle needs gas, the driver is sent to that specific station and can purchase the fuel without having to deal with petty cash and receipts. However, using petty cash for this purpose is also done.

At the end of the day, the coordinator or captain knows to have vehicles standing by to transport crew back to the hotel. Then, once all the production vehicles are loaded, they are returned to their overnight parking, which could be at the hotel if there is enough space, or to a parking garage.

PICTURE VEHICLES

Picture vehicles are any vehicles that appear onscreen. As such, your script determines the kind of vehicles that you need. The script, however, might state that an actor drives his car to the store. Perhaps no specific kind of vehicle is mentioned. This is where the transportation coordinator has creative input. After discussions with the director, the coordinator will venture to find the perfect vehicle that fits that character. In motion pictures, as in life, the kind of vehicle a person drives reflects his character and style, as well as economic status.

In some cases a picture vehicle may not exist. I once worked on a show that needed an armored truck. Since renting an existing armored vehicle from a company such as Brinks or Purolator was impractical, the transportation team bought an ice cream truck and worked with the art department to turn it into an armored truck for the film. In other cases, entire vehicles are constructed from scratch, such as the Batmobile. Sometimes picture vehicles are not covered by the transportation department. Vehicles such as spacecraft are covered by the special effects department, which uses models or CGI.

PRODUCTION VEHICLES

Following is a list of some of the production vehicles that would be found on a medium- to high-budget project. As previously stated, in lower-budget projects usually only one or two trucks would be used to transport all the equipment to and from set. One rule on union shoots is that no one except teamsters is authorized to drive or move trucks.

> *Camera truck:* The camera truck is used to house the camera equipment and film stock. The truck also has a darkroom that the loader uses to change film magazines.
>
> *Grip truck:* Houses the grip equipment.
>
> *Lighting truck:* Houses the electrical equipment. Depending on how involved the lighting is for the project, there may be more than one lighting truck.
>
> *Honeywagon:* A trailer that contains dressing rooms and bathrooms. The number of rooms that you need depends on the number of union cast that will be on set at one time. SAG has a rule that each actor must have a dressing room while shooting. Sometimes one of the dressing rooms is used for the AD team as an office. The honeywagon also has separate bathrooms on one side of the vehicle that can be used by crew.
>
> *Makeup trailer:* Used for the makeup team and is outfitted with mirrors, sink, and makeup chairs.
>
> *Wardrobe trailer:* Used for the wardrobe team and is outfitted with dressing areas and wardrobe racks.
>
> *Production office truck:* If not using a honeywagon room, a separate truck is used as an office for the AD team, where they work on call sheets and production reports, and communicate with the production office.
>
> *Prop truck:* Houses all props needed for the show.
>
> Set dressing truck: Houses all set dressing needed for the show.
>
> *Generator tow:* This vehicle tows the generator.
>
> *Stake bed:* This vehicle is a pickup with an extra large bed and is used for hauling anything as needed.
>
> *Minivans:* Used for transporting cast and crew to and from the set.

Star trailers: Nicely outfitted recreational vehicles (RVs) for stars. The number of trailers varies depending on the budget and the caliber of stars on the shoot.

Director's trailer: Another nicely outfitted RV, which may be used also by the producer.

Water truck: This vehicle is needed in case you need to shoot with rain.

Special effects truck: This vehicle may be needed for any special effects equipment.

SUMMARY

The transportation department, also called transpo, handles all production and picture vehicles. The transportation coordinator works with his captain and drivers to make sure all vehicles are on set as needed and to transport cast and crew as needed. When working with picture vehicles, the transpo coordinator may work with other departments to coordinate special effects or stunts. The number of production vehicles on a show varies with the size of the show. A low-budget production may have only one vehicle in which to store all of the equipment, whereas a higher-budget show may have numerous vehicles.

Post-Production

Editing Picture and Sound

Post-production in the entertainment business is one of the fastest changing fields in the industry. New software and techniques are developed each year that have an impact on the process of post-production. The purpose of this chapter is to describe the people that work in post-production and to describe the process. Because of changing technology, this process varies greatly for different production levels. It should be noted that this chapter does not attempt to provide the technical aspects of post-production such as what editing program to use and how that system functions. There are many books that cover those subjects in great detail. These books also quickly become dated as the process changes. This chapter concentrates more on the people and the process. Figure 17.1 illustrates the post-production hierarchy.

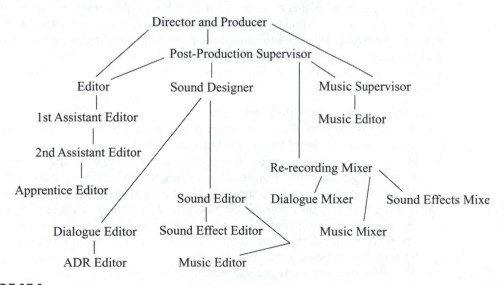

FIGURE 17.1

Post-Production Hierarchy.

POST-PRODUCTION SUPERVISOR

The post-production supervisor is the person who makes sure that everything in the post-production process is coordinated and completed on time. This person tends to the details of each point in the process, ensuring for the producer that the project is proceeding well and on time. This person may begin work during principal photography or shortly after principal photography is completed. A general list of duties follows:

- Meets with the producer to discuss a possible post-production schedule and delivery date.
- Creates and publishes a post-production schedule (in consultation with the director and producer). This schedule articulates deadlines for different steps in the process.
- May arrange for picture and sound editing facilities.
- May coordinate the **scoring sessions,** including communicating with the composer and renting the stage.
- May rent a sound mixing facility for the final **sound mix.**
- Provides communication between the editors and producer or production staff.
- May work with film labs to ensure timely transport and delivery of materials.
- May work with the special/visual effects team to coordinate delivery of the effects.

EDITOR

The editor's job is to cut the picture together. In low budget this could mean that the editor not only cuts the picture but also cuts and mixes the sound. In medium to higher budget projects the editor will only cut the picture, along with the help of a few assistants. In this case, the editor's job is highly creative. He or she not only cuts a scene according to the footage that was shot but also uses the shots to tell the story. As the head of the editing department the editor is also in charge of and responsible for the editing budget. The editor starts work as soon as footage is returned to the production from the lab. Following is the process the editor may go through to accomplish a final edit:

- Receives dailies from the production office.
- Receives notes from the script supervisor. These notes tell the editor how a scene was covered and how each shot was named.
- Has one assistant or more to digitize or load the footage into the editing system. Digitizing is the process of recording the dailies into the computer. This is used when you have shot on film and transferred the film to a digital format. The only time digitizing is not needed is when you shoot with a camera that records your footage on a hard drive. In this case, the drive is hooked up to your computer and the footage is placed in the editing program as files, with each take being a different file.
- May look over the footage to see what has been shot.
- Begins to choose takes, either with the director or alone (depends on the director).

- Once takes are chosen, may herself or have an assistant assemble the footage into a first cut.
- As further footage is sent to the editor, repeats the process of cutting together scenes.
- May then edit a first cut of the film, either alone or with the director. Different producers and directors have varying styles when it comes to their involvement in the editing process: Some directors and producers prefer to sit in on almost every editing session, influencing how each scene takes shape from start to finish. Other directors only prefer to sit in on the editing process after the first scenes are cut together.
- Each time a cut is ready, the editor will arrange for a screening with the producer and director.
- Continues with further cuts of the picture until the final cut is achieved.
- May need to edit a **television version,** if applicable.
- Sends the cut picture, or **edit decision list** (EDL), to the negative cutters (if shooting film). The EDL is generated by an editing system and shows the exact time code location of each picture cut. The negative cutters use this list to cut and conform the negative to your cut project.
- Turns the final picture over to the sound editors and composer.
- May in some cases cut the trailer.

ASSISTANT EDITORS

The **first assistant editor** on a project assists the editor. Depending on the personal style of the editor, these job duties may vary. For instance, one editor may be comfortable with letting the assistant editor put a first cut of a scene together. Some editors may even give certain scenes to an assistant to take to the first or second cut. Another editor may only want the first assistant editor to log and digitize footage.

The **second assistant editor** on a project assists the first assistant editor. Having any assistant editors on a project at all has become more of a luxury because of faster and easier-to-use editing systems. There is always an assistant needed, though, to digitize footage. In this case, that task usually falls to the second assistant editor. If there were no second, this duty would fall to the first. The second may also be asked to put first assemblies of the footage together, or even first and second cuts if there is a time factor.

The **apprentice editor** is much like a production assistant in other departments. His or her main job is to assist the other members of the editing team. This may include getting them coffee, retrieving tapes, logging footage, and, depending on skill level, digitizing footage. The apprentice is usually someone with little experience who is looking to move up the editing ladder. This position is sometimes paid and sometimes not, depending on the budget of the production.

SOUND DESIGNER

The **sound designer** is the person responsible for the aural concept of a project. The aural concept is a kind of **aural vision** for the film. If you listen to different films, you will notice that some projects may sound grittier and noisier; some may sound quieter and more peaceful. This is not by accident. The sound designer has created an aural concept (in consultation with the director) of how the final film will sound. It is then his or her job to see that vision realized on the sound track. To do this, the sound designer discusses the vision with the director and producer. Then he or she supervises all aspects of the sound track, from hiring a post-production crew to supervising the sound editing and mixing. The sound designer oversees the creation of sound effects tracks, **Foley tracks,** and especially the music track. He may also work with a **music supervisor** to ensure that the aural vision and the vision of the director are accomplished on screen.

The sound designer is a position mostly seen on high-budget films. In high-budget projects you would have a sound designer, possibly an assistant, and an array of sound editors. In very low budget, you may have one person who records the location sound. You then may have only one other person who completes the entire sound edit and mix. In medium budget you may have more than one person working on your sound in post-production, and one of them may be given sound designer credit (mainly because it looks good on the resume).

SOUND EDITOR

The description of the sound editor varies greatly on projects because of budget. In low budget your sound editor may be the person who performs the duties of the sound designer, **dialogue editor, sound effects editor, automated dialogue replacement (ADR) editor,** and **music editor.** In medium to higher budget projects the sound editor may work on putting together the tracks that other editors have built and supervise the other sound editors (in this case, he or she would be called the supervising sound editor). The process for the sound editor is as follows:

- May receive a first cut of the picture. Often the post-production schedule dictates that sound editing needs to begin before a final cut of the picture is achieved. In this case, as the editor finishes final scenes, they are sent to the sound editor(s) until the final cut of the picture is achieved (which is then sent to the sound editor).
- May receive a final cut of the picture to begin working on. This option is ideal for the sound editor.
- Receives original sound recordings and sound reports. These recordings may be needed because they contain room tone, which is placed under scenes to provide a consistent background ambience.
- Holds **spotting sessions** with the director. A spotting session is a meeting between the sound editor and the director. In this meeting they watch the film and discuss possible problems with the sound, placement of sound effects, Foley, and sometimes music. See Figure 17.2 for an example of a spotting sheet.
- Begins **building the sound tracks,** including the dialogue track, sound effects track, and ADR and music tracks. Individual dialogue, sound effects, ADR, and music editors may also do this job.
- Brings in the director and producer at various points to listen to the tracks and discuss changes.

SPOTTING SHEET

MUSIC   (SND FX)   **DIALOGUE**   **AMBIENCE**

PROJECT TITLE   "Regina of Icelandia"   **PAGE NUMBER**   1 OF 16
SPOTTER   Audrey Snyder   **DATE PREPARED**   August 8, 2002

ITEM	sync/non	IN TC	OUT TC	DESCRIPTION
wind	n	00:01:30:00	00:01:35:00	howling, over desert
cranial computer	s	00:01:10:10	00:01:10:10	over Gerie's dialogue
footsteps	s	00:01:32:06	00:01:33:04	climbing over rocks
crowd	s	00:01:40:00	00:01:42:20	gasp
scrape	s	00:02:00:00	00:02:00:00	finger slides across screen
crowd	n	00:02:05:10	00:02:15:00	claps & cheers
wind	n	00:02:30:17	00:02:31:00	howling over Regina's CU
crowd	n	00:02:45:00	00:02:50:00	cheer to hush
sky tubes	s	00:02:59:00	00:03:10:03	fly away, engines soaring
cranial computer	s	00:03:34:00	00:03:35:00	on Uomo
footsteps	s	00:03:56:03	00:04:07:12	Uomo & Donato down hallway
Wochera tower	n	00:04:30:00	00:04:35:00	night sounds
Regina's feet	s	00:04:10:10	00:04:10:10	twitch on floor
blue haze	s	00:04:32:06	00:04:33:04	electronic buzz sound
cranial computer	s	00:05:40:00	00:05:42:20	on Margee
screen	s	00:06:00:00	00:06:00:00	soft electronic buzz
door	s	00:06:05:10	00:06:15:00	slams
sky tube	s	00:07:30:17	00:07:31:00	starts up, flies away
guests	n	00:07:45:00	00:07:50:00	hushed conversation
gong	s	00:07:59:00	00:08:10:03	heavy, deep
crowd	n	00:08:34:00	00:08:35:00	laughing
double doors	s	00:08:56:03	00:08:07:12	creak open
crowd	n	00:09:00:00	00:09:30:10	clapping
crowd	n	00:10:00:00	00:10:14:01	hushed conversation
double doors	s	00:10:45:12	00:10:49:20	slam shut

FIGURE 17.2
Spotting Sheet.

- Continues to work on the tracks until the director and producer are satisfied.
- Once the tracks are finished, prepares the tracks for the sound mix. The process of preparing usually means making sure all the tracks are in proper order, labeled properly, and volume levels are consistent.
- May then output the tracks to another format to send to the mixing session. This may not need to happen if the project will be edited and mixed on the same sound editing system, such as **Pro Tools,** which has both sound editing and mixing functions. Note that in lower budget productions the audio is sometimes edited and mixed by the picture editor. In this case, the tracks merely stay in the original editing program and are built and mixed there.

DIALOGUE EDITOR

The dialogue editor heads up the sound editing team. His or her main job is to take the dialogue that has been recorded on a project and clean it up. The dialogue editor adds **crossfades** to smooth out the ambience differences of different takes and removes unwanted background noises. The editor may edit ADR into the main dialogue (if there is no ADR editor) or replace lines with alternate takes of the original production track dialogue.

The dialogue track of a film is usually the prominent track. Filmmakers know that if the dialogue of the actors cannot be heard clearly, you will lose your audience. Dialogue editors are knowledgeable about speech patterns and speech rhythms. Subsequently, dialogue editors are extremely meticulous people, having to deal with the minutiae of a sound track in order to make it sound its best. Following are some general guidelines for the process of dialogue editing:

- Listen to the dialogue track.
- Complete a spotting sheet, making notes of items that need improvement. For instance, you have a scene with two actors talking. In between their dialogue a bang is heard off set (someone dropped something during shooting). The dialogue editor makes a note to remove that sound. On the other hand, perhaps in the same scene that bang is heard on top of an actor's dialogue. The dialogue editor would make a note that ADR will need to be recorded for that line.
- Add crossfades between dialogue cuts to create smoothness.
- Fill in any missing ambiences between words.
- Adjust levels and pitches of voices so they are consistent.

SOUND EFFECTS EDITOR

The sound effects editor is the editor that adds or creates sound effects that are then added to the picture. Sound effects editing is arguably the most creative of the editing jobs. These people are known for creating something out of nothing. For instance, the sound of a waterfall can be recreated using tissue paper. Sword fight sounds can be created using two kitchen knives. Whatever the scene calls for, or whatever effect might add sonic quality, it is the sound effects artist who can provide. The sound effects artist also uses sound effects to define space, establish locale, and create humor or counterpoint. The purpose of sound effects is to direct a viewer's emotion and enhance the dramatic impact of a scene. Following is a list of general guidelines for the sound effects editor:

- Hold spotting sessions with the director and/or producer.
- Insert any needed sound effects via a sound effects library.
- Record any effects that cannot be found in a library. An assistant or a **Foley artist** may also accomplish this job. A Foley artist is a person who performs actions to create sounds such as footsteps or any sound that needs to be synchronized to the picture.
- If necessary, hold **Foley sessions** to get needed sound effects.
- Continue to build the sound effects tracks until all are completed.
- If applicable, send the sound effects tracks to the main sound editor.

MUSIC EDITOR

The music editor is the editor who adds music to the picture. While music itself has many purposes in a project, the placement of that music also has a purpose. Music is used to intensify action, depict identity, establish place, and recall or foretell events. There are certain guidelines for a music editor when placing or using music. These guidelines are as follows:

- Music can be used to overlap or **segue** between scenes.
- If a piece of music starts within a scene, it should play all the way through (there are exceptions to this based on artistic choice).
- Music should start only when the dramatic emphasis of a scene changes.
- Music should always reflect the emotional state of the character.
- If the music does not have a purpose, you do not need it.

The music editor will follow some of the same procedures for the music editing process, as follows:

- Hold spotting sessions with director or music supervisor. At this session, the placement of each piece of music is chosen.
- As pieces of music are received, place them accordingly.
- Hold meetings with the director or music supervisor to adjust music as needed.
- If applicable, send the music tracks to the main sound editor.

ADR EDITOR

The ADR editor is the editor who records and then adds the ADR to the picture. ADR is needed when an actor's dialogue either was not recorded well on set or is bad because of some unwanted background noise. Sometimes, though it is not advisable to do too much of this, ADR will be recorded because the director wants a different "read" on an actor's line. In low budget, because of scant resources, it is not always advisable to do much ADR. This is especially true if your **re-recording**

mixer is inexperienced. Combining ADR with production dialogue and making it sound seamless is an art, often acquired only by years of experience. Too much ADR that does not match the production dialogue will make your project sound amateurish. Alternately, if your production sound is unintelligible, you may have to do ADR. Sometimes the choice is the lesser of two evils. The ADR editor will go through the following process:

- May hold spotting sessions with the director, dialogue editor, or main sound editor.
- Will work with the post-production supervisor to schedule ADR recording sessions.
- Records actors' dialogue at the session.
- Edits the ADR into the ADR tracks.
- May send the ADR tracks to the sound editor.

RE-RECORDING MIXERS

The re-recording mixer, also known sometimes as the sound mixer, is the person who mixes all the tracks of a project together to reach a final mix. In low-budget pictures, the re-recording mixer mixes all of the tracks, including dialogue, sound effects, ambience, and music. In higher budget productions, the dialogue editor may become the main re-recording mixer, accompanied by two other mixers who all work together in one mixing session. One will mix the sound effects, and the other will mix the music.

The purpose of the mixing session is to sweeten the sound, or, in other words, blend the sound tracks and adjust levels and add digital signal processing (DSP) so that the final sound of the picture is achieved. **DSP** is the practice of processing different sounds with effects such as **reverb** or **equalization** (EQ). For instance, if a person's voice is heard over a telephone, the sound mixer will "EQ" the voice (decreasing the mid-frequency range) to make it sound electronic. Generally, the sound mixing session would be attended by the mixer(s), producer, and director and could take anywhere from 1 week to 1 month, depending on the complexity of the picture. The session could proceed as follows:

1. All parties watch the project scene by scene and give notes, and the sound mixer makes adjustments.
2. The re-recording mixer adds digital effects to certain sounds as needed, or directs the dialogue or music mixer to do so.
3. The re-recording mixer adjusts volume levels so they are consistent throughout the piece and the dialogue is prominent.
4. The director and/or producer add suggestions throughout the session. These suggestions are talked about and implemented as needed.
5. The mixer(s) proceed through the show until all scenes are completed.
6. The parties will then listen to the project one last time to determine if any adjustments need to be made.

LOOPING/ADR

Looping, also known as ADR, is a process in which the actors come in during post-production and redo their dialogue in a looping facility. There are several reasons why this may be necessary. First, perhaps an actor's dialogue was recorded poorly on set, or because of conditions beyond control, the actor's dialogue sounds bad because of the location (planes overhead, nearby construction, etc.). Second, the director may want a different read on a certain line. In low budget, be careful of redoing a lot of dialogue. Only do what is absolutely necessary. The reason for this is that often in low budget you cannot afford an expensive sound mix with an experienced mixer. The ability to replace location dialogue with ADR and make it sound seamless is an art, acquired over years of experience. If you do not have a mixer with much experience or skill, your project could end up sounding amateurish. Looping is usually part of an actor's contract. Looping sessions involve the following:

- After principal photography, the producer, director, and sound editor determine how much and which lines of dialogue will need to be looped.
- The producer or UPM books a post-production facility that does ADR.
- The producer or UPM contacts necessary cast and arranges for a looping schedule.

Following are the steps to take to achieve a successful ADR session.

What to Do Before the Session

1. Hold a spotting session with your director or producer to determine exactly which lines need to be recorded.
2. Have the production call and schedule each actor; you should allow approximately 10–15 minutes completing the ADR for each line.
3. Make sure your spotting sheet tells you at what time code each line exists.
4. If you don't already have one, create a new track in your session that will contain only ADR.
5. Arrive at least a half-hour before the session is to begin.
6. Test the microphone in the booth and test recording into your computer or recorder.
7. Double-check to make sure all of the lines to be recorded have a memory location.
8. Make sure the producer provides script pages for each actor.

What to Do During the Session

1. Once the producer and actor arrive, make the actor feel comfortable; actors are often nervous and inexperienced at this.
2. Place the actor in front of the microphone at the proper position.
3. Have the actor read a few lines, and adjust the level on the mixing board for optimum recording.
4. If using computer software, call up the first memory location.

5. Select the line and let the actor rehearse.
6. When the actor is ready, begin recording.
7. Keep recording until you feel proper synchronicity (sync) has been achieved.
8. Be sure to make a note on the ADR cue sheet about which take the director/producer liked the best.
9. Repeat the above steps until all lines are recorded.

THE SOUND MIX

Once your sound is mixed, usually in a mixing studio using sound mixing software, the mix needs to be sent to your film lab. When your mix is complete, your sound mixer may "**bounce,**" or combine, all of your sound tracks to achieve the number of tracks that will accommodate your format. Again, the format of the mix that you send to the lab depends on your capabilities and your lab. The goal is to have your mix at the lab at the same time that the cut negative is being sent to the lab from the negative cutters. This way the lab does not have to wait for one or the other and can proceed with striking your prints.

The kind of mix your re-recording mixer completes depends on the format and distribution of your piece. In the past if your show was shot on 16mm film and intended to be projected that way, you will do a **mono mix.** A mono mix has all of the sound tracks combined into one channel. That channel is the white squiggly line you see on a 16mm film print.

If your piece was shot on another film format or shot digitally for theater release and will be projected on film, the mixer will complete a mix for 5.1, 7.1, or 10.2 surround sound. This kind of mix directs different channels to different speakers. Surround sound is now found in most theaters and is the kind of mix that is used on DVD.

If your project will be shown internationally, the editors will also create music and effects (**M&E**). Completing the M&E is the process in which any sounds from the dialogue track that are not dialogue are moved or reproduced onto another track. This leaves one track of dialogue only and other tracks filled with all of the M&E. Then, when a different country wants to create a different language version of your piece, they can lay down the dialogue in their language that they will then combine with the other M&E tracks.

THE POST-PRODUCTION PROCESS

The post-production process is an ever-changing practice. What was done as recently as 10 years ago no longer exists. What follows is a description of the various ways to shoot and edit a project. These descriptions are not meant to be exhaustive in the technological sense (there are many sources with updated technological practices, such as trade magazines and editing textbooks), but are meant to be a thorough treatment of the steps of the process.

When I talk about "finishing on" a certain format, I am referring to the final format of the piece. A work may be finished on film because it will be projected in a theater on film. A project may be finished digitally, either because it is going straight to DVD or Blu-Ray for distribution or because it will be projected digit-ally. Each production is different. The finished format of your piece is determined by what kind of distribution you have. If your project is not going for theatrical distribution, it may be shot on film, edited by computer, and then directly output to the current format, DVD (SD or Blu-Ray), for distribution.

Shooting Film for Release on Film

In previous years, film projects would be edited on film, and sound would be edited on magnetic stock (sound film). The process was cumbersome and lengthy. No one does this anymore. Today, there are film projects that are still shot on film, but are then edited on a nonlinear editing system by the following process:

1. The film is transferred to a digital format, which is digitized into the computer.
2. The original sound files, disks, or DVDs that were recorded on set are also digitized and synchronized to the picture.
3. Then, sound and picture are edited inside the computer.
4. Next, the project outputs lists that the negative cutters use to conform the original picture negative to what was edited by the computer.
5. Meanwhile, the sound tracks have been moved to a sound editing system (un-less sound will be cut in the original picture editing program).
6. The dialogue, sound effects, ambience, and music are all cleaned up and added to the picture.
7. Then, the tracks are mixed and the final sound mix is output to whatever format your lab requires.
8. Once the negative is cut, it is sent to the lab, where it is combined with the final sound mix and prints are made. The first print is called an answer, or check print. The producer, director, and DP view the answer print and make changes to the colors as needed. Many directors and producers are also at this point going to a digital intermediate. This is a digital form of check print where colors are corrected.
9. The lab then strikes **release prints.** Release prints are what are shown in the theaters. To strike a print means to make a print of your show. In the high-budget world, the release prints may be ordered and paid for by the distributor.

WORKING WITH THE LAB

What lab you choose to process your film is an important choice. Not all labs are the same. Many labs have the ability to process film, transfer, and return dailies to you. Some labs may need to send your film out for a transfer. Sending the dailies out for transfer may take longer, which may or may not be an issue for you. It is important that the turnaround time of the lab (the amount of time the lab takes to return dailies to you) fits your schedule. You do not want to be waiting more than 1 or 2 days for dailies to come back to you, especially if you have a tight post-production schedule. Traditionally, projects would have their footage processed and then watch the footage on film with a projector. Now, many are opting to watch dailies digitally or through the internet.

The process of working with a lab begins by getting information from other industry people regarding what labs they have used and what labs they like or avoid. The location of the lab could also be important. If you are shooting on a distant location, then your footage and dailies will need to be shipped. This is fine, as long as your budget can handle the shipping charges. You also need to find out what times or what days the lab processes film. Some labs process 24 hours a day, 7 days a week. Some smaller labs may process only on several days per week. Again, the choice of the lab must fit your schedule.

Next, call the lab and check with it about turnaround, the bath, and its capabilities. Once you have chosen a lab, call and set up an account. The lab will want to know the following:

- The time frame in which it will receive footage.
- The title of the project. Labs traditionally refer to a project's title when referring to a show.
- How quickly dailies need to be turned around.
- The format on which the transfers need to come back.
- Where and to whom the dailies will be sent. Often dailies are sent not only to the production but also to an executive producer or studio executive. The lab will duplicate the dailies if you request and send them wherever you need.
- Who will be the contact person to receive dailies or address concerns?

After receiving dailies, the lab will process the film, strike dailies, and return them to you. It will also retain your film negative until you need to send it to the negative cutters.

NEGATIVE CUTTING

Traditionally negative cutting was the process of taking the original negative of your footage and cutting it to conform it to an EDL. This cut negative was later sent back to your film lab so the lab could marry this cut negative to your sound mix and strike answer-and-release prints. To marry in this sense means to combine picture with sound on one piece of film. Currently, negative cutters will remove selected takes that are chosen from the dailies and then resplice them into new rolls. These rolls are then scanned to form the digital intermediate. There are many companies in the business of cutting negative. Many specialize in certain formats: 16mm, 35mm, or 70mm. Be sure that the cutting house you choose has experience with the format you are using. Following is a checklist regarding your cutting house:

- In pre-production, call cutting houses to get rates. Their rates usually include a setup fee and cost per cut.
- Check with your contacts to find the cutting house that best fits your needs.
- Call the company to discuss cutting your picture.
- Make sure that it will not be too swamped. If you are dealing with a deadline for delivery, you do not want to be slowed down by your post-production houses.

- The house will work with you to make sure you send it the proper materials.
- Notify your processing lab as to when it can expect to receive the cut negative, so it will be ready to strike your prints in a timely manner.

Shooting Digitally

Some projects that would normally be shot on film are now being done digitally because of the cost savings. Even a couple of feature films have been shot digitally and shown in major theaters. Shooting and finishing digitally has fast become the way many projects are done. Many projects today are still shot on film but finish digitally because they are never intended to be shown in theaters. The process, staying in the digital realm, might seem easier, but is not without its bugs. You may shoot on a digital format such as HD, only to find out later that the format is incompatible with your editing system. Be sure to know exactly what technologies work together and those that do not.

The process here is relatively simple:

1. Shoot with a digital camera.
2. Import the files into your editing system (if the system does not already do that automatically).
3. Input the sound and synchronize to the picture.
4. Edit your piece.
5. You can then, on some systems, edit your sound on the same system.
6. Alternatively, you can output your cut sound to a sound editing system for more precise sound editing.
7. Conduct a sound mix and then output from either system to your final format.

MAIN TITLES AND END CREDITS

The process of putting together the final credits of a film can be very complicated. Many of the film's main titles and end credits are determined contractually. Stars may have a certain size font that must be used or a specific placement where their names must appear. Unions have rules about credits for the director, UPM, assistant directors, director of photography, editor, art director, set decorator, costume designer, and makeup artist. For instance, the **Director's Guild of America** (DGA) requires that a director's credit appear last in the opening credits and not be smaller than 50 percent of the size of the project title. It also requires that a producer send the guild a copy of the main and end titles so the DGA can review them for compliance to guild rules.

Some unions are more specific than others when it comes to defining how their members receive credit. It is wise to always check with each union for its specific rules. If your show is nonunion, you may choose to write your credits however you see fit. There is a general guideline for the order of main and end credits: see Figure 17.3 for an example. Keep in mind that the example credit list may have more than or not all of the personnel in your project. Each credit list is particular to each show. Furthermore, many projects could have multiple people in one position.

Frame Right Films, Inc., presents
A J Darin Wales Film
Regina of Icelandia

Starring
Jing Lei Wales
Zane Duran
Lindsey Snyder

and
Julia Marie

Costumes Designed by
Carolyn Margaret

Production Designer
Elizabeth Stahl

Director of Photography
Reagen Beard

Special Visual Effects by
Danielle Kirsten

Music by
Matt Brinkman

Casting by
Smith and Jones

Written by
Keenan Beards

Executive Producers
Margie Guerrera
Albert Jose

Produced by
Belinda Smith

Directed by
J Darin Wales

End Credits
A J Darin Wales Film

*At this point some projects will relist the main cast members, then,

Associate Producer
Joe Smithy

(example names excluded from this point forward)

Unit Production Manager	**Clapper/Loader**	**Assistant to "Name of the Star(s)"**	**Supervising Sound Editor**
First Assistant Director	**Additional Operators**	**Assistant to "Name of the Producer"**	**Sound Editors**
Second Assistant Director	**Gaffer**	**Assistant to "Name of the Director"**	**Dialogue Editor**
Second Second Assistant Director	**Best Boy Electric**		**Sound Effects Editor**
	Electricians	**Receptionist**	**ADR Editor**
DGA Trainee	**Generator Operator**	**Runner**	**Music Editor**
Art Director	**Key Grip**	**Wardrobe Supervisor**	**Music Supervisor**
Set Decorator	**Dolly Grip**	**Costumers**	**Re-recording Mixer**
Set Dresser	**Best Boy**	**Seamstress**	**Special Effects Supervisor**
Lead Man	**Company Grips**	**Key Makeup Artist**	(List as appropriate)
Swing Gang	**Rigging Crew**	**Assistant Makeup Artist**	**Visual Effects Supervisor**
Art Department Coordinator	**Striking Crew**	**Additional Makeup**	(List as appropriate)
Assistant Art Director	**Sound Mixer**	**Special Makeup Effects**	**Catering by**
Props	**Boom Operator**	**Key Hair Stylist**	Craft Service Person
Assistant Props	**Playback**	**Assistant Hair Stylist**	**2nd Unit**
Script Supervisor	**Cable Person**	**Additional Hair**	(List as appropriate)
Location Manager	**Production Accountant**	**Transportation Coordinator**	**Negative Cutter**
Assistant Location Manager	**1st Assistant Production Accountant**	**Transportation Captain**	**Titles by**
Location PA	**2nd Assistant Production Accountant**	**Drivers**	**Lenses and Camera Equipment by**
Location Scout	**Production Coordinator**	**Stunt Coordinator**	**Grip and Lighting by**
Camera Operator	**Assistant Production Coordinator**	**Stunts**	**Re-recorded at**
1st Assistant Camera Person	**Office PAs**	**Post-Production Supervisor**	**Copyright**
2nd Assistant Camera Person	**Key Set PA**	**Assistant Editor**	**All Rights Reserved**
Camera PA	**Set PAs**	**Apprentice Editor**	(A list of sound format such as DTS or DTTS)
			(MPAA Seal)
			(Production Company Logo)

FIGURE 17.3

Main Titles and End Credits.

For instance, a show may have more than one assistant props person. In this case, each of the assistants' names is grouped under the assistant props credit.

Aside from union rules, the order of the credits can be at the discretion of the producer. As such, usually someone will be given a credit that has not existed before. I once worked a show where I was the director's assistant in pre-production. I was moved to doing travel for the run of the show, and then returned to being the director's assistant in post-production. The producer of the show gave me an option as to what credit I could have. We settled on "production associate." In addition, each person's name in the credits must be spelled correctly. This is accomplished by using the crew deal memos and cast contracts. These contracts have a section where the person prints his or her name as he or she would like it to appear in the credits. If during the course of your show someone is fired, he or she may or may not receive screen credit. Generally, producers will still give that fired person credit but put his or her name second, after the person who completes the project.

Other credits that may appear in a project are specific to that piece. For instance, I worked once on a feature film that used military equipment and vehicles, so there were numerous credits for military advisors, consultants' drivers, and pilots. Essentially, anyone who has helped in the making of a picture could receive screen credit at the discretion of the producer.

The process begins in the production office, generally at the end of principal photography.

1. The UPM will have one of the coordinators type a preliminary list of credits based on the crew list. The UPM will inform this person what order and what names go in the main titles.
2. Once completed, this first draft is sent to the producer for approval.
3. Changes are made as necessary. The final credits are not completed at this time, because other personnel, such as sound editors, may still need to be hired in the post-production process.
4. Once the film is closer to completion, a final list of credits will be generated and approved.

Because some editing systems have the capability, some credits in low-budget projects can be done in the editing system. These types of main titles and end credits may be limited by the scope of the software. If you are shooting film and finishing on film, the credits can still be done on an editing system, output, and then transferred to film.

Some main titles require that you see moving picture under the titles. If you are shooting digitally and outputting to a digital format, it is fairly easy to accomplish this with editing software. If you are shooting film, however, the process is more involved. Be sure to check with your lab for what they might require.

SUMMARY

The post-production process continues to change as new technologies are developed. It is important early in production to know what your delivery format is, as this will affect the steps of post-production. Your post-production supervisor will monitor the post-production process, ensuring that all deadlines are met. Your editor works to edit the picture while your sound team works to build the sound tracks and complete a final sound mix. The involvement of the producer and director in this process varies. Some directors prefer to sit in on most editing sessions, while others prefer to come in only when scenes are completed. Finally, the choice to shoot on film or a digital format is determined by your director and/or producer. This choice depends on the aesthetics of the show, its budget, and the final delivery format.

Music

The use of music in a project is an important issue because it usually involves questions of copyright and ownership. You may use music for your project that is pre-recorded, which means someone owns the music and the copyright. Or, you may hire someone to compose original music for you. In this case, the music is a "work-for-hire," which means that the producer or production company may own all the rights. Whatever kind of music you plan to use in your project, it is always wise to obtain the services of a lawyer or music clearance company. They will know the intricacies of copyright law and the procedure for **licensing.**

Three kinds of music appear in a project. First, there is **source music.** This is music that comes from a specific source onscreen, such as a car radio or a jukebox. Then there is **production music,** which is music that may come from a singer or musician. Finally, there is **underscore.** This is the music that plays under each scene, adding dramatic impact.

Music functions in a show to intensify action, unify transitions, or foretell events. It also serves to set the mood or atmosphere of a piece. Just think of any western you ever saw and the distinctive country-style twang comes to mind. The number one rule when placing music in a piece is the following: the music must reflect the state of mind of the character.

LICENSING RIGHTS

Obtaining music for a piece can be done many ways. First, let's say you want a song from the 1950s for a particular scene. That song, already published, has an owner who owns all the copyright. This owner may be the original artist or a record label and is entitled to a royalty if the work is used. To find out who the owner is, you need to do a copyright search. This search can be done with the U.S. Copyright Office (www.copyright.gov).

Alternately, you can contact the **American Society of Composers, Authors, and Publishers** (ASCAP). This society is made up of composers, songwriters, lyricists, and music publishers and functions to protect their rights. ASCAP monitors all licensing and royalties for public performances of copyrighted works. In addition, other music clearance companies will do much of the legwork for you. Another licensing company is Broadcast Music Incorporated (BMI).

Once you find the owner of a copyrighted piece of music you then contact him or her or ASCAP to obtain licensing rights. There are different kinds of licensing rights:

> *Music or public performance rights:* These rights include **public performance rights** and the right to recite, play, sing, dance, or broadcast a composition in public.
> *Synchronization or reproduction rights:* **Synchronization,** or sync, rights are paid for by one fee in one license. These rights allow a person to produce the music in sync with a certain picture.
> *Adaptation rights:* **Adaptation rights** allow a producer to alter the music as needed.
> *Dramatic rights:* **Dramatic rights** allow someone to use the story or title set forth in a song.

Of all these rights, you will certainly need music and sync rights if you want to use a piece of copyrighted music in your show. The other rights would only be needed in special cases.

The cost of licensing rights varies from piece to piece. A very popular song from the 1950s may cost more than a less popular song from the 1940s. The key to this process is starting early. A copyright search may take weeks. Obtaining licensing rights may take even longer. Furthermore, an early search may reveal that a song is too expensive or not available.

MUSIC IN THE PUBLIC DOMAIN

Another way of obtaining music for your film is finding pieces that are in the **public domain.** This means that anyone may use the music. However, you have to be careful. Let's say you want to use a Mozart piece. Certainly, his music is in the public domain; however, a recording of his music probably is not. The record company that created and paid for the recording would own that recording. You can have someone play Mozart's music and record your own version. Essentially, at what point a piece enters the public domain is based on copyright law. Check the U.S. Copyright Office website for a full description.

MUSIC SUPERVISOR

Having a music supervisor on a show is mostly seen in medium- to high-budget projects. In low budget, the producer usually will pick up these duties, or may delegate them to the UPM. The music supervisor of a project supervises all aspects of music in a show. He or she may be the person hiring a music clearance company, or working with a project's composer. The music supervisor will create a breakdown of the script and make notes on any references to production or source music. Then, if reference is to a well-known song, the music supervisor will work to obtain licensing.

COMPOSER

The composer of a film or digital project composes the underscore. However, it is not out of the realm of possibility that he or she be called on to compose a song that will be performed in the show. The composer begins his or her job in post-production, usually shortly after the first cut of the project has been completed. The composer will watch the first cut and begin creating melodies for certain characters and certain scenes. At this stage the director may also be involved, discussing key points where he or she may want music to enhance a certain moment. The composer will continue to create pieces of music until the final cut of the picture is completed. Once the final cut is sent to the composer, he or she will compose sections of music with specific music cues, starting and stopping the music to intensify dramatic impact. At this point the director will come back and view the composer's work. They will discuss the cue points and make adjustments as necessary. Once the underscore is complete, you are ready to proceed to a scoring session.

MUSIC PACKAGE FEE

A music supervisor or composer may also be available to provide a **music package.** This package would include everything involved with the music, from composing to recording to delivery. The final delivery is the music that is turned over to the music editor to synchronize to the picture.

CONDUCTOR

If you are using a score that requires the services of an orchestra, a **conductor** is hired to conduct them. A **conductor** in this kind of application is experienced in conducting an orchestra while watching the project on a screen. This way the conductor can make sure the timing of the music matches the picture.

ARRANGER/ORCHESTRATOR

Arrangers and **orchestrators** help to write the music for different instruments, based on the composer's score. Some composers will do this; others may prefer to have an arranger handle it. A time factor may determine the necessity for an arranger. An orchestrator specifically writes out the score in orchestral form. The arranger may enhance the piece with countermelodies, harmonics, and variations of theme.

COPYIST

A **copyist** is the person who takes the arrangement from the arranger or orchestrator and separates out individual pieces for each musical instrument. This allows each musician to have a music sheet written for his or her instrument only. The copyist is also expected to catch any mistakes the arranger may have made. Traditionally the copyist may also write a condensed score that will be used by the conductor. As technology develops, this task is being completed more frequently by computer software, from either handwritten or computer-generated scores.

THE SCORING SESSION

The scoring session is the session during which the score is played and recorded. This is usually completed on a **scoring stage**. A scoring stage is a specific kind of recording studio. This studio is able to fit and mic an entire orchestra, with the picture projected behind the orchestra. The composer, director, producer, and music supervisor usually attend this session along with the conductor, orchestra, arranger, and copyist. Scoring for a project could take anywhere from several weeks to several months, depending on the amount of score to be recorded.

If a full professional orchestra is unaffordable, some productions opt to hire an amateur orchestra, perhaps from a young artists' school. The quality of orchestras certainly varies, so it is wise to listen to an orchestra first before hiring it. In very low budget, the score may be performed by novice composers or musicians and recorded in a recording studio. Most recording studios can provide a pseudo-sync setup with picture, which produces a score that may not be frame accurate but can be revised in the sound editing system to match the picture.

SOUND TRACK ALBUM

If a project warrants, a sound track album of the score may be constructed. The decision to produce a sound track album is based on the notoriety of the score's composer and/or the popularity of artists that may have songs in the sound track of the film. The process begins when the producer of a project makes an agreement with a record label. The record company produces the CD (or digital download) and gets revenue from the sales. The company then pays the studio or production company a royalty. Royalties can range from 10 to 19 percent of the CD retail price. The record company may also ask the studio to put up matching funds for promotion. It is advantageous to both parties in this arrangement to produce a CD. The record company receives revenue from sales as well as more exposure of their artists. The production company receives revenue and more exposure for their project.

SUMMARY

In this chapter attention is paid to the residual areas of completing a film. Music for a project might come from re-recorded songs or may be originally composed. Copyright of the music is an important issue, best handled by a lawyer or music clearance company. If an original score is commissioned, it is written by a composer and performed by musicians in a scoring session. The scoring session allows the composer to match each piece of music to the picture. After the scoring session, the music is sent to the music editor, to be edited into the sound track. Finally, if desired, the music for a project may be turned into a sound track, which provides revenue and exposure to the record company and the production.

The Rest
of the Story

Contractuals & Other Matters

This chapter outlines the important legal and financial issues that come with producing a show. The following sections cover areas that require the filmmaker to enter into contracts. The purpose of the insurance discussion is to simplify the subject for many readers who might find it intimidating. The legal section explains how having a lawyer, though it may be expensive, may save money in the end. Publicity is also discussed in terms of the importance of getting good stills that can be used to help present and sell the film. The completion bond, a lengthy agreement, is broken down and explained.

INSURANCE

There are a couple of different kinds of insurance that are necessary on a project. These include **errors and omissions** and a traditional **production package.** You purchase this insurance from insurance companies that specialize in entertainment insurance. When you apply for insurance, the insurer will want to know what your experience is, if you have had insurance before, and if there were any previous losses. The insurer will also want you to outline any stunts or use of animals, vehicles, explosives, or fire.

Errors and Omissions

Errors and omissions is a type of insurance that covers the production if anyone tries to sue you. The intention of errors and omissions is to cover only cases in which you inadvertently infringed on someone's copyright or committed **slander, invasion of privacy,** plagiarism, **unfair competition,** or **defamation** (see "Glossary" for full definitions of these terms). If there is willful infringement, the insurance may not cover legal costs. For instance, if someone claims that you stole a story idea, he or she could attempt to sue you. This type of insurance helps pay legal costs to resolve the matter.

Production Package

Production package insurance is a type of insurance policy that is specifically written for projects in the entertainment industry. This package typically contains four different kinds of insurance: cast, negative, third party, and **faulty stock.** Each policy for a production will differ depending on who or what is being insured. For instance, shooting at a person's house that may have expensive furniture or artwork might require higher liability coverage on the policy.

Cast

Cast insurance covers costs incurred if for some reason a cast member is injured or killed on set or in post-production. These costs could go for reshooting or using CGI to cover the scenes that the actor had yet to shoot. The decision to reshoot or use CGI is usually based on how much of the actor's scenes have been completed. If only one or two scenes were left, the producer may decide to rewrite the scenes, omit them, or use CGI.

Equipment

Equipment insurance covers any rented or owned equipment such as the camera, grip or electric equipment, etc.

Negative

Negative insurance covers your film negative (if there is one). If your negative is somehow lost or destroyed, insurance would cover the cost of replacing this negative. This translates into the amount it would cost to reshoot those scenes. Negative coverage also includes items related to your negative, such as audio disks, tapes, or DVDs. Recently, negative insurance has also been expanded to include the loss or damage of most formats.

Third Party

Third-party insurance covers items that are rented or borrowed from a third party. For instance, if you were to rent an expensive fur coat for a scene, and someone spills a bucket of paint on it, then this insurance covers the cost of replacing the coat.

Faulty Stock

Faulty stock insurance covers the cost of replacing and reshooting scenes from any film or tape stock that may become lost or damaged. Damage to film stock includes that which occurs if the film is fogged or ruined by a camera and any damage that may occur at a lab.

Auto

Production insurance for vehicles will cover **nonowned,** or **rented, vehicles.** These vehicles could be picture cars or production vehicles.

Money and Securities

Money and securities protection covers any losses to a production's money and securities during the course of the production.

Extra Expense

The miscellaneous category in insurance would cover a few items common to all productions as well as items specific to your production. Common items include any loss or damage to props, sets, wardrobe, instruments, or owned or rented equipment. Items specific to your production may be added in this column. For instance, let's say your script calls for a scene where a herd of horses is used. You might add to your policy animal mortality insurance, which would cover the loss or injury of the horses.

WORKERS' COMPENSATION

Workers' compensation is a contractual that you pay to cover any cast or crew who may become injured or ill during your shoot. This insurance pays for medical, disability, death, and lost wage benefits. Workers' compensation will also cover benefits for dependents if a person is killed while working. Some states require that you purchase workers' compensation insurance from their state insurance program. Currently these states include Nevada, North Dakota, Ohio, Washington, West Virginia, and Wyoming. Others do not, but all states require some type of workers' compensation. This applies to all employees, even independent contractors, unless they provide proof that they carry their own workers' compensation.

COMPLETION BOND

A completion bond, also known as a completion guarantee, is a kind of insurance that guarantees investors that, should a production go over budget or fall to pieces, either they will get their money back or the film will be completed. Most investors or banks would not even consider giving money to a venture without a completion bond. When you procure a completion bond, you are also agreeing that the bond can monitor the production. This means that the bond company will receive copies of the call sheets, production reports, and weekly cost reports from your accounting department. A representative from the completion bond company (most are located in California) will review them closely, looking for any indications that the film is in trouble. One indication may be that too much film is being shot or that too many hours are being accrued by the crew. If your project looks like it may go over budget, you can seek additional financing from your investors. However, the bond company must consent to this extra funding.

The process for getting a completion bond is as follows:

1. You send a script, shooting schedule, and budget to the bond company. It is important that your budget have a 10 percent contingency. Most bond companies will not insure a project without this.
2. The bond company meets with the producer and/or director. At this meeting, the bond company will want to see acquisition documents. These documents include the rights to the story (if applicable) and the script. The bond company may also request that additional personnel attend this meeting, such as the art director or production accountant.
3. If the bond company deems the project feasible, it sends a **letter of intent** to guarantee the film, subject to availability of financing and personnel. This letter of intent can then be used to secure financing.
4. Once financing is secured, the producer and bond company sign a completion bond agreement, provided by the bond company. The completion bond company will also sign a completion guaranty with the financer. At this point, the completion bond company is paid a fee, which is usually a percentage of the budget minus the contingency.

It is important to understand what a completion bond will cover, and what it won't cover. A completion bond generally will *not* cover or insure the following:

- The cost of the MPAA seal
- The quality of picture
- Any defects in copyright
- Overbudget costs due to currency fluctuations
- Costs not covered in the budget
- Distribution expenses
- Additional shots for a television version
- Anything after delivery of the film

The delivery of the final film is based on specifications set out in the completion bond agreement. These specifications include, but are not limited to, the following:

- The film must be produced in accordance with the budget and production schedule. This does not include minor changes to the production schedule. Rather, this refers to major changes in the time frame of shooting the picture.
- The film is based on the screenplay.
- The film qualifies for an MPAA rating.
- The final film has the agreed-upon length, including titles.
- The final film is in the agreed-upon format, such as 35mm.
- The film must be first-class quality.
- The film must have had the agreed-upon cast in certain roles, as well as the expected producer and director.

THE LEGAL DEPARTMENT

One of the first and most important people for you to employ is a lawyer. It is especially important to hire an entertainment lawyer, because this type of attorney will be familiar with the various kinds of contracts that are used on a production. Entertainment lawyers are also well versed in copyright laws, which will help you if you are shooting a project that is not originally yours, as well as when it comes to adding music to your picture.

Why You Should Get a Lawyer

You should get a lawyer for a couple of reasons. First, let's say you do find an investor who is willing to give you money for your project. The next step is to sign an agreement between you and the investor. Do you know what kind of agreement needs to be signed? You could find a standard contract in a book and use that. Do you understand every clause in the contract? The lawyer is there to ensure that your interests are guarded, to make sure you aren't "taken to the cleaners."

Furthermore, some investors would prefer to work with someone who has a lawyer. Investors like to know when they are funding a project that they are dealing with someone who fully understands the laws and contracts in this situation.

Getting the Right Lawyer

Getting the right lawyer is crucial to the smooth running of any of your negotiations. Many lawyers will know the law. Many lawyers will know contracts. It is important that you find the lawyer that also suits you and your project personally. Some lawyers will charge you to sit down and talk with them first; they call this a consultation fee. Other lawyers may not charge you a fee until you agree to do work with them. If you are hiring a lawyer for the first time, make sure you hire one who is willing to work with someone with little or no experience. Your relationship with your lawyer should be based on respect and trust. At first, you want to find a lawyer who will not mind walking you through some of the contracts so you can understand them. While you should him or her never completely entrust all decisions to your lawyer, you should be able to trust him or her enough for what you do not know.

CLEARANCES

A clearance is legal permission to use an item that appears in your project. If you are using copyrighted music, you will need permission to use, or license, that music. If you plan to show some brand-name soda in a scene, you may need clearance from the soda company. Any product that has a brand name, including wardrobe labels, food, beverages, cigarettes, and cigars, may require clearance if it is clearly visible and identifiable in the frame. However, in most cases, as long as the product is being used for its intended use, you may not need to contact the company. However, even if the product is being used for its intended use, the company may not appreciate being in the type of film you are making and have concerns about the image of the company being shown in your film. If you are not sure, check with your lawyer or representative.

Clearances may be handled by a studio representative whose job is to find possible clearance problems in a script, bring them to the attention of the director and producer, and either obtain clearance or suggest their removal from the script. If there is no studio representative, a **script clearance company** could compile clearance reports. These reports point out possible problems. Some of these companies will also work to obtain any permissions needed. Other items that may require clearance include the following:

- Stock footage.
- News footage.
- Film clips.
- Television clips.
- Excerpts from published written works.
- Portrayal of well-known celebrities or politicians.
- Names of characters, businesses, products, artwork, and state and government officers.
- Derogatory references in dialogue. A derogatory reference could be a character referring to an actual, known person as racist or a pedophile, something that would be injurious to this person's reputation.
- Inaccurate factual statements. These statements not only may be inaccurate but also could qualify as defamation. For instance, a character could say that a known company knowingly manufactures products that are addictive, deceiving the public. If that statement is untrue, the production company could be sued for slander.
- Statements that might constitute invasion of privacy, **libel, trademark,** or copyright infringement.
- Telephone numbers. Most productions use the typical "555" prefix, with the rest of the number being above 4000, which is not used by any telephone company.

RELEASES

Releases are agreements between you and another party, in which the party agrees to let you photograph or record him or her (see Figure 19.1 for an example). Releases are typically necessary for actors, animals, or stunt people, those that are seen on the screen. If photographs of a person are used, releases are also necessary for the people in the photograph. Other releases are needed for locations (see Chapter 15 for an example). In higher budget shoots, a production will post a notice if they are shooting in an area where a crowd will be used. The notice states that, by being in the area, the people are granting the production the right to photograph them. Thus, no individual releases are needed. If, however, a large number of extras are employed to work as background, then individual releases are obtained for each person.

In low budget, where hiring extras is a luxury not many can afford, some projects will use their crew and anyone they can grab for background. Many low-budget deal memos contain a release in them so that the crew member can be placed at any time in front of the camera. If the production is grabbing people for the background on the spot, release must be obtained, but only for those people who are recognizable. A person walking far in the background, where you cannot make out his or her face, would not need a release.

RELEASE

AUTHORIZATION TO REPRODUCE PHYSICAL LIKENESS

For good and valuable consideration, the receipt of which from ____Joe the Actor____ is knowledged. I hereby expressly grant to said ____Frame Right Films, Inc.____ for ____"Regina of Icelandia"____ and its employees, agents, and assigns, the right to photograph me and use my picture, silhouette and other reproductions of my physical likeness (as the same may appear in any still camera photograph and/or motion picture film), in and in connection with the exhibition, theatrically, on television or otherwise, of any motion pictures in which the same may be used or incorporated, and also in the advertising, exploiting and/or publicizing of any such motion picture, but not limited to television or theatrical motion pictures. I further give the said company the right to reproduce in any manner whatsoever any recordations made by said company of my voice and all instrumental, musical or other sound effects produced by me.

I hereby certify and represent that I have read the foregoing and fully understand the meaning and effect thereof and, intending to be legally bound, I have hereunto set my hand this ____22____ day of ____June____ 20 ____02____ .

SIGNATURE _____

ADDRESS AND TELEPHONE _____

WITNESS:

FIGURE 19.1
Example Release Form.

CONTRACTS FOR CAST, CREW, AND SERVICES

The basic contract for a crew member is called a deal memo. This deal memo is an agreement that states that you hire the crew member for a specified amount of time and for a certain rate. There are other clauses as well. See Figure 19.2 for an example.

Other contracts include agreements for equipment and services. An equipment agreement (see Figure 19.3) states the items to be rented, how long they are to be rented, and at what cost. This kind of agreement may be contracted with a company or an individual who may own certain equipment. An Intern Release is shown in Figure 19.4.

PUBLICITY

While the process of production is highly creative, it is also part of a business. While there is a place for film to be art for and of itself, most often the art is meant to be seen, and if it is to be seen, people have to know about it. There will be advertising eventually, but in the meantime, to take the most advantage of the time you are shooting, a publicist is hired to create and handle all publicity. Unit publicists are most often seen only on medium- to high-budget productions, but it is important to know and understand their function.

Daily Crew Deal Memo

Producing Company	Frame Right Films, Inc.	Picture Title	Regina of Icelandia
Employee Name	Sandy Buttons	Position	Costumer
Employee Address	38927 Circle Drive	Account #	7082
	Trinkle, PA 17653	Start Date	7/8/02
Employee Telephone	872-555-6898	Rate	$___/day or (flat)
Loan Out Company* ("Lender")	N/A	Studio (___) Location(__X__) (Check One)	
Federal I.D.#	N/A	Guaranteed Work Hours___10_____/day	
Social Security#	999-888-888	Travel: Yes, all locations	
Hotel:	Regular room		

For Equipment Rental, see agreement on reverse side. *See Separate Loan Out Agreement.

Per Diem: $62.00/day

In accordance with the Immigration Reform and Control Act of 1986, any offer of employment is conditioned on satisfactory proof of applicant's identity and legal ability to work in the United States (I-9 form attached).

Employment hereunder is of an "at will" nature and subject to termination without notice by either party. While employed hereunder, Employee's services shall be on an exclusive basis to ___Frame Right Films, Inc.___ (Employer).

1) Services are for a minimum period of one day. There is no other guarantee of the period of services unless otherwise specified.

2) All purchases and rentals must be by cash or Purchase Orders. Procedures governing purchase orders, petty cash expenses, and inventory of purchases are subject to approval by the Producer.

3) Petty cash expenses not accompanied by receipts will not be reimbursed. There will be no reimbursement of any cellular phone charges without prior approval.

4) Employee is responsible for all recoverable items purchased. These must be reconciled with accounting during the last week of principal photography. All recoverables will be collected at wrap.

5) No sixth or seventh day or Holiday work will be paid unless authorized in advance by the Unit Production Manager. Only the Unit Production Manager may authorize overtime work.

6) All employees agree to submit an invoice for services on completion of principal photography. Employee agrees to be paid within 30 days of employment.

7) Employee hereby expressly authorizes the company to deduct any unsettled hotel incidentals incurred by the Employee or any unreconciled petty cash advances from the Employee's paycheck.

FIGURE 19.2

Daily Crew Deal Memo.

8) The production office may help you with certain personal arrangements, (e.g. personal travel or shipping), but any service will have to have payment arrangements made in advance by check or credit card.

9) Transportation to and from distant location will be provided by Company. Employee is not to drive to a distant location unless approved by Company.

10) The services hereunder are subject to the applicable terms of such collective bargaining agreement, if any, which by its terms are controlling with respect to the services hereunder.

11) Employer reserves the right to discharge Employee at any time, subject only to the obligation to pay the balance of any earned and accrued compensation due. This agreement is subject to termination in the case of any suspension or postponement of production because of labor controversy, strike (or threat thereof), act of God, or any other customary "force majeure" reason.

12) Employer shall own all rights in and to the results and proceeds of Employee services on and in connection with the picture as a "work made for hire."

13) Employer may assign, transfer, license, delegate and/or grant all or any part of its rights, privileges and property hereunder to any person or entity. This agreement shall be binding upon and shall inure to the benefit of the parties hereto and their respective heirs, executors, administrators, successors and assigns. Employee hereunder may not assign this Agreement and Employee's rights and obligation.

14) Unless subject to any other applicable written agreement, screen credit is at the producing company's sole discretion. If credit is granted, the name should read <u>Sandra Buttons</u>.

15) The Employee understands that there is an injury and Illness Prevention Program in place on the production and confirms that he/she has read and understands the Safety guidelines for Production. Any Employee found in violation of a safety rule or guideline may be subject to disciplinary action, up to and including termination of employment.

Accepted and agreed to: _____   Date _____
(Employee)

Approved by: _____   Date _____
(Unit Production Manager/Producer)

Box/Equipment Rental Addendum

The following equipment (itemized list attached) will be rented from the undersigned employee for the amount of $_____/day.

Rental (circle one)   is   /   is not   paid for preparation time.

Agreed to by: _____   Date _____
(Employee)

FIGURE 19.2
Continued

Approved by: _____ Date _____
(Unit Production Manager/Producer)

Product Placement Addendum

The undersigned represents, warrants, and agrees the undersigned will not enter (and/or authorize the entering of) any agreement with respect to any placement of products for on-screen exposure of any such product, item, and/or logo in connection with the picture, it being understood and agreed that any such agreement or arrangement shall be solely made by Employer and/or Production Resources department of Employer and/or the Distributor of the picture unless otherwise specifically requested and authorized in writing by such Production Resources Department.

Agreed to by: _____ Date _____
(Employee)

Approved by: _____ Date _____
(Unit Production Manager/Producer)

FIGURE 19.2
Continued

The Unit Publicist

The unit publicist is a person who handles all publicity for a show. He or she may be hired by a studio or production company and usually has contacts with industry press such as trade publications and entertainment broadcast shows. The unit publicist answers to the production executive of a studio or the production company owner. The unit publicist is the point person for all publicity associated with a show. The unit publicist's general duties are as follows:

- Works with the studio or production company to decide what to publicize. Each show is different. A show might decide it is more advantageous to push the star of a show or may decide to publicize the latest special effects that will be used on a show.
- Sets up interviews with the producer, director, and stars with print and broadcast.
- Sends stories about the project to print and broadcast.
- May be needed to handle bad publicity situations.
- Oversees the still photographer to make sure the proper stills are being taken and are of good quality.
- Coordinates press day.

The Still Photographer

The still photographer works on set to capture stills that will represent the project visually. The still photographer comes to set each day to shoot. He or she has read the script and has reviewed it with the unit publicist. The publicist guides the photographer in what scenes might be better for shooting. The photographer usually comes to set at the shooting call, after all preparations for the first scene have been made. In low-budget projects, the photographer shoots the rehearsals. This is because he or she doesn't want the click of the camera shutter to interrupt actors or get on the sound track. What some photographers also do in this case is time the shot either right before the director calls action or right after the director calls cut. Some photographers in high budget have special cameras with silent shutters and can proceed to shoot during a scene. At the end of the day, the photographer delivers the rolls of film to the unit publicist. Many photographers today are shooting digitally and will download the pictures at the end of the day and give them to the publicist on a CD or thumb drive.

EQUIPMENT RENTAL AGREEMENT

__Frame Right Films, Inc.__   __"Regina of Icelandia"__   __6/23/02__
Production Company   Production Title/No.   Date

__Acme Grip and Lighting__
Renting Company

__9790 Garner Lane, Dallas, TX 87992__   __469-123-4567__
Company Address   Phone No.

__Todd Hioupee__
Employee Name

__1898 Tree St., Florence, TX 89279__
Employee Address

__Sound Mixer__   __89078097890__
Position   S.S. No./Employer I.D. No.

EQUIPMENT

__20 Walkie-Talkies, 20 chargers__

I, __Todd Hioupee__ warrant that I am the owner of the above described equipment and that I have the right and/or authority to rent or lease same to **Frame Right Films, Inc.** and/or the Producer, Production entitled **"Regina of Icelandia."**

Daily Rate or __Weekly Rate__ or Flat Rate of __$2600.00__ beginning on __6/30/02__ delivered to __162 Rajlim St., Bend, GA__ premises on __7/22/02__ (Date).

I understand and agree that **Frame Right Films, Inc.** and/or the Producer shall have full responsibility and liability for the safekeeping of the equipment, and they shall be responsible or liable for the replacement of the equipment or any part thereof.

_____   _____
Renter's Signature   Producer

FIGURE 19.3
Equipment Rental Agreement.

INTERN RELEASE

Ladies and Gentlemen:

In consideration for Frame Right Films, Inc.'s utilizing the services of the undersigned, while rendering any services hereunder, the undersigned agrees that in the event of any injuries sustained during the course of such services, the undersigned will look solely to Frame Right Films, Inc.'s Workers' Compensation insurance. Frame Right Films, Inc., hereby agrees to provide Workers' Compensation insurance to cover injuries that the undersigned may sustain while rendering services hereunder.

Very truly yours,

Frame Right Films, Inc.

By: _____

(Producer)

AGREED & ACCEPTED:

_____

(Intern)

FIGURE 19.4
Intern Release.

Following is a guideline for what to have your photographer shoot on set:

- Director "directing" actors.
- Director next to the camera, "working."
- Camera operator with his or her eye to the lens.
- Sound mixer, with a good view of the DAT or other recorder.
- Medium to wide shot with the camera and operator, boom, actors, and director watching.

What Not to Shoot

- Crew members smiling at the camera (these are useless).
- Crew members doing anything but working.

Shooting the Action

- Get as close to the film camera as possible and try to replicate what the camera shoots. Shoot only rehearsals unless the shot is MOS. Sometimes good shots can also be taken immediately before "action" and after "cut."
- Try to catch emotional moments between the characters or shots that showcase the emotional state of the character.

- Try to catch action shots, if applicable.
- Think about what might be a good shot for the film poster or DVD cover, or a shot that tells what the story is about (without giving away too much).

PRESS DAY

Press day is a day during your shoot when you invite print and broadcast press to your set. You should pick the most exciting day of shooting. That way, the press gets good footage or stills for their publications or broadcast. The unit publicist coordinates who will come and helps them secure lodging. Before press day, the publicist arranges a schedule for the press to have sit-down interviews (some on camera) with the producer, director, and lead actors. The publicist also coordinates with the 1st AD to schedule these interviews so as not to interrupt shooting. On press day the unit publicist notifies all press of what will be happening and when their interviews are scheduled. The publicist also works with the 1st AD to find a location for any on-camera interviews. The idea is for the interviewee to be available yet not too far from the set. Usually the interview location is arranged so that the crew or a set can be seen in the background.

SUMMARY

Every production from low to high budget should have insurance. This insurance guarantees compensation for the loss or damage to equipment, stock, props, wardrobe, and sets. In addition, some cast must be insured in case of loss, injury, or illness. Another type of insurance is the completion bond. This bond guarantees an investor that an independent entity will either finish a troubled project or return that person's investment. There are many contracts associated with a show, so it is wise to retain the services of a good lawyer. Finally, hiring a unit publicist ensures that your production will receive proper exposure to the industry.

Miscellaneous

This final chapter covers a few subjects that contribute to the smooth running of a production. From making sure your craft services will satisfy a crew to providing proper medical attention in case of an emergency, these extra items are sometimes afterthoughts, but contribute to the morale of a crew.

Finally, this chapter includes a brief discussion of unions and guilds, what they are for, and how to become a member.

CRAFT SERVICES

Craft services are the foods you provide your crew throughout the day. This food could range from potato chips to hot hors d'oeuvres. The quality of this service can either raise or lower the morale of your crew. Skimpy craft services may leave your crew feeling cheated, while abundant and wisely chosen craft services keep the crew happy and productive.

THE CRAFT SERVICE PERSON

Craft service people vary in experience. The craft service person could be someone looking for a way to break into the industry or a union member who does craft services for a living. In very low budget, when paying a craft service person is a luxury, this job may unfortunately fall to the producer. In not-so-low to medium budget, usually one craft service person will suffice. On higher budget shoots, a few craft service people are hired to ensure each unit and location that is shooting will be covered. Make sure there is enough of the right kind of craft services for the specific location. For instance, I once worked a shoot in the Mojave Desert that shot on a dry lakebed, in August (not the greatest scheduling!), so we made sure that craft services had an overabundance of water to keep the crew hydrated. I also worked a shoot once in the summer. It was over 90 degrees outside and the crew shot outside all morning. Around midmorning the craft service person came to set with a snack: homemade, piping hot chocolate pudding. While the thought was appreciated, the choice was not.

It is a good idea to make sure your craft service person is familiar with the Industry Wide Labor Management Safety Committee Safety Bulletins, which has an addendum called the "Guidelines for Food Service Providers and Craft Services." The duties and responsibilities of the craft service person are as follows.

Pre-Production

- Checks with heads of departments for specific requests such as vegetarian preferences or favorite foods.
- Purchases craft service supplies.
- Rents craft service supplies such as a coffeemaker, hot plate, etc.
- May need to rent a vehicle to transport craft services (low budget). In higher budget shoots, craft service companies own vehicles for transporting equipment and food.

Production

- Arrives on set a half-hour before crew call to set up. Craft services should always be ready when the crew arrives, not just setting up.
- Works with the 2nd AD to determine the location for the craft services table.
- Prepares any mini craft services. For instance, the director may send the cameraperson off to get some shots, or a small crew may need to travel to get driving shots. The craft service person always makes sure a small cooler of drinks and snacks can go with them.
- Replenishes craft service supplies throughout the day.
- May bring snacks to the set periodically.
- At the end of the day, wraps out the craft services table.
- Prepares craft services for the next day.

Choices for Good Craft Services

- Always have coffee ready when the crew arrives. Also, make sure coffee is available throughout the day.
- On hot days, supply more salty snacks, juice, and water. The salty snacks help the body retain fluid better, which fights against dehydration.
- On very cold days, provide hot chocolate and have the craft service person bring it to set periodically.
- Choose foods appropriate to the season, such as fruits and vegetables.
- High-energy drinks are expensive, but crews love them.
- With the low-carb craze still going strong, having these items is a good idea.

- All snacks should be finger foods, easy to eat on the run.
- While some crew claim that they want healthy foods on set (and some will actually mean it), most really want the Twinkies and cookies. Provide both to keep them happy.
- Vary the selection of snacks from day to day so the crew will not become bored.
- Always keep the craft services table neat and clean. Presentation makes a difference.

CATERING

Catering, as opposed to craft services, is used when you provide your crew with a meal. This meal could be lunch, breakfast, or dinner, depending on what time you begin shooting. Quite a few catering companies specialize in providing food for production crews. These caterers understand that they might be called on to provide a hot meal for over one hundred people in the middle of the night (because shooting began at 6 p.m.!).

Hiring Catering Companies

Catering on a production is used for the one sit-down meal of the day. This meal may come at any time of the day, depending on when you start shooting. A general rule is that the crew will have this meal no more than 6 hours after crew call. You may sometimes run into a situation where you will shoot overtime. Six hours after the crew has come back from lunch, if you do not wrap, you must offer them a **second meal.** In most cases, this is considered a **walking meal.** In low budget, this could consist of pizza or hoagies. In higher budget projects, you have the option of having the caterer do the second meal.

There are many catering companies across the nation that specialize in catering for film crews. An Internet search will reveal many that you could contact. In low budget, if you cannot afford a catering company, you might hire individuals as independent contractors who will handle both craft services and the catering. The best way to make your choice is through personal reference. If you don't know anyone who has used a specific company, then go with the caterer who best fits your budget and food style. Most caterers feature their chefs on their website and in their promotional materials. Many caterers own mobile kitchens so they can prepare the food on site. Subsequently, some caterers serve only a certain area of the country, although some larger caterers will go anywhere.

Contact the caterer and he or she will send you sample menus to give you an idea of what can be done. Once you choose the caterer, sign a contract for the duration of the shoot. Caterers generally charge by the person, so one piece of information they will need is the average number of crew and cast they will serve. This information will give them a better idea of what they can provide. During production the 2nd AD will call the caterer each day with the exact number of people to expect the next day.

The Last Supper

Traditionally, the last day of shooting warrants a big last supper for the crew. Many producers splurge for a special meal such as steak or lobster. The meal becomes a small celebration for the crew and cast. This meal can be ordered at any time during production. However, be sure to give your caterer plenty of notice in case the food has to be imported.

SET FIRST AID

First aid on a set is crucial. Accidents happen frequently, and immediate and appropriate first aid may save a life. I once worked on a shoot in Oklahoma where I was hit by a car almost head-on during the lunch break as I was crossing the street. A witness told me I flew and flipped approximately 20 feet into the air. Luckily, the nurse on set knew enough not to move me until the paramedics arrived. She attended to me and kept me calm. Fortunately, I escaped the incident with only minor cuts and bruises. There are a few ways to ensure that you have proper first aid. In very-low-budget productions, you may only have a first aid kit. If you can't hire a first aid person, it's a good idea to poll your crew and find out if anyone has experience in this area. Furthermore, make sure the crew knows who is in charge of administering first aid, to avoid confusion if something happens. In medium to high budget, you can hire a nurse or emergency medical technician (EMT) to cover first aid on set. You can find EMTs through the National Registry of Emergency Medical Technicians (NREMT, www.nremt.org). This registry represents members of the National Association of Emergency Medical Technicians (NAEMT), an association for EMTs, paramedics, and emergency medical service educators and administrators. NAEMT holds educational programs for its members, coordinates liaison activities with different industries, and works to develop national standards of emergency medical care.

Emergency Procedures

If an emergency were to occur on set, there should be standard emergency procedures in place, regardless of whether you are shooting a low-, medium-, or high-budget project. Events that would qualify as emergencies include, but are not limited to, equipment or vehicles that injure a crew or cast member, sudden illness of a crew or cast member, stunts or special effects that go wrong, and any other kind of accident. Following is a general guideline for emergency procedures:

1. Notify the EMT or nurse that an event has occurred.
2. Allow the EMT or nurse to evaluate the person's condition.
3. On the advice of the EMT or nurse have the 2nd AD call 911.
4. Keep other crew and cast from surrounding the event.
5. Pull the person's emergency form (see Figure 20.1) from the set box.

EMERGENCY INFORMATION - EXAMPLE "Date"

NAME: Joe Thegrip
ADDRESS: 34 Smith St., City, State, Zip
HOME Phone: 555-555-4433
CELL: 555-555-8883
Email: joethegrip@email.com

PERSON TO NOTIFY IN CASE OF EMERGENCY: Janie Thegrip
Address & Cell #: 34 Smith St., City, State, Zip 555-555-5555
Relationship to you: Wife

PLEASE STATE ANY MEDICATIONS THAT YOU
ARE TAKING, OR ARE **ALLERGIC** TO: (i.e. bee stings, penicillin, insulin, etc.)
Allergic to bee stings and penicillin

LOCAL PHYSICIAN INFORMATION: (Address, phone & after hours #)
Dr. Fred Jones
43 Smithton St., City, State, Zip
555-555-3333 After Hours: 555-555-4883

Figure 20.1 Emergency Form.

6. Cease all shooting until appropriate aid is given to the person.
7. If the person does not require an ambulance but needs to be escorted to a hospital, provide a crew member with a map to the nearest hospital so he or she can transport the person.
8. Make sure the crew member calls the production once the status of the person at the hospital is determined.
9. Notify the person's emergency contact person (found on the emergency form).
10. Note the event on the production report.
11. Report the event to the insurance company using an accident/injury report (Figure 20.2).
12. Be sure to follow up with the person's condition the following day and/or until the person is able to return to work.

ACCIDENT/INJURY REPORT

Date of Accident: _____

Name of Injured Party:Phone: _____

Address: _____

_____

_____

Production Title: _____

Producer: _____ EP: _____

Director: _____

Witness	Address	Phone
_____	_____	_____
_____	_____	_____
_____	_____	_____
_____	_____	_____

Provide a description of how the accident occurred. Be specific.

_____

_____

_____

_____

Provide a description of any first aid administered and the outcome.

_____

_____

_____

_____

Signed:

Figure 20.2 Accident/Injury Report.

SET MASSAGE THERAPIST

Crews work long hours in often stressful situations. Some productions, high budget mostly, will hire a **set massage therapist** to minister to crew members throughout the day or for a couple of hours per day. Again, this is a luxury, but your crew will love it.

PRODUCTION ETIQUETTE

Every production is different. Because each script is unique, new situations arise that lead to varying confrontations, conflicts, and procedures. However, some guidelines are common to most productions, from low to high budget.

- Unless you are the director or 1st AD, always work quietly and keep personal conversations to a minimum. Professional sets are kept very quiet.
- Do not bother the director with problems, suggestions, or unnecessary questions.
- If you are new to production, always ask for clarification if you do not understand an instruction. Pretending to know more than you do only makes you look foolish.
- Never make assumptions; clear communication is crucial to the smooth running of a set.
- Humility works better than pride. People will respect you more if you don't try to be something you're not. Don't go around dropping names and credits. There will always be someone who has more experience than you.
- Follow-up is very important. If you give someone a task, check with him or her to make sure it is done. This is not an insult but competent production behavior.
- On professional sets, there should be a sense of urgency. People who work slowly will not survive a shoot trying to get twenty scenes in 1 day (low to medium budget).
- Make sure the crew knows its jobs. Most problems come from either someone not doing his or her job or someone doing someone else's job.
- There are three kinds of people in the industry: those that work well, those that work fast, and those that work well and fast. It's the last category of people that keep getting work.

UNIONS, GUILDS, AND ASSOCIATIONS

Many unions and guilds may be associated with your shoot. Generally, union crew members are employed on productions that shoot in states that are not "right-to-work" states. Right-to-work states are states that guarantee that any person has a right to work in that state. Thus, no one can be excluded from employment by the presence of a union. Often, medium- to high-budget shoots will have union crew members. Low-budget shoots may not. It is always wise to check with the local film office in the area where you are shooting to find out if unions need to be involved in your shoot. Each union has its own governing rules, by which a production must abide. When using union crew, you must become signatory to that union for the duration of the shoot.

Guilds and associations are organizations to which crew members may belong. Each organization has rules regarding employment for its members. Most associations are a place for members to network and take part in workshops and seminars that are intended to keep them updated on the state of the industry or to discuss certain issues. An outline of the various unions, guilds, and associations follows. As membership requirements can change over time, they are not included here. Visit their websites for the most updated information on membership.

American Society of Composers, Authors, and Publishers (ASCAP)—www.ascap.com

ASCAP is the association that protects the rights of composers, lyricists, songwriters, and music publishers. It should be contacted if you are using the music owned by any of its members. Royalties may be necessary for the artist if you use his or her music.

- Has over 100,000 composers, songwriters, lyricists, and music publishers.
- Licenses and pays royalties (minus their operating costs) for public performances of copyrighted works, including on the Internet.
- Gives out scholarships, grants, and awards.
- Provides health, life, long-term care, instrument, equipment, and studio insurance.
- Provides access to a credit union.
- Provides online registration of music titles.
- Has a database (called ACE) of song titles, including information regarding the publisher of the song along with contact information.
- There is no cost to join, just annual dues of $10. These dues have never increased since the association began in 1914.

International Alliance of Theatrical Stage Employees (IATSE)—www.iatse-intl.org/home.html

IATSE is a union for crew members. Nearly all below-the-line personnel on a production would belong to IATSE or National Association of Broadcast Employees and Technicians (NABET), another union described later.

- Exists to protect laborers' work rights.
- Provides health benefits, vacation pay, and a pension plan.
- Requires contractual contributions from employers. In other words, the production pays for benefits for the crew member.
- Holds production seminars for its members.
- Publishes a quarterly magazine called *The Official Bulletin*.

International Brotherhood of Electrical Workers (IBEW)—www.ibew.org

IBEW represents workers in utilities, construction, telecommunications, broadcasting, manufacturing, railroads, and government, with members in the United States and Canada. Membership includes workers in radio, television, and recording.

National Association of Broadcast Employees and Technicians—www.nabetcwa.org

NABET is a union for people employed in broadcasting, distributing, telecasting, and cable, and sound recording. It is the broadcasting and cable television workers' sector of the Communications Workers of America (CWA). The CWA is a union for communications, broadcasting, cable, television, journalism, publishing, electronics, and manufacturing.

- Provides wages and benefits such as health and pension.
- Monitors working conditions and employment security provisions.
- Headquartered in Washington, DC.

Casting Society of America (CSA)—www.castingsociety.com

The CSA is an association for casting directors in film, television, and theater. It has more than 350 members throughout the world, including the United States, Canada, England, Australia, and Italy. Membership can have the following benefits:

- Use of the CSA designation in screen and print credits.
- Awards such as the "Outstanding Contributions in Casting Award," the "Casting Society of America Award," and the Method Fest "Heart of Performance Award."
- CSA-sponsored events.
- Mail forwarding.
- Business contact referral service.
- Posting of members' resumes, the CSA Episodic Assignments List, and a membership directory online.
- Access to a CSA publicist.
- CSA-sponsored committees.

Actors' Equity Association (AEA)—www.actorsequity.org

The AEA is a labor union for actors and stage managers in the professional theater.

- Publishes an equity booklet.
- Membership requires a fee and previous employment under an equity contract or prior membership in various performing arts unions.
- Provides email services, a production rulebook, and a document library.
- Provides pension and health benefits.

American Federation of Television and Radio Artists (AFTRA)—www.aftra.org

AFTRA is a union, affiliated with the AFL-CIO, representing actors in news and broadcasting, entertainment programming, recording business, and commercial and nonbroadcast industrial and educational media. Members include actors, announcers, news broadcasters, singers, dancers, sportscasters, disc jockeys, talk show hosts, and others. They have their national headquarters in New York and an office in Los Angeles.

- Negotiates bargaining agreements.
- Provides health and retirement benefits.
- Gives out scholarships through the AFTRA Heller Memorial Foundation.
- Holds seminars and training programs.
- Provides access to credit unions, low-fee credit cards, and financial services.

International Documentary Association (IDA)—www.documentary.org

The IDA supports documentary filmmakers with a variety of services. Its members include producers, directors, writers, editors, camera operators, musicians, researchers, technicians, journalists, educators, distributors, cable and broadcast executives, film festivals, and members of the public in forty countries and forty-six states. Membership includes:

- A subscription to the IDA magazine, published ten times per year.
- Discounts on the Millennium edition of the *IDA Survival Guide and Membership Directory*.
- Discounts on seminar transcripts, books, and audiotapes.
- Discounts on admission to events such as the annual Awards Gala and the annual celebration for documentaries that have been nominated for "Best Achievement" at the Academy Awards.
- Discounts on health insurance, a credit union, post-production services, transcription services, and tape-to-film transfers.

    IDA also does the following for its members:

- Holds the InFACT Documentary Showcase, which shows documentaries to various venues.
- Provides support and information on fiscal sponsorship of documentaries for nonprofit organizations.
- Posts jobs.

Directors Guild of America (DGA)—www.dga.org

The DGA represents directors, unit production managers, assistant directors, technical coordinators, associate directors, stage managers, and production associates.

- Monitors guild requirements for directors, such as having the director's name appear in all advertising and publicity associated with a project.
- Provides legal information, representation, and **arbitration.**
- Monitors **residuals.**
- Holds seminars for its members and programs for its minority members.
- Instituted the Artists' Rights Foundation.
- Has minority committees such as the African American Steering Committee, Asian-American Committee, Ethnic Diversity Steering Committee, Independent Directors Committee, Latino Committee, and the Women's Steering Committee.
- Provides networking through events and meetings.

Writers Guild of America (WGA)—www.wga.org

The WGA is a labor union that represents writers of motion picture and television screenplays. It also has a widely used script registration service, open to anyone. The WGA will register your script with the guild for 10 years. Some of the services WGA provides include:

- Contract negotiation.
- A WGA newsletter.
- Health and pension benefits.

Screen Actors Guild (SAG)—www.sag.org

SAG is the union for actors in television and motion pictures. Some of their membership benefits include:

- A national newsletter, *The Screen Actor Magazine,* published quarterly.
- The John Dales Scholarship Fund, which is a grant for members and their dependents to go to college or graduate school.
- A Membership Assistance Fund, which provides emergency financial aid to eligible SAG members in need.
- Catastrophic Health, which provides financial assistance in the event of a life-threatening illness.
- A speaker series.
- Financial seminars.
- Pension and health insurance.
- A credit union.
- Eligibility for an annual SAG award.

Academy of Motion Picture Arts and Sciences (AMPAS)— www.oscars.org

The **AMPAS** exists to advance the arts and sciences of motion pictures. The membership includes executives, producers, directors, writers, actors, art directors, cinematographers, editors, music producers, publicists, and animation, sound, and visual effects personnel. In addition to holding the annual Academy Awards, the academy has other functions:

- Recognizes outstanding achievements of its members.
- Fosters educational activities such as workshops and seminars.
- Owns film research facilities.

Membership is by invitation of the board of governors for those who have achieved distinction in their field. Two members must sponsor a new membership.

Academy of Television Arts and Sciences (ATAS)—www.emmys.tv

The ATAS is a national organization dedicated to various pursuits in the professional advancement and education of television. Membership consists of executives, producers, performers, announcers, newscasters, writers, craftspeople, directors, artists, designers, photographers, editors, academics, and entertainment attorneys. In order to join, you must have 1 year of professional television experience. ATAS also has associate memberships for academics and students. Some of the academy's activities and benefits include:

- The annual Emmy awards.
- A subscription to *Emmy* magazine along with newsletters of ongoing activities.
- Internships for students.
- A yearly faculty seminar that brings faculty from around the country to meet with industry professionals.
- Support with insurance and job listings.
- Various seminars and screenings.

Producers Guild of America (PGA)—www.producersguild.org

The **PGA** is made up of executive producers, producers, and associate producers. Most producers belong to this guild.

- Provides networking opportunities.
- Allows its members to put PGA in their credits.
- Provides a pension plan.
- Holds arbitration seminars.
- Provides copyright services.
- Publishes a news magazine.
- Sponsors screenings.
- Gives out producer awards each year.
- Provides access to a credit union.
- Provides opportunities to network with other industry personnel.
- Holds quarterly meetings.
- Provides discounts to trade shows.
- To join you must provide two industry references, an application, and resume.

American Federation of Musicians (AFM)—www.afm.org

The **AFM** represents the interests of professional musicians. The organization works to negotiate fair agreements, protect ownership of music, and lobby legislators. AFM believes in the fight against online music piracy and is dedicated to protecting artists in record deals and recording contracts. Some of its membership benefits include:

- Health and pension plans.
- A part of the AFL-CIO union privilege program, which helps members with loans, credit, cars, legal services, and pet insurance.
- Free music contracts.
- A booking program that provides employers with information on artists.
- A subscription to *International Musician*.

The Film Foundation—www.film-foundation.org

The Film Foundation is an organization of industry personnel interested in preservation and restoration of films. It merged with the former Artists Rights Foundation to form the Artists Rights Education Legal Defense Fund, which advocates for artists' rights by holding public events, national campaigns, and educational programs.

- Publishes a newsletter with special events listings.
- To join, contact the Foundation and provide a donation of $50 or more.

National Association of Broadcasters (NAB)—www.nab.org

NAB is a full-service trade association that represents radio and television broadcasters. Their memberships include radio stations, television stations, cable and satellite companies, international broadcasters, and equipment manufacturers. Membership is also available to international broadcasters, educators, and students. Some of its benefits include:

- Technical, research, and information resources.
- A career center, newsletters, convention and conference discounts, and publication discounts.
- A benefits program.
- Discounts on insurance, car rentals, and credit cards.

American Film Marketing Association (AFMA)—www.afma.com

The **AFMA** is for makers of English-language independent films and television. This includes independent projects even if a major studio distributes them. AFMA is made up of over 130 production and distribution companies worldwide and promotes the idea that its producers retain ownership of a project.

- Provides marketing support services.
- Helps with government relations for international projects.
- Has the **American Film Export Association** (AFEA), which is a division dedicated to opening new markets in Europe.
- Can help provide arbitration for dealing with licensing disputes across borders.

- Monitors box office data for independents.
- Provides informational services. The AFMA sets standard definitions for licensing rights and territories.
- Provides information for producers regarding financing and distribution companies.
- Wrote the *Producer's and Distributor's Guide to Product Delivery*. This is a 150-page guide for independent filmmakers that provides information on film and trailer elements, delivery material, product protection, and critical records. The guide also includes templates for bank financing, certificates of origin, lab access letters, and a compilation of formats used worldwide.
- Participates in the **Federation of Independent Film Producers**. This is a Paris-based association that protects and promotes the interests of the global feature industry.
- Participates in the **International Intellectual Property Alliance (IIPA)**. This is a Washington, DC–based trade association of the U.S. core copyright industries. The IIPA provides access to government agencies for trade discussions.
- Has contact with over twenty financial institutions that support the independent film industry.

The **American Film Market** is an event where independent filmmakers can attempt to secure distribution for their projects. Filmmakers, production companies, and distributors from over sixty-five countries attend the market. They hold over six hundred screenings during this 9-day event. The market is usually held in late February in Santa Monica, California. During this time, the AFM holds luncheons and seminars for industry personnel. AFM also presents the AFM Independence Award to a producer who has exemplified the independent spirit.

Motion Picture Association of America (MPAA) — www.mpaa.org

The **MPAA** was founded in 1922 to restore a favorable image for movies and now works to protect content for filmmakers as well as deal with the American rating system and research. They have offices in various countries around the world.

SUMMARY

Craft services are a small but important part of your production if you want to keep a crew happy. Make sure your craft service people know and understand the specific needs of a production crew. Just as important is hiring the right catering company that understands the proclivities of a production schedule. First aid on set is necessary in any budget level. Make sure your EMT or nurse is licensed and understands the rigors of a production day. While all sets are different, there are certain aspects of production etiquette common to most productions, which include proper behavior on set and knowing one's job. Finally, many different unions and guilds might be associated with your show. Each one provides networking opportunities, some provide benefits, and most help to monitor and protect their members.

Guide to The Production Forms Online

The online forms for this book contain all of the forms presented in the preceding chapters, as well as many more forms that are needed on a production. The files are set up so that if you are looking for the kind of forms the location department uses, just look in the folder titled "Locations." If you are looking for a specific form and do not know what department it might fall under, open the section titled "Complete Alphabetical List of Forms," where you will find all of the forms in alphabetical order. All forms were generated in either a word processing or spreadsheet format, so that you may adjust them for your needs. Also, for the reader's convenience, all forms are repeated in a fillable pdf format.

In addition, many forms have "Example" versions. These forms are already filled out, and some have explanations as to how they were written. A list of the forms follows. Finally, a number of lists, such as pre-production or post-production are included to help remember all that needs to be done.

LIST OF FORMS ONLINE

Accident Injury Report
Actor's Deal Memo Non-Union
ADR Cue Sheet
Animation Budget Template
Animation Crew Plan
Animation Feature Production Schedule
Animation Feature Schedule
Artwork Release Form

Box Rental Agreement
Budgets (Various examples and blank forms)
Call Sheet – Commercial
Call Sheet – Legal
Call Sheet – Letter
Camera Report
Cash Advance Request
Cash Flow Weekly
Cash Flow Worksheet
Cash Receipt Full Page
Cash Receipt Small
Cast Addendum
Cast List
Cell Phone Log
Certificate of Insurance Application
Check Request
Composer Agreement
Cost Report
Crew Time Card
Crowd Release Notice
Dailies Shipping Log
Daily Script Report
Deal Memo Daily
Deal Memo Weekly
Delivery and Production Files Checklist
Distribution Log Crew
Emergency Form
Equipment Rental Agreement
Example Accident Injury Report
Example Breakdown Sheet
Example Cash Flow
Example Cast List
Example Contact List
Example Crew List
Example Daily Script Supervisor's Report
Example Day Breakdown
Example Day-Out-Of-Days
Example Emergency Form
Example Film Stock Summary Report
Example Final Budget Report
Example Hotel Log
Example Line Items
Example Location List
Example Low Budget 20000
Example Low Medium Budget 10 mil
Example Medium Budget 30 mil
Example One Liner

Example Page Breakdown
Example Post-Production Calendar
Example Production Report
Example Production Strip Board
Example Scene Log Film
Example Shooting Schedule
Example Shot Coverage
Example Student Film Budget
Example Weekly Deal Memo
Expendable Supply List
Extra Talent Voucher
Film Stock Summary Report
Foley Cue Sheet
Hotel Log
Intern Release
Location Agreement
Location Neighborhood Filming Notification
Location Release Agreement Non-Filmed
Loss and Damage Report
Meal Allowance Sheet
Mileage Log
Minor Permit Application
Player's Engagement Agreement
Post-Production Checklist
Pre-Production Checklist
Private Vehicle Release Forms
Product Placement Release Form
Production Report Digital
Production Report Legal
Production Report Letter
Purchase Order Log
Purchase Order Log
Revision Colors
Safety Checklist
Safety Guidelines Acknowledgement
Safety Report
Scene Log Digital
Scene Log Film
Script Clearance Checklist
Script Coverage Form
Script Distribution Checklist
Script Distribution Log
Shipping Log
Sound Report
Spotting Sheet
Spreadsheet Budget Template Feature Film
Still Photograph Release

Storyboard Form
Student Film Budget Template
Synchronization License
Talent Release for Minors
Talent Release Form
Travel Log
Travel Transport Request Sheet
Vehicle Rental Agreement
Walkie Talkie Sign Out Sheet
Weekly Production summary Digital
Weekly Production Summary Film
Wrap Checklist
Wrap Sheet
Writer's Agreement

GLOSSARY

2D animators   Personnel who composite images.

2nd assistant editor   A member of the editing team. Assists the 1st assistant editor. May log and digitize footage or cut scenes.

2nd Team   A term referring to the stand-ins on a set.

2nd Unit   An extra unit of crew that may shoot beauty shots, extra scenes, or specialized footage such as aerial or underwater footage.

2nd Unit director   The director for the 2nd Unit.

3D animators   Personnel who use software to create original animation of characters, buildings, or sets.

5.1 surround sound mix   A sound delivery format used for DVD and theatrical applications that uses six speakers to aurally envelop the audience.

A list   A list of actors who are "hot."

Above-the-line (ATL)   Refers to the creative personnel who appear in the first section of the budget. ATL includes categories such as story, writer, talent, producer, and director.

Academy of Motion Picture Arts and Sciences (AMPAS)   An association that exists to advance the arts and sciences of motion pictures. Gives out the Academy Awards (Oscars).

Accounting apprentice   A member of the accounting team. Usually someone with little experience who desires to move into the entertainment accounting field.

Accounting department   The department that handles funds for the production, including purchase orders, check requests, cash advances, payroll, and petty cash.

Actors Equity Association   An association for actors and stage managers of the professional theater, based in New York City.

Actual   Refers to the column in a budget report that shows the actual amount of funds spent on a particular line item.

Adaptation rights   Rights that allow a person to alter a piece of music when used in conjunction with a production. Also refers to rights to taking a story from an original source such as a book.

Additional labor   Any labor that is used for a department in addition to the regular crew, such as additional makeup artists needed for a large cast.

ADR   Automated dialogue replacement. The process of re-recording dialogue or narration for a production. Also called *looping*.

ADR editor   The editor in the audio post-production team who records and then may add ADR to the picture.

Aerial and underwater units   Additional units hired to attain aerial or underwater footage for a production.

Ambience   An audio term that refers to the background sound of a scene, such as crickets in a nighttime scene.

American Association of Producers (AAP)   An association for executive producers, producers, production executives, associate producers, segment producers, production managers, post-production supervisors, and coordinators.

American Federation of Musicians (AFM)   A union that represents the interests of professional musicians.

American Federation of Television and Radio Artists (AFTRA)   A union for actors in news and broadcasting, entertainment programming, recording business, commercial and nonbroadcast industrial, and educational media.

American Film Export Association (AFEA)   A division of the American Film Marketing Association dedicated to opening new markets in Europe.

American Film Market   A film market event where independent filmmakers attempt to secure distribution for their projects.

American Film Marketing Association (AFMA)   An association for makers of English-language independent films and television that promotes the idea that ownership of a project is retained by its producers.

American Humane Association   An association for the protection of animals from abuse.

American Society of Composers, Authors, and Publishers (ASCAP)   A society that monitors licensing and residuals for composers, songwriters, lyricists, and music publishers.

Amount column   The column in a budget that shows the number of units for that line item.

Animal handler   Person who is hired to monitor animals on set.

Animation supervisor/director   The person on a production who oversees the animators and will work with the visual effects supervisor if animation is to be combined with any visual effects.

Animators   Members of the visual effects team who create animation.

Answer print   Also referred to as a check print. The first film print with picture and sound, used to check colors and print quality for each scene.

Apple boxes   Wooden boxes in varying sizes (pancake, quarter, half, and full) used by the grip and electric department for various tasks.

Apprentice editor   A member of the editing team in an entry-level position. The apprentice position is usually unpaid and for someone who wants to work his or her way into editing.

Arbitration   The legal process for determining ownership of a work or authorship of a script.

Arranger   A member of the music department who helps to write music for different instruments based on a composer's score.

Art department coordinator   A member of the art department who coordinates work for the department and handles the processing of funds.

Art director   A member of the art department who executes the look of a film for the production designer. He or she also supervises the construction of the sets.

Assistant casting director   A member of the casting department who assists the casting director with auditions, cast lists, and communication with actors.

Assistant location manager   A member of the location department who assists the location manager in securing, coordinating, and monitoring locations.

Assistant makeup   A member of the makeup team who assists the key makeup artist in preparing actors for the set.

Assistant production office coordinator (APOC)   A member of the production staff who assists the production coordinator with communication and support for the cast and crew. May also handle travel for the cast and crew.

Assistant to the costume designer   A member of the wardrobe department who assists the costume designer in wardrobe matters.

Assistant to the producer   An assistant for the producer who handles tasks, such as screening telephone calls, scheduling appointments, taking notes at meetings, and sometimes running personal errands.

Associate producer   A title for a member of the producing team who can occupy various roles on a production.

Atmosphere   A term that refers to extras or background actors on a production.

Aural vision   The concept or vision of the sound for a film or video.

Axis   Refers to an imaginary line that exists between actors or between the camera and an actor. The axis serves to keep screen direction among actors consistent and logical.

B list   A list of actors who are not currently "hot."

Back matching   The process of identifying references in a script to past or future actions.

Background   Actors on a set who occupy the background of a scene. Also called atmosphere or extras.

Background coordinator   A person hired by an extras casting agency who coordinates background actors on set.

Banded   Electrical cables used to connect the generator to lights on set.

Beauty shots   Shots of scenic panoramas, sunrises, or sunsets, usually shot by 2nd Unit.

Below-the-line (BTL)   Refers to the section of a production budget that contains crew and equipment.

Best boy electric   A member of the electric department who is in charge of the lighting truck.

Best boy grip   A member of the grip department who is in charge of the grip truck.

Big production meeting   A meeting held in pre-production, approximately a week before principal photography, during which the script is read scene by scene and issues are discussed.

Black wrap   A material made of blackened foil used by the grip and electric departments for various tasks such as blocking portions of a light beam.

Body makeup   Makeup that is applied when an actor has to appear nude or semi-nude in a scene.

Boom operator   A member of the sound team who places the microphone in the optimal place for recording.

Bounce   Combining audio tracks in audio post-production.

Breakdown   The process of identifying elements in a script.

Breakdown sheet   A form used to categorize elements in a script.

Breaking film   A production term that refers to the process of taking a film magazine and cutting off the amount that is exposed so that it can be sent to the film lab.

Budget report   A report that shows how much of each line item has been spent in a production budget.

Budget structure   The structure of a budget, including divisions such as Above-the-Line, Below-the-Line, Post-Production, and Other (contractuals).

Building the microphone   The process of preparing the microphone for shooting, involving placing the microphone in a housing called the sound blimp and attaching cables and a boom pole.

Building the sound tracks   The process of creating sound tracks such as sound effects, music, and ambience to complete the final sound track of a project.

Bumped   Refers to the process of paying an actor or extra more money for a special skill or characteristic.

Bureau of Alcohol, Tobacco, and Firearms   The federal agency that, among other things, licenses special effects personnel for pyrotechnics.

Buyer   A member of the art department whose main responsibility is to purchase items for the set.

C-stand   A metal stand that is used to hold nets, flags, silks, and other grip items.

Cable person   A member of the sound department who carries and distributes the cable between the boom operator and sound mixer.

Call sheet   A form that informs cast and crew of the content and schedule for the following day's shooting.

Call time   The time that an actor or crew member is required to arrive on set.

Callback   A second audition for cast.

Camera car   A vehicle that provides a platform for placement of the camera.

Camera operator   A member of the camera team who operates the camera.

Camera package   The equipment that is ordered for the camera department. The package includes the camera, tripods, lenses, filters, and other items.

Camera reports   A report that shows the footage count and amount of footage for each filmed take. The camera report is attached to and sent in with exposed film.

Cash advance   A form to request a particular amount of cash to pay for various items.

Cash flow worksheet   A worksheet that shows when, how much, and to whom cash will be distributed.

Cast insurance   Insures actors for a production. Cast insurance requires that each covered cast member complete a physical before shooting.

Cast numbering   The process of assigning numbers to each character in a production, which are used on the cast list, production schedule, shooting schedule, and one-liner.

Cast release   A form that allows a production to reproduce the likeness of a cast member.

Casting director   The head of the casting department, who supervises the casting of all speaking cast on a production.

Catering   Meals provided to crew while on set.

Certificate of insurance   A form that outlines insurance coverage for a production, required by most locations.

Character breakdown   A list of characters from a script, with their general physical, age, and personality characteristics, used to help cast a project.

Check request   A form used to request a specific amount of money.

Checking the gate   The process of inspecting the film gate behind the lens of the camera for obstructions such as hair and dirt.

Child Performers Education and Trust Act of 2003   The updated form of the original Coogan Law, guaranteeing that a portion of a minor's wages (15 percent) must be set aside in a trust that he or she can draw on when he or she turns 18 and that a child's earnings are property of the child.

Choreographer   A person who choreographs dancers or musical production numbers on a project.

Clapper   A member of the camera team who operates the clapper, or slate, for the camera.

Clearance   The process of obtaining permission on a project to use a company or person's trademark, product, or name.

Closed dailies   Refers to only a few people watching a day's footage because the footage is either sensitive or confidential.

Closed set   Refers to a set on which only a few people are allowed because the shooting is either sensitive or confidential.

Cloud tanks Water-filled tanks that are injected with a liquid to create cloud effects.

Cold reading When an actor must read a scene immediately after receiving it.

Company grips Members of the grip department who provide support to the camera and electric departments.

Completion bond An insurance document that guarantees an investor a full return on his or her money if a production is unable to finish.

Composer The person who writes the underscore for a project.

Compositing lead The person who oversees the compositors and answers to the compositing supervisor.

Compositing supervisor The person who oversees all composites that may be used to create an effect.

Compositors Computer artists who combine different footage and computer elements to create composites.

Computer-generated images (CGI) Images created on a computer.

Computer graphics supervisor The person responsible for choosing software that may be required for an effect, for the process by which the effect will be achieved, and for overseeing all graphics for a project.

Conductor The person who conducts the orchestra for the recording of a score for a project.

Construction coordinator A member of the construction team, under the art department, responsible for coordinating and overseeing the building of all the sets for a project.

Construction foreman A member of the construction team, under the art department, responsible for the day-to-day operations of the construction crew and who answers directly to the construction coordinator.

Construction labor Members of the construction team who build the sets.

Contingency fee A portion of the budget (10 percent) that is set aside for unforeseen or unexpected production costs.

Continuity Refers to keeping track of consistency among the elements of a shot and of screen direction.

Contractuals Line items in a budget that are contracted, such as the completion bond, insurance, and legal costs. Contractuals usually are expressed as a percentage of the overall budget.

Coogan Law A law that came about when child actor Jackie Coogan turned 18 and found that he had no money in his trust fund. The Coogan Law provided that 15 percent of a child's earnings be set aside in a trust fund until the child turns 18. The rest of the earnings was community property between the child and the parents.

Copyist The person who takes the arrangement of a score from the arranger or orchestrator and separates out individual pieces for each musical instrument.

Cost report A report completed by the accounting team that shows current spending of the budget.

Costume designer The head of the wardrobe department, who designs the wardrobe looks for each cast member of a project. May design original wardrobe or oversee the purchase or rental of existing wardrobe.

Counter-to-counter service A service provided by some airlines through which a package can be brought to a counter at the airport, flown on a flight, and received at the counter of another airport.

Courtesy credit A main title or end credit given to someone as a courtesy or favor.

Cover sets Locations that are set aside to shoot at in case the originally scheduled location, usually an exterior, becomes unavailable because of bad weather.

Craft service person The person who sets up and maintains the craft service table throughout the day.

Craft services A table of snacks that is replenished throughout the day for cast and crew.

Creature manufacturer A person who is in the business of creating creatures for motion pictures. This person usually works for a special effects house and is hired out by the company to create creatures.

Crew gifts Gifts given out at the end of a production from the producer or production company to the cast and crew.

Crew packets Packets given to cast and crew on their arrival to the area of shooting (city, town, etc.) containing information such as a production schedule, shooting schedule, contact list, crew list, new script pages (if any), hotel information, new memos (if any), film commission information, brochures, and recreational information about the area.

Crosses Refers to the actions that extras will take in the background of a shot, when extras cross the frame.

Crossfades A term used in audio post-production. A crossfade may be created when two sounds are adjacent to each other. The first sound is faded out as the second sound is faded up.

Dailies The footage that is shot in 1 day.

Daily progress report A report prepared by the script supervisor that summarizes the scenes, minutes, pages, and setups accomplished for the day.

Day breakdown A form completed by the script supervisor that shows on which story day each scene occurs.

Day-out-of-Days A chart that shows what days an actor starts work, works, is on hold, is dropped, is picked up, and/or finishes.

Day players A term referring to actors or crew who work and are paid by the day.

Deal memo An employment contract for cast and crew that stipulates rate and term of employment.

Defamation The making of false or injurious statements about someone, statements that present a person as immoral or expose a person to hatred or ridicule. Libel is written defamation, and slander is verbal defamation.

Delivery The date on which a project is delivered, for either airing on television or distribution to theater or video.

Development budget A budget, separate from a production budget, that covers the costs to develop a project. This may include costs for research, script writing, and/or packaging a project with cast and key personnel.

DGA trainee An apprentice in the Directors Guild of America, hired out to train on the director's team of a production.

Dialect coach An expert in one or more dialects who trains actors how to perform their roles in that vernacular.

Dialogue editor An editor in the audio post-production department who takes dialogue that has been recorded on a project and cleans it up. He or she adds crossfades to smooth out the ambience differences of different takes, gets rid of unwanted background noises, and may edit ADR into the main dialogue.

Digital audio tape (DAT) A digital sound tape used to record sound on location.

Digital cinematographer/shader The person who works by computer to alter angles, color, and lighting that appear on digital or animated creatures or objects.

Digital modelers Members of the visual effects team who construct creatures and sets on the computer to create an effect.

Digitize The process of recording footage, either analog or digital, onto a computer for editing.

Director The person who creates a vision for a project, constructs shots, and directs actors.

Director of photography The head of the camera, grip, and electric departments, responsible for the photographic look and lighting of a production.

Director's assistant An assistant who works solely for a director managing schedules and providing personal assistance.

Director's Guild of America (DGA) The union for directors, unit production managers, assistant directors, technical coordinators, associate directors, stage managers, and production associates.

Dispatcher A person who coordinates the vehicles, drivers, and movements of a large transportation department.

Distant A term referring to any crew or location that is greater than 60 miles from the production office or main area of shooting. A distant crew member receives per diem and hotel.

Distribution The venue at which a project is played.

Distributor The company that distributes a project. Distributors can be for either theatrical or video release, domestically or worldwide.

Dolly A platform that rolls on wheels or track. The camera is placed on the dolly to achieve moving shots. This kind of dolly usually has a hydraulic lift for the camera, along with seats for the camera operator and director.

Dolly grip A member of the grip department who operates the dolly.

Dolly track Six- or 9-foot sections of attached metal poles on which the dolly rides.

Doorway dolly A flat platform dolly with its own wheels. The camera sits on its tripod on top of this type of dolly, which is narrow enough to fit through a doorway.

Dramatic rights Rights that allow someone to use the story or title from a song for a production.

Drop–pickup Refers to the status of an actor who may work 10 or more days on a union shoot. After 10 nonworking days, an actor is dropped from contract and then picked up at a later date.

DSP (Digital signal processing) Refers to the process of applying digital effects to audio.

Edit decision list A list created by a nonlinear editing system that shows the time code address of each cut on a project.

Editor The head of the editing team, who is responsible for achieving the final cut of a picture.

Eighths (1/8s) The minimum unit of measurement on a script page (measuring vertically). Used to determine the length of a scene.

Electricians Members of the electric department who place lights and cable to light a set. Also called electrics or lamp operators.

Electronic press kit (EPK) A videotape or digital package of press materials for a project. The EPK usually contains featurettes, behind-the-scenes footage, and interviews with stars, directors, and/or producers.

Element A category that is identified from a screenplay in a script breakdown. Major elements include speaking cast, extras, stunts, vehicles, animals, props, special effects, wardrobe, makeup, visual effects, and set dressing.

Emergency form A form filled out by cast and crew in pre-production that contains information about whom to contact in case of emergency and about any medical allergies or conditions.

Encumbered A column in a budget report that shows amounts for items or services that have been ordered but not fully paid for at the time the report is written.

Equalization (EQ) The process of increasing or decreasing certain frequencies from a sound to correct or create an effect.

Errors and omissions A form of insurance that covers legal costs if a production is sued for issues such as infringement of copyright, slander, invasion of privacy, plagiarism, unfair competition, or defamation.

Exhibit G A sign-in and sign-out sheet for actors who belong to the Screen Actors Guild.

Expendables Items such as gaffer's or camera tape, batteries, canned air, and grease pencils used on a production that are expendable, meaning they are used up during the course of a production.

Expense report A report that shows a receipt-by-receipt accounting of a cash advance or petty cash.

Exteriors Locations that are outside.

Extras Actors without dialogue who usually appear in the background of a scene. Also called atmosphere or background.

Extras casting coordinator The head of the extras department who casts extras for a production.

Extras release A form for extras that allows the production to use their likenesses.

Faulty stock A form of insurance that covers the cost of replacing and reshooting scenes from any film or tape stock should they become lost or damaged. Damage to film stock includes that which occurs if the film is fogged or ruined by a camera and any damage that may occur at a lab.

Featurette A behind-the-scenes short documentary about the making of a film or video.

Federal Income Compensation Act Also known as the Federal Insurance Contributions Act. A federal tax taken out of a person's pay for social security.

Federal Unemployment Insurance A federal tax taken out of a person's pay for unemployment insurance.

Federation of Independent Film Producers A Paris-based association that protects and promotes the interests of the global feature industry.

Film courier A company that specializes in transporting exposed film to and from a lab.

Film magazine The compartment on a film camera that houses the film.

Film office An office, of a city or of a state, that provides production support.

Film stock summary report A daily report filled out by the 2nd AC that shows an inventory of short ends, wasted film, no-good film and printed film and a total amount of film for the day.

Final crew list The crew list that is distributed at the end of a production, showing every crew member who ever worked. This crew list is coveted by crew members for networking.

First assistant accountant A member of the accounting team. Assists the head accountant with purchase orders, check requests, cash advances, and possibly payroll.

First assistant cameraperson (1st AC) A member of the camera team. Assists the camera operator, measures and pulls focus, and levels the tripod.

First assistant director (1st AD) A member of the director's team. Runs the set, responsible for making the day.

First assistant editor A member of the editing team. Assists the main picture editor. May digitize footage and/or cut scenes together.

First shot call The telephone call placed by a set PA or assistant director to the production office with the time that the first shot of the day was achieved.

First team on set A phrase called out by the 2nd AD when actors are arriving on set.

Flags Metal frames of different sizes (18" by 24" or 24" by 36") and covered with black material that are used by the grip department to block flares in the camera lens or to redirect or block light.

Flare A reflection on the camera lens from a light.

Flat fee One fee paid for all of a person's work on a show, as opposed to a daily or weekly payment.

Fogger A device used by the special effects department to create fog or smoke effects with liquid nitrogen, oil, kerosene, or dry ice.

Foley artist A person who re-creates sound effects on a stage in audio post-production. Foley effects may include footsteps and opening or closing doors.

Foley sessions Sessions held for recording Foley effects.

Foley tracks Audio tracks in an audio session that contain sounds recorded in a Foley session.

Form 1099 A form from the Internal Revenue Service given to an independent contractor that shows his or her nontaxed earnings for the year.

Freelancers People who work from production to production as opposed to working on salary for one company or production.

Fringe benefits Benefits paid to employees, such as vacation, health insurance, and pension. Also called fringes.

Full-scale physical effects Special effects that are created on set. These kinds of effects usually happen in real time and on an actual-life scale; they include explosions, crashes, squibs, or weather effects.

Gaffer The head of the electric department, in charge of lighting the set and responsible for executing the look the director of photography wants.

Garage sale A sale held after a production has finished principal photography where items such as props, set dressing, or vehicles are sold to the public.

General expenses A section of the budget that contains line items for telephones, postage, office supplies, office equipment rental, office meals and sometimes legal fees, the MPAA seal, post-production accounting, bank fees, and interest.

Generator A transportable device that provides electricity for lights.

Generator tow A vehicle that is used to tow large generators.

Genny operator The person who operates and maintains the generator.

Glidecam A portable rig that holds a camera that an operator uses to achieve moving shots. It is like a steadicam but does not attach to the operator's body.

Greenery Any foliage that is used as set dressing on a production.

Grip A member of the grip department who provides support to the camera and electric teams through the use of grip equipment or any rigging of anything.

Grip package The equipment and truck that is used by the grip department, which comes in 2- to 10-ton sizes.

Ground squibs An electrical device that is placed on the ground or on an object to simulate bullet hits.

Hair and makeup tests Filmed or videotaped trial in pre-production to test hair and makeup looks for particular actors.

Hair breakdown A breakdown of various hair looks for characters in a script, scene by scene.

Head accountant The head of the accounting department, responsible for the actual disbursement of funds to vendors, cast, and crew. Also known as the production accountant.

Header board A section of the production strip board that shows character names and their cast numbers.

Headshots Photographs of themselves that actors use to get work.

High budget Varies greatly, but usually a budget of $50 million or more.

Hold days The number of days an actor is under contract with the production but not shooting.

Honeywagon A vehicle used in production that contains dressing rooms for actors and bathrooms for cast and crew.

Hotel log A log, kept by the APOC, that shows the departure, arrival, and room number of each cast and crew staying at a particular hotel.

House power The electricity that comes from the actual location.

IATSE (International Alliance of Theatrical and Stage Employees) The union for below-the-line crew.

Independent contractor A person who works for a production and does not get taxes taken out of his or her pay. An independent contractor pays taxes quarterly directly to the government.

Industry Code of Conduct A guideline for crew behavior written by the Industry-Wide Labor Management Safety Committee, a committee under IATSE.

Industry-Wide Labor Management Safety Committee Safety Bulletins Safety guidelines distributed by IATSE that promote safety on sets. These guidelines cover the proper handling of firearms, water hazards, pyrotechnics, vehicles, food, etc.

Interiors Locations that are inside.

International Intellectual Property Alliance (IIPA) A Washington, DC–based trade association of the U.S. core copyright industries. The IIPA provides access to government agencies for trade discussions.

Invasion of privacy   Occurs when a person's right of privacy has been infringed upon. See *"Privacy."*

Investors   People who provide financing for productions.

Jib   A rig on wheels that has a long extension-type pole, at the end of which the camera is attached. A jib provides height that can range from 2 to 7 feet, along with a 5- to 8-foot reach.

Key grip   The head of the grip department, responsible for providing support to the camera and electric teams.

Key hair   The head of the hair department, responsible for styling actors' hair.

Key makeup artist   The head of the makeup department, responsible for the makeup and hair budget and for applying makeup to cast.

Key PA   A production assistant who is put in charge of the other set production assistants.

Last supper   Production slang for the meal that is served on the last day of shooting. Traditionally it is an upscale meal to celebrate the end of shooting.

Lead man   A member of the art department in charge of transporting set dressing to and from a set. Also in charge of the swing gang.

Letter of intent   A letter that states a person's intention to work on a production, usually based on particular conditions such as achievement of financing.

Libel   When someone commits defamation through the printed or written word.

Licensing   The process of permitting someone to use copyright protected work for a fee.

Lighting grid   A diagram showing the placement of lights on a set.

Lighting package   The equipment and truck used by the lighting team. A lighting package includes lights, stands, scrims, etc.

Line item production budget   The type of budget used for productions.

Line producer   The person who is responsible for the budget and running of a production.

Lining the script   The process of identifying shots on a script page as they are being taken on set.

Local   A person is local if he or she resides in the area in which the production is shooting. Local crew typically does not receive per diem or hotel.

Local production coordinator   A person who is hired to set up a production office at a particular location. This person is usually local to the area and answers directly to the main unit production coordinator.

Location fee   A fee paid to a location's owner for use of the facility and the right to film there.

Location list   A list of locations being used for the production, along with contact information.

Location manager   The head of the locations department, responsible for finding locations for the production.

Location map   A map constructed by the location team that shows the area of shooting and has directions from the production office to the location.

Location release agreement   An agreement between the production company and the owner of the location granting to the production the right to film there.

Location scout (event)   An event where heads of departments travel to possible locations to discuss the viability of using a particular site.

Location scout (person)   A member of the location department, usually a local, who goes out and photographs potential locations.

Lock-up   A term referring to a situation on set in which all possible passersby are stopped and asked to wait until the shot is over. Production assistants usually provide lock-up.

Locked   A term referring to the status of an item when most changes for that item are complete or that item is secured. Items include the script, cast, locations, and picture.

Looping   The process of re-recording an actor's dialogue or narration. Also called automated dialogue replacement.

Loss and Damage   A line item in a production budget that allows for the loss of or damage to any equipment in that category.

Low budget   Varies greatly but could signify a budget of less than $10 million.

M&E   Music and effects. This identification is used for a type of mix in which the dialogue track is stripped of any effects, leaving other tracks having all music and effects. This is done so that the dialogue track can be easily removed from the tracks and replaced with a foreign language track.

Make the day   A phrase that means to shoot all scenes that were scheduled for the day.

Makeup breakdown   A breakdown completed by the makeup department that shows each character's makeup requirements and choices scene by scene.

Martini   An industry slang term referring to the last shot of the day.

Matte painting A hand-painted background of a scene that could not be found in the real world or is not convenient to shoot at.

Meet-and-greet A party held a day or so before principal photography where crew members can meet and socialize.

Men's costumer/women's costumer Member of the wardrobe department who dresses the actors.

Miniature pyrotechnics A form of special effects where miniatures are in some way destroyed.

Miniatures Small models of aircraft, creatures, or almost anything.

Minor permit A permit that allows a production to use a minor. Also known in some states as a theatrical permit.

Modelers The craftsmen who construct physical models of creatures with wire frames, latex, and paint.

Money and securities A form of insurance that covers any losses to a production's money and securities during the course of the production.

Mono mix A mix intended for a mono format medium such as 16mm.

MOS Stands for "mit out sound." To shoot MOS means to shoot without recording any sound.

Motion control camera A camera that allows computerized positioning. The camera has the ability to move into exactly the same position or in exactly the same direction, whether panning or tilting, take after take.

Motion Picture Association An international arm of the MPAA, formed in 1945 after World War II to re-establish films in the worldwide market.

Motion Picture Association of America (MPAA) An association founded in 1922 to restore a favorable image for movies. The association keeps seven studios on their board of directors and issues the Academy Awards yearly.

Movie Magic Budgeting A software program for writing a production budget.

MPAA seal A seal given by the Motion Picture Association of America.

Multiple elements An element that may contain many items, such as extras.

Music editor The person who edits music into the sound tracks of a production.

Music or public performance rights Rights that include the right to recite, play, sing, dance, or broadcast a composition in public.

Music package fee A fee paid to the music supervisor or composer to provide a package that would include everything involved with the music for the production, from composing to recording to delivery.

Music supervisor The person who supervises all aspects of music in a show. He or she may be the person hiring a music clearance company or working with a project's composer.

Nagra A 1/4-inch analog tape recorder used for recording sound on location.

ND stunt/ND stunt people A stunt that happens with background in a scene, such as a crowd of people diving away from a speeding car.

Negative cutter The person who cuts the negative of a picture to conform it to a workprint or edit decision list.

Negative insurance Insurance that covers the cost of replacing your film negative due to loss or destruction.

New deal A term used on set to alert crew that the current shot is completed and they are about to move on to another shot.

Nonowned or rented vehicles A section of coverage under production insurance that covers picture cars or production vehicles.

O.S. Stands for offscreen. This usually refers to a speaking actor who is in a scene but not seen in a shot.

Office production assistant An entry-level job assisting the production coordinator in the production office.

One-liner A schedule that lays out production schedule information in scene order.

Optical effects Traditionally refers to effects created with an optical printer. Currently also refers to any effects that are created in post-production.

Orchestrator The person who helps to write music for different instruments, based on the composer's score. An orchestrator specifically writes out the score in orchestral form.

Overhead A line item in a production budget that refers to the cost of running a production company.

Padding Adding additional funds to a production budget, "just in case."

Parent's consent form A form signed by the parent of a minor that allows the production to reproduce the likeness of the minor.

Partial A term referring to a scene that is only partially completed at the end of a shooting day.

Payroll fee A fee paid to a payroll company for that company to handle payroll for a production.

Penalties Monetary fines levied against a production for violating union rules.

Per diem A daily monetary allowance given to distant cast and crew to pay for meals.

Permits Permission from a city that allows a production to film in public areas.

Petty cash An allotment of cash to pay for minor items.

Physical effects Special effects that are created on set.

Pickup report A report given to drivers in the transportation team with information about whom to pick up at the airport and when.

Picture vehicles Vehicles that appear on camera. Also called picture cars.

Post-production supervisor The person who makes sure that everything in the post-production process is coordinated and completed on time.

Press day A day during shooting when print and broadcast press are invited to come watch shooting and conduct interviews with actors and, sometimes, the director or producer.

Previous A term found on various reports that refers to what was previously shot.

Principal photography The period of time when a production is shooting.

Prints and advertising budget A budget used in the distribution process to pay for advertising costs and the cost of theater prints.

Privacy The right for a person to live his or her life in seclusion, without unwanted publicity.

Pro Tools A sound editing and mixing software program sold by Digidesign.

Producer–Screen Actors Guild Codified Basic Agreement of 1998 An agreement that states that the producer of a show will notify the AHA if using animals.

Producer's and Distributor's Guide to Product Delivery A document published by the American Film Marketing Association providing production support for independent filmmakers.

Producers Guild of America (PGA) A union made up of executive producers, producers, and associate producers.

Product placement Placing a brand-name product in a shot so that it is clearly visible and recognizable.

Production assistants (PAs) Assistants for various departments. Many departments have their own assistants such as camera PA, wardrobe PA, and set PA.

Production board A document that shows the order of scenes in strips. Each strip contains information on each scene.

Production designer (PD) Head of the art department, responsible for the look of the film in terms of everything the camera photographs.

Production interns Interns that work on set or in the production office.

Production music Music that may come from a singer or musician on set.

Production office coordinator The liaison between the studio and set and the person who oversees the running of the production office.

Production package A type of insurance package specifically written for projects in the entertainment industry. This package typically contains four different kinds of insurance: cast, negative, third party, and faulty stock.

Production report A report completed after a day's shooting that shows what happened that day in terms of cast and crew work times, hours of shooting, location of shooting, amount of the script that was shot, and the amount of footage shot.

Production schedule A schedule that shows what scenes are shot on what days.

Production staff People who work for the producer, typically the UPM, POC, APOC, office PAs, and accountants.

Production vehicles Vehicles that are used to transport equipment, such as the grip truck, or provide support services, such as a honeywagon.

Props person The person who creates and/or acquires props for a show. Also called the prop master.

Prosthetics Latex appliances used by the special effects makeup department for effects, such as a large nose.

Public domain Refers to material that is no longer protected by copyright and is freely usable by the public.

Pulls focus The process a 2nd AC performs to keep a subject in focus when either the subject or camera is moving.

Pyrotechnics Effects that include fire, such as explosions.

Quarterly dues Money paid to a union for the benefits of membership.

Rain tower/stand A device used by the special effects department to simulate rain.

Re-recording mixer The main sound mixer in a mixing session who mixes all the tracks of a project together to reach a final sound track.

Release print A print that is shown to an audience in a theater.

Remote camera system A camera system that allows the operator to turn the camera on and off remotely.

Rendering A computer function that occurs when effects are finalized and processed.

Residuals Additional money paid to actors or writers based on a percentage of the total actual compensation they received on a project.

Reverb Short for reverberation. Refers to the sound created by natural audio reflections of a room.

Revision colors The colors that code each revision that a document goes through. The standard colors are white, blue, pink, green, and yellow.

Rigging crew A lighting crew that works one set ahead of the main unit, prelighting the set.

Right-to-work state A state that guarantees that any person has a right to work in that state.

Room tone The sound of a room while quiet, recorded on set after shooting is completed.

Rough cut Traditionally the first cut of a film or video.

Run of show Refers to people or equipment being employed for the entire production.

Rushes Another term for dailies.

Safety manager The person who is responsible for all safety conditions on the set. Also called the safety officer.

Sandbags Small bags filled with sand, used by the grip and electric departments for various tasks such as securing light stands.

Scale The minimum amount of payment for a cast or crew member based on union rates.

Scene log A log filled out by the script supervisor that shows for each shot how many takes were shot, how long each take was, how much footage was used, which sound roll the take occurs on, and which lens was used.

Scoring The process of writing a musical composition, called the underscore, that will play underneath a scene.

Scoring sessions The sessions in which the underscore is recorded.

Scoring stage The studio where a score is recorded. A scoring stage typically has room for an orchestra, a theater-sized screen, equipment for synchronized projection of the picture, and a control room for recording.

Screen Actors Guild (SAG) The union for actors.

Script breakdown The process of breaking down a script into elements.

Script clearance companies Companies that specialize in, for a fee, identifying items that may require clearance via a clearance report.

Script supervisor The person in charge of the continuity of the film and recording what is shot each day.

Second assistant accountant A member of the accounting team. Assists the first assistant accountant.

Second assistant cameraperson (2nd AC) A member of the camera team. Assists the 1st AC. May load film magazines, carry camera boxes, and operate the slate.

Second assistant director (2nd AD) A member of the director's team. Assists the 1st AD in running the set, keeps the set quiet, coordinates cast movement on set, writes the call sheet and production report, and may direct background.

Second meal A meal given to cast and crew 6 hours after the first meal, if necessary.

Second second assistant director (2nd 2nd AD) A member of the director's team. Assists the assistant directors in the running of the set. May handle SAG paperwork and the production report and assist in lock-ups.

Second team The stand-ins.

Segue A transition between scenes, for either picture or sound, in the form of a hard cut, dissolve, or crossfade.

Sequence A group of scenes that share a common theme or time.

Set box A box of files kept on set that contains various paperwork that might be needed on set, such as blank call sheets and production reports, emergency forms, production schedules, and location documents.

Set designer The person who works directly under the art director to draw any sets that may need to be constructed from scratch.

Set dresser A full-time on-set art department person. He or she is on set to make sure that all set dressing is placed correctly and maintains continuity.

Set massage therapist A person hired to provide massage therapy to tired cast and crew.

Set production assistants Assistants who work on set directly under the assistant directors.

Shipment log A log that shows when and where all shipments to and from the production office go.

Shooting schedule A schedule that shows what is being shot on a particular day along with what props, special effects, actors, and set dressing may be required.

Short ends The amount of film left over on a spool after the exposed portion of the roll is shot.

Shot list A list handed out at the beginning of the day to heads of departments that shows the number and order of shots for the day.

Side A copy of a scene from a script, used to audition actors.

Signatory Signing on with a union to employ members of that union and abide by its regulations for rates and work hours.

Silent bit An extra with some sort of physical characteristic or special ability. Also known as special ability extra.

Silk A typically white piece of silk that is placed on a metal frame and hung to block out harsh light.

Site fee A fee paid to the owner of a property for use of the location. Also known as a location fee.

Slander When someone commits defamation through the spoken word.

Slate A rectangular sign that shows the names of the director and producer and the name and number of the shot. The slate is photographed at the beginning of a shot so the shot can be identified in post-production. Also known as a clapper.

Sound designer The person responsible for the aural concept of a project.

Sound editing The process of building dialogue, ADR, sound effect, and music tracks to achieve the final sound track of a project.

Sound editor The person who oversees the sound editing of a project. May also edit the tracks. Sometimes synonymous with supervising sound editor.

Sound effects Sounds that occur in a scene, such as walking, items touching, or items hitting each other. Sound effects can be descriptive or connotative, meaning they either identify objects in a scene or enhance the dramatic impact of a scene.

Sound effects editor The person who builds the sound effects tracks in a sound track.

Sound mix A session in which all of the sound tracks are blended to form a complete sound track.

Sound mixer The person who records sound on location.

Sound package The equipment needed to record sound on location. A typical package includes the recorder, microphones, cables, and boom poles.

Sound report A form the sound mixer fills out that identifies each take and gives its length, whether it is sync or wild, its time code, and comments about how the take sounded.

Source music Music that comes from a specific source on-screen, such as a car radio or a jukebox.

Speaking cast Any cast member who has lines.

Special effects coordinator The person in charge of the coordination and execution of all special effects for a project.

Special effects makeup A makeup artist who specializes in creating special effects makeup such as bullet wounds, bleeding, sores, growths, or prosthetics.

Special equipment A piece of equipment that is not traditionally needed for shooting, such as a rainmaker or aerial camera.

Special or visual effects unit A unit of crew that shoots separately from the main unit to work solely on special or visual effects.

Speed The term the sound or camera operator uses after turning on the recorder or camera and giving the machine a few seconds to get to full running capacity.

Split calls Giving different calls to different members of the cast and crew. There is one crew call for most crew, but some members of the crew, such as the still photographer, might have a later call.

Spotting session A session in which the sound, ADR, sound effects, or music editor sits down with the director and/or producer to watch a show and identify points at which sound will be added, deleted, or changed.

Spreadsheet budgeting Using a spreadsheet program such as Excel to write and work in budgets.

Squib An electrical charge that creates a small explosion; used to simulate someone being shot by a gun.

Staging area Areas on a set where various departments, such as grip, lighting, camera, and sound, place a small amount of their equipment for easy access. Also refers to a place where actors or extras are held until needed on set. Also called a holding area.

Stake bed A pickup truck with an oversized, flat bed, used to haul anything.

Stand-in A person who has the same general physical characteristics of an actor—height, weight, and coloring—and who stands in his or her place on set, in a scene, while the electric department lights the scene. This is done to see how the lighting will look on the actor.

Standard screenplay format A format for writing screenplays that is standard in the industry, with guidelines to margin size, spacing and placement of dialogue, scene numbers, scene pages, and descriptions.

Standby greensperson A member of the art department who creates, places, and dresses foliage on the set.

Standby painter A member of the art department who paints sets and set dressing.

State Unemployment Tax A tax taken out of a person's pay for state unemployment insurance. The amount taken out varies from state to state.

Steadicam A camera mounted on an apparatus that is attached to a person's body. Used in filming for smooth movement of the camera.

Stereo mix A sound mix where dialogue, music, and ambience are routed to two speakers.

Sticks Another term for the camera tripod.

Still photographer The person who takes still photographs on set for use in publicity and advertising.

Stock footage Prefilmed footage that is cut into a picture, such as city skylines or historical news footage.

Storyboard artist A person who draws storyboards for a director.

Storyboards Sketches of all shots in a picture, drawn in pre-production and distributed to heads of departments so they can see what each shot will look like.

Strike To tear down a set after it is no longer needed.

Strip board A document that shows the order of scenes in strips. Each strip contains information on each scene. Also known as a production board.

Strips A graphic representation of a scene that shows the names of the actors involved and the name, location, and time frame of a scene. Used in the strip or production board.

Stunt coordinator The head of the stunt department. Budgets, coordinates, and executes all stunts for a project. Also responsible for the safety of each stunt.

Summing tool A tool (Σ) in spreadsheet software such as Excel that will calculate columns of numbers; used in spreadsheet budgeting.

Swing gang Members of the art department, answering directly to the lead man, who work to move heavy set dressing to and from the set.

Synchronization or reproduction rights Music rights that allow a person to reproduce music in sync with a certain picture.

Taft–Hartley A situation/contract where a nonspeaking actor on an SAG show is given lines in a scene and thus becomes eligible to join SAG.

Tagging The process of completing a script breakdown by identifying elements in a scene using computer software such as Movie Magic Screenwriter.

Tech scout An event that takes place after a location is locked, in which heads of departments go to the location and discuss any unresolved matters regarding shooting in that specific place.

Technical advisor A person with a certain expertise who is hired by a production to advise on technical matters of shooting a scene, such as a lawyer, doctor, or military person.

Television version The version of a project that is suitable for showing on television. Television versions must go through the standards and practices department, which checks the program for objectionable content not suitable for the general public.

The Blue Book A set of guidelines for working with minors, published by the California union for studio teachers.

The Film Foundation An organization of industry personnel interested in preservation and restoration of films. They merged with the former Artists Rights Foundation to form the Artists Rights Education Legal Defense Fund, which advocates for artists' rights by holding public events, national campaigns, and educational programs.

The Official Bulletin A quarterly magazine published by IATSE.

Theatrical permit A permit for the use of minors on a production. Also known in some states as a minor permit.

Third man A term used historically for the cable puller, or cable person, in the sound department.

Third-party insurance Insurance that covers items rented or borrowed from a third party, such as a wardrobe or prop house.

Timing the script The process of reading a script and timing each scene, usually performed by the script supervisor in pre-production.

Trademark The name of a product or logo that identifies a specific product and distinguishes it from other products.

Transfer The process of taking film and transferring it to a video format for editing.

Transportation captain A member of the transportation team who assists the transportation coordinator in running the transportation department.

Transportation coordinator The head of the transportation department who oversees the acquisition of all picture vehicles, coordinates the movement of all production vehicles, and coordinates airport pickups and deliveries.

Travel allotment The amount of funds allotted to a distant crew or cast member to travel to and from a location.

Travel/movement The process of transporting all cast and crew on a daily basis to and from the location.

Traveling matte A painted or computerized background that is specifically created to be combined with a moving image.

Turnaround The amount of time between camera wrap and crew call the next day.

Two-point system The system used for loading a production vehicle, which involves two people working in tandem to load the truck as quickly as possible.

Tying in The process of hooking up lights to an electrical source such as a generator or power box.

Underscore The musical piece that plays under a scene to heighten dramatic impact.

Unfair competition A section of the Lanham Act, which states that a person cannot use the name or title of an existing product that would cause the public to confuse that name with the trademarked product.

Unit production manager The person who oversees the day-to-day running of the crew and set.

Unit publicist The person who handles all publicity for a show.

Video assist A person who provides for the director a monitor that will show what was just shot.

VIP office A nondescript office set aside for any "VIP" that might visit the production, such as an executive producer or studio executive.

Visual effects Effects that are created inside a computer.

Visual effects producer The person, working either independently or for a visual effects house, who oversees the creation and delivery of all visual effects.

Walking meal A meal given 6 hours after the first meal. It is called a walking meal because it usually consists of foods that a person can eat while continuing to work. Also called a second meal.

Wall of envelopes A wall that is set aside in a production office and covered with envelopes for each department, used for the distribution of paperwork.

Wardrobe breakdown A breakdown written by wardrobe personnel that shows each wardrobe look for each actor, scene by scene.

Wardrobe supervisor The person who oversees wardrobe operations on set and answers directly to the costume designer.

Wedges Small triangular blocks of wood that are used by the grip department for various tasks, including leveling the dolly track.

Weekly player Refers to actors or crew who work, and are paid by, the week.

Wescam A camera rig that is attached to a helicopter, used for getting aerial shots.

Writers Guild of America (WGA) The union for screenwriters.

Wild sound Refers to audio recorded on set, but that is not synchronized to any picture.

Work-for-hire Terms by which any work a person produces while in the employ of a production is owned by the production.

Workers' compensation A form of insurance that covers any cast or crew who may become injured or ill during a shoot. This insurance pays for medical, disability, death, and lost wage benefits.

Wrap The period after shooting is finished at the end of the day when remaining cast is dismissed and crew puts away all equipment. Also refers to the period after principal photography is finished and the production office is closed out.

Wrap party Party after principal photography is finished to celebrate the production.

INDEX